ANTILOGIC

ANTILOGIC
Why businesses fail
while individuals succeed

Bruce McComish

JOHN WILEY & SONS, LTD
Chichester ● New York ● Weinheim ● Brisbane ● Singapore ● Toronto

Other Wiley Editorial Offices

John Wiley & Sons, Inc., 605 Third Avenue,
New York, NY 10158-0012, USA

WILEY-VCH Verlag GmbH, Pappelallee 3,
D-69469 Weinheim, Germany

John Wiley & Sons Australia, Ltd, 33 Park Road, Milton,
Queensland 4064, Australia

John Wiley & Sons (Asia) Pte Ltd, 2 Clementi Loop #02-01,
Jin Xing Distripark, Singapore 129809

John Wiley & Sons (Canada) Ltd, 22 Worcester Road,
Rexdale, Ontario M9W 1L1, Canada

Library of Congress Cataloging-in-Publication Data
McComish, Bruce.
    Antilogic : why businesses fail while individuals succeed / Bruce McComish.
    p. cm.
    ISBN 0-471-49451-8
    1. Small business–United States–Management. 2. Success in business–United States.
    3. New business enterprises–United States. I. Title.
    HD62.7.M388 2001
    658.02′–dc21

                                                                                    2001026859

British Library Cataloguing in Publication Data

A catalogue record for this book is available from the British Library

ISBN 0-471-49451-8

Typeset in Times by Deerpark Publishing Services Ltd, Shannon, Ireland
Printed and bound in Great Britain by Biddles Ltd, Guildford and King's Lynn

This book is printed on acid-free paper responsibly manufactured from sustainable forestation, for which at least two trees are planted for each one used for paper production.

CONTENTS

PREFACE

I HAVE had the good fortune to be the Chief Financial Officer of a couple major international companies. Chief Financial Officers are in a privileged position as the shareholders' friend. They are the conscience of the organization and act as the bridge to the shareholder. They talk to management of course and analysts, institutions, bankers, journalists, economists, politicians and individual shareholders. In short, they hear the inside story from those who ought to know, from the opinion-formers and the movers and shakers. It is all very interesting but they need to be quick off the mark to keep up with the logic of business and the financial markets. Being so close to the action should make it all clear but it so often seems to be insubstantial or inexplicable. The results are so perverse that perhaps Einstein was right when he said that reality is merely an illusion, albeit a very persistent one. He could have gone further and said that persistent illusion is the only reality.

Perhaps the curious logic of business is really a paradox. This is where things do not turn out as you expect, where contradictions turn out to be true and opposites can in fact be very close to each other such as love being close to hatred, cruel to being kind, appeasement leading to war and deterrence leading to peace. It is the same in economics. Consider the fallacy of composition. An increase in individual savings in a recession leads to a decline in total savings. Another example, this time from economic history, is of the mercantilists. These rulers sought to build up wealth for their Kingdoms in the form of gold. They did this to such effect that their subjects starved, whereas their spendthrift neighbours ended up with all the beef and wine, but none of that indigestible gold.

Paradox, or what appears to be a paradox is alive and well in the world of business and investment today. It reaches its highest art form with the brokers' analysts, although the economists generally do a very good job. Often the same argument is used to explain contradictory events and different arguments to explain identical facts.

The announcement of an accretive take-over causes the price to go down because the market expects there to be a share placement. Bad news is good news because interest rates will go down. High profits and low unemployment is bad because interest rates will go up. We see bizarre reactions in the market to profit announcements when better than expected results are greeted by a fall in the share price.

Keynes encountered the same phenomenon. This was not a real paradox but something pseudo driven by one investor racing to beat the others.

> The social object of skilled investment should be to defeat the dark forces of time and ignorance which envelop our future. The actual, private object of the most skilled investment today is to 'beat the gun'…to outwit the crowd, and to pass the bad or depreciating, half crown to the other fellow… We have reached the third degree where we devote our intelligences to anticipating what average opinion expects the average opinion to be".[1]

Keynes grappled with the temptation of going with the herd, and was forced by his own investment performance to change his views of the market. The investor should buy, not sell on a falling market. The expectation of picking up bargains was more rational than yielding to the panic psychology of the crowd. This would avoid the problem of believing in the consensus. Keynes wrote to his friend Labordiére.

> But whether for the slow going or the quick going, is not the rule to be in the minority? It is the one sphere in life and activity where victory, security and success is always to the minority and never to the majority. When you find anyone agreeing with you, change your mind. When I can persuade the Board of my Insurance Company to buy a share, that, I am learning from experience, is the right moment for selling it.[2]

In other words it can be better to go in the opposite direction, to go against, to be Anti the herd. We can take this philosophy one step further by looking at the old rule that if your broker offers you a slice in a float you can tell that the float will not be successful. This clearly relates to Internet public offerings. Although the market capitalization of Internet stocks is very large, the free float is very low. If you can get the stock you ask for, then you know you don't want it. This is the current manifestation but the rule applies generally to the share market. Why would I want to buy a share that you want to sell?

These surprising outcomes have become ever more prevalent despite the advance of the study of financial markets. There has to be an explanation that has escaped the theory thus far. One reason for some of these unexpected financial outcomes stems from the emergence of large organizations where wage employees and bureaucrats make the investment decisions instead of entrepreneurs. Now people are motivated by how good they look rather than by their ability to generate cash value. They are more concerned about the elegance of the impression they create.

Big corporations and especially those in regulated industries find it comforting to have certainty and continuity. When achieved this can lead to self-delusion and wishful thinking. Naturally, management expects the market to acknowledge the excellence of their results and reward them with an increase in the price of their shares. However, if the market is expecting the result it will have already anticipated the price and alert investors will now sell and move on to the next opportunity causing the price to fall.

The market confuses winners and losers when it comes to rewarding management. Good management often goes unnoticed while in contrast the non-performers so weaken their enterprise that it is taken over. The resulting increase in share-price through take-over, rewards the work of the incompetent with an upward spurt in the value of his options as well as the solace of compensation from the change of control clause in his employment contract. There is also a particularly stylish market non-performer who is able to repeat the process and create the perpetually upwardly mobile golden parachute. The parachute is made of gold, yet defies gravity so as to go up and not down. Again this is a sort of reverse logic at work. It is certainly not nonsense as that would be the absence of sense. Rather it is a contrary logic or logic with different objectives. This reverse logic I call Antilogic.

Now why would any board employ such a person? The answer is clear. A true incompetent will so weaken the organization as to bring on a take-over and the release of true shareholder value. The efficient market that is supposed to foresee all somehow always fails to anticipate the take-over. The justification for the resulting share price lift is the control premium. This is the premium the market demands of acquirers for the right to take over a company. Acquirers are willing to pay the premium and accept the task of earning it back. Some Chief Executives are convinced of their company's ability to transform the value of the acquired company despite evidence of plenty of previous failures. Oh well, practice makes perfect. It is the poor performer that gives the acquisitive executive his chance to try again.

We might think that the advance of scientific management techniques would reduce the scope for business uncertainty about true value. But it has not, as evidenced by the periodic violent crises that continue to trouble the world. Various explanations have been provided by noted authorities that

have suggested complexity, lax regulation, impact of program trading, hedge funds and cultural impacts. Several economists have noted the transfer of economic activities from the ownership of entrepreneurial owners and small firms to the bureaucratic clutches of the major corporations. There is probably some validity in all these reasons but the major question remains. These are very strange events and certainly not what we were trained to expect. No explanation is to be found in the classic textbooks or even given by the television pundits. This is not a random outcome. It is so pervasive that it must be effective for someone. Other influences must be at work, but what?

Gradually during my many years as Chief Financial Officer working for multinationals in several countries I came to identify the nature of these other influences. Sharing this discovery is the goal of this book.

INTRODUCTION

ANTILOGIC, VAPOURCASH, ANTICASH AND THE STRUCTURE OF THIS BOOK

GENERATIONS OF economists, accountants, statisticians and share analysts built up the theoretical basis for markets, the performance of the corporations and all other forms of financial activity. The working of markets had been ascribed to *the invisible hand* or the autopilot of the *efficient market*.

Now the power of the computer and the Internet has brought together the world's information and the power to process it into the definitive understanding. With this knowledge we might expect a greater efficiency and certainty in markets. Investors could now expect predictable returns but the super returns and unexpected crashes would be things of the past. Recent market uncertainty has demonstrated that this utopian expectation was ill founded. The global village promised by the Internet has become the global jungle. We are assailed with floods of information, much of it contradictory. Rather than fading away, the pundits of the media and the financial intermediaries have greatly expanded their futile efforts to analyze this burgeoning data to explain what is happening and perhaps influence the observer if he is minded to invest.

If the market is efficient and well informed, and if management is better educated than ever, supported by advanced management analytical techniques and enormous computing power, how is it possible such market volatility and major corporate errors are so prevalent? Some extra factor is needed to explain this situation of the market knowing everything at the same moment that management apparently knows nothing or has forgotten everything. How can we reconcile this growth of capability with the disappointing reliability of the output? Much is written about financial booms and busts but there is no consensus about what has happened or why.

One view is that we see and hear only a series of snap shots taken from a myriad of events. No one can judge the overall picture and so the apparent

discrepancies are just a sort of white noise that obscures the sound funda-
mentals. The theory stated by these advocates is that the ups balance the
downs. The winners and losers must even out overall. There may be
discrepancies at the detail level but the total level is assumed to confirm
the robustness of the financial system.

This view is comforting but unfortunately not supported by the
evidence. The world financial system is actually not in balance at all!
There is a persistent systemic problem. This is true for all three major
measures; balance of payments, balance of capital payments and balance
of portfolio investments. All have persistent imbalances in the same
consistent direction and the discrepancies are not trivial. Our certainty
about the validity of our corporate and financial market systems has existed
only because we did not take the trouble to check if they balanced on a
global scale.

The International Monetary Fund has the mandate to try and achieve
balance in world economic affairs. This is balance in many senses of the
word. The IMF is trying to encourage balanced economic growth so that it
advances steadily without too many violent fluctuations of boom and bust.
It is also trying to achieve balance in the economic aspirations of both the
rich industrialized countries and the poor developing nations by balancing
the needs of each category. It is trying to aid these objectives by improving
the equality economic policy making by providing statistics that are clear,
consistent and reliable. This is the acid test of world financial flows. Do
they balance on a global basis and is this consistently the case over time?
There is bad news here.

The world does not balance and it has not done so for years or perhaps
ever. This cannot be as is explained in the 1998 *Balance of Payments
Statistics Yearbook*

> In principle, the combined surpluses and the combined deficits arising from
> the current account transactions of all countries should offset each other
> because one country's credits are the debits of another. The same principle
> applies in the recording of world capital and financial transactions. However
> in practice sizable statistical discrepancies are evident.

The implications for the reliability of all economic and financial theory
are so serious the IMF retains a heavyweight Committee on Balance of
Payments Statistics that publishes an annual report in which it comments
on the statistics and the work of the committee. Unfortunately the results
are worse than ever and indicate that the world has a structural surplus
with itself. The IMF is very concerned about this and through the Working Party on the Statistical Discrepancy in World Current Accounts and

the Working Party on the Measurement of International Capital Flows embarked on repeated well resourced and very serious professional campaigns over several years to remedy the situation. A specialist task force worked for seven years to investigate and eliminate the problem and has addressed all likely sources of statistical error. The titanic struggle to wrestle the world back into balance can clearly be detected between the lines of the cool professional text of each annual report but nothing seems to work.

1995. Balance of payment statistics reported to the Fund and published in Volume 46 (1995) of the *Balance of Payments Statistics (Yearbook)* continue to show large statistical discrepancies in the global current account and the global capital and financial accounts, each of which should, in principle, sum to zero at the world level.

In the global current account, the excess of debits over credits, which had averaged about $US110 billion in 1990–1992 narrowed in 1993/1994 to about $US80 billion. The imbalances on trade, income, and current transfers, however all increased. Most noticeably, in 1994, the imbalance of credits over debits in the trade account widened for the fifth consecutive year.

1996. The *Balance of Payments Statistics Yearbook* continues to reveal sizable discrepancies in global summations of current, capital, and financial account transactions. Although the overall imbalances in the world current and financial accounts have been trending downward in recent years, they mask rising imbalances and erratic swings in several standard components that make up the aggregates.

1997. In financial account transactions, the discrepancy in portfolio investment was unusually large in 1996; recorded transactions in portfolio investment liabilities exceeded portfolio investment assets by more than $US200 billion.

1998 Balance of payments statistics reported by the IMF's Statistics Department and published in the 1998 *Balance of Payments Statistics Yearbook* continues to reveal sizable discrepancies in global summations of current, capital and financial account transactions.

Economists I have questioned are very uncomfortable with evidence that the world does not balance. This outcome is not predicted by their theory and therefore should not happen. They have set out their theory, defined the criteria for accepting or denying the hypothesis, gone out and collected the data, checked and refined the data and finally when the results contradict the hypothesis, they deny the data.

Or rather, they find someone else to blame for the data. When the evidence is put under their noses they are unanimous that the accountants are to blame. Their reasoning goes like this. The numbers are not consistent with the theory. The accountants prepare numbers and balance the books. These books do not balance and therefore the accountants must have done it or not done it as the case may be. Eloquent economists, who are prepared to justify any other theory from first principles, and who are capable of making any forecast and explain why their forecast was appropriate even in the face of a different outcome, are united in their speed to blame the accountants.

Their over-hasty conclusion would not pass muster with any self-respecting auditor let alone with a forensic accountant. Although the world is a very big place the nature of the global balance problem he confronts is conceptually no different than that of the accountant undertaking the consolidation of the accounts of a multinational.

In the case of the whole world imbalance, the economists diagnosis of the problem does not tally with the symptoms. Confronted with the same evidence the forensic accountant would proceed in a manner totally different to the economists, not least because his experience is that he is only called in when things are not right or do not feel like they are right. His first presumption is that there is a problem to be solved but he has to investigate to find what that problem is. He will discover that there is a material variance of long standing with a tendency to go in one direction. Not only does this suggest a structural problem but also that the variance is cumulative and if followed through to a world balance sheet will have created extremely large discrepancies. He would then apply double entry accounting.

The strength of double entry is to ensure that there is no escape. If the item is not in one place, it must be in another. If it is not in one period it must be in another. If it is not an asset it must be an expense and so forth. Given enough time and resources our diligent accountant will be able to verify all of these significant items, one way or the other. He begins with a discrepancy and it has to find a home. If he then checks all of the possible material causes and does not resolve the discrepancy then he has disproved the comfortable assumption that all those quirky business and financial market differences balance out overall. In fact, the Statistical Task Force will have carried out a process very similar to our forensic accounting hero but the discrepancy has only worsened.

It is only too easy to dismiss the discrepancy as a technical imperfection. It is much more serious than that. It implies that the whole structure of economic theory applied to financial markets has not and apparently cannot be verified at the global level. There are many explanations of these market differences but they do not meet the test of conventional logic let alone the most fundamental of accounting verification. Something has to bridge the gap to explain what is happening. I call it Antilogic.

In this book we will examine the influence of Antilogic on the behaviour of corporations and financial markets. My primary focus is on the world of business and finance but we will find that the practical examples are not adequately explained by conventional finance theory and I borrow from the worlds of physics and mathematics. I suspect that the influence of Antilogic is just as strong in other aspects of society.

What is Antilogic? In subsequent chapters we will explore its nature and development but first we need to be very clear as to what is meant by the word Antilogic. I searched *The Macquarie Dictionary* for guidance. The Anti- prefix gives the important clue as this has the core meaning; 'against' or 'opposed to'. Particularly relevant additional meanings are; rival or spurious, pseudo, the opposite of or reverse of, not, un, placed opposite, moving in the reverse or opposite direction.

So, there is nothing random or uncontrolled about Antilogical. It may be just as elegant as logic but simply comes from a different direction, possibly or even probably the opposite direction. We will also see that sometimes the direction is not as important as the motivation of the perpetrator. I will show that Antilogic need not be ineffective for the perpetrator, simply that it is not at all in line with the conventional expectations of organizational or financial market theories.

Antilogic is to be strictly distinguished from nonsense. Nonsense is defined as that which makes no sense or is lacking in sense, words without sense or conveying absurd ideas, senseless or absurd action, foolish conduct, foolish notions, etc., absurdity. Nonsense may share some of the whimsical features of Antilogic but it is fundamentally different because nonsense reflects a lack of sense. Nonsense is not sense or the absence of sense. It is a sort of sense vacuum.

A possible alternative label might have been unlogic (or even unreason as used by management pundit Charles Handy) but I have rejected this as being too restrictive. The prefix *un* means *not* giving a negative or opposite force comes close to what I have in mind but although it captures the idea of opposite it fails to include the concept of rival or spurious.

Antilogic has logic but of a different kind. In this regard, its relation to logic is very similar to the relation of antimatter to matter (a subject we will pursue in Chapter XII). *The Macquarie Dictionary* defines antimatter as 'matter (sometimes hypothetical) consisting of antiparticles, contact between antimatter and matter results in the annihilation of both with the production of gamma radiation'. So, we see clearly that antimatter is a sort of matter but of a fundamentally different, indeed conflicting, kind.

The whimsical, unfamiliar or even extraordinary nature of Antilogic can prompt the impolite categorization as Bull. Again, this is a definitional mistake. Bull is defined by *The Macquarie Dictionary* as 'excessive talk, which is usually boastful, exaggerated and unreliable'. This confusion is related to the style of delivery and the temptation to forcefully reject the unfamiliar. But there is nothing inherently boastful, exaggerated or unreliable about Antilogic.

Antilogic, therefore in summary, is very much the opposite of logic. It may look logical but in fact is not. It is logic through the looking glass, just like logic but reversed. Just as with vision, if the image and its mirror image meet there is nothing to see. It is also close to being the opposite of paradox. As mentioned in the preface, paradox looks strange but is valid. Antilogic looks valid but actually is strange.

The use of the word Antilogic has very early origins, being associated with a group of philosophers in ancient Greece who were known as Sophists. Their most prominent member was Protagoras and they often found themselves in competition with Plato and his followers who did not appreciate the Sophists' success in argument. The Platonic writings make frequent reference to what Plato calls 'eristic' (Greek eristikos, fond of wrangling) and 'antilogic'. Ever since, the two often have been incorrectly treated as identical. Eristic, for Plato, consists in arguments aimed at victory rather than at truth. Antilogic involves the assignment to any argument of a counter argument that negates it, with the implication that both argument and counter argument are equally true. We will take this concept further and explore whether argument and counter argument negate each other or whether one prevails. We will discover that Antilogic can have an existence independent of its matching logic. We will also discover the Ancient Greek contribution to corporate governance, forecasting, banking methods and debt restructuring.

There are many sorts of Antilogic in the modern world of finance. It is frequently the inappropriate application of logic or application in the wrong situation or wrong direction. This inappropriate application often stems from use of conventional wisdom to such an extent that the financial cliché can be seen as the essence of Antilogic. Antilogic is pervasive, takes many forms and is continuing to evolve. It is a mystery how this happens, as there do not seem to be any new financial clichés these days. Practitioners often do not realize that the actual situation has changed and so Antilogic can be created inadvertently or by habit.

Because of the tendency of groups to seek consensus it is quite common for the position of logic and Antilogic to reverse. I have provided many intriguing and whimsical examples of Antilogic both because they are entertaining in themselves but also in the hope that humour will serve to point out these logical flaws in a pleasant manner. Antilogic is the counter position to logic but is not just the application of reverse logic. It very much includes rival logic demonstrating individual actions clearly against the stated objectives of the organization but supportive of the individual's logic and objectives. This is a rival or spurious logic according to the theory of the firm or of the market but it may be appropriate for the individual. As it turns out, Antilogic indeed does have a tendency to eliminate logic when the two come in contact.

It is difficult to be comprehensive but the common characteristic of Antilogic is the explanation that looks better than the ultimate outcome. The purpose of Antilogic is to explain an action or to prompt an action by the audience. The success of Antilogic depends on the audience and their reaction. Inherent to the effectiveness of Antilogic is the willingness of the audience to accept the argument made. This is, in turn, greatly influenced by the performer and the circumstances of the performance. The creators of Antilogic would not bother unless they anticipate some advantage from an approving audience.

Rank and file practitioners may not be able to distinguish logic from Antilogic and for many it no longer matters. Often the explanation can be found in human nature but a pattern emerges of Antilogic being associated with particular professions, market circumstances and economic theories.

This book describes the background conditions that encourage the creation of Antilogic. A process of categorization gives an insight into the main types of Antilogic, the conditions that favour its occurrence, how it may be recognized and explores the world of cash based on Antilogic.

Chapter I explores those beliefs we hold for things the way they are and always have been. Curiously, although it seems that things have always been the same there are fashions that cause the immutable to change quite often and unpredictably. We are often aided in this transition by our willingness to be influenced by the judgement of the larger group. Our participation with the group may be to provide us with a simple alternative to decision making but is often to provide the protection found in large numbers. None of this aids the quality of the decision making, as we will find that the outcome is the result of persuasion by important people who do not take kindly to disagreement. In financial circles this importance comes from existing success as measured by corporate size or personal wealth. The ability of the important to justify their good fortune in terms of social virtue can be taken to the extent of being quasi-religious dogma.

Chapter II shows how business personalities and corporate governance generate the Antilogic concept in the business environment. The corporations are the prize business exhibits of the democracies. Yet the functioning of the corporation itself owes little to principles of democracy. And the theory assumes that, contrary to their self-interest, management is expected to work diligently in the interests of the shareholder. In this chapter we will explore the inner working of the corporation and try and find out whether it is the inherent decision making expertise of the corporation that permits the markets to function efficiently. We discover that the CEO credibility cycle provides a predictable financial dynamic within companies. There are a few exceptional personalities who can escape the gravitational pull of the efficient market as manifest by the CEO credibility cycle and these form a class of their own.

Chapter III explores whether the perfect market compensates for the imperfections of the corporation. The efficient market theory rejects the impact of personalities in determining the outcome of business and markets. We will explore the fatalistic expectations of those who believe in the invisible hand of the market. Chapter IV describes how some Antilogic is created when words are mistaken for action or when the objective is mistaken or reversed. An easy way for making our decisions is to accept the views of others. In Chapter V we explore the Antilogic created by accountants and, in Chapter VI, further Antilogic created by statisticians.

The expected outcome of action causes the need for predictions about the future as we strive for competitive advantage ahead of the perfect market. Some forecasts are better than others are as we see in Chapter VII when we consider non-forecast-forecasts.

Antilogic can flourish easily when there is a widespread willingness to accept a plausible label without much concern as to the contents it supposedly describes. In Chapter VIII, The Amazing Role of Cash we make the important discovery that much of Antilogic stems from accepting as money something different and less substantial. I define this to be Vapourcash and its special form, Anticash. The presence of Vapourcash and Anticash are good clues to Antilogic and so we explore how these commonly occurring forms of unofficial money come about and the role they play with Antilogic.

What is Vapourcash? As the name implies it is something that looks and sounds impressive but lacks substance and drifts away and upward when you try to grasp it. Vapourcash is explained in Chapter IX. It is created in a wide range of circumstances and for a wide range of motives. It can be general and neutral in manner with the individuals not conscious that they are generating Vapourcash. Consequently they need have no specific motivation relating to its use. For many, their actions are prompted by habit, by political pressure or an honest wish to do the right thing.

Anticash is a special form of Vapourcash created at or near the moment of bankruptcy when the normal rules of accountancy are abandoned during financial crises. This is explained in Chapter X together with its role in the history of money. The bankers are the high priests in the creation of money of all sorts and their role is revealed in Chapter XI together with the inspired support they receive from the accountants.

Once we understand what the label really is covering we can explore in greater depth the role that money plays in perpetuating Antilogic. The concepts are not widely publicized as yet due to the persistent but simplistic reliance on the tangible comfort of so-called real cash. A digression into the history of money quickly reveals that there is nothing very real about real cash. Vapourcash may sound insubstantial but it cannot be less substantial than cash itself.

Adding the parallels gleaned from the physicists about Antimatter in Chapter XII will permit us to solve the logical imbalance of the world in the closing recapitulation and advice.

Our references to experts often include particular terminology that is translated, where necessary, into the language of Antilogic. By its nature, Antilogic in the financial world is presented as self evidently correct and expressed in positive terms. In pointing out the traps of Antilogic the experts I quote sometimes express their examples in negatives. Consequently we must be alert to the switch between positive and negative description. I provide a commentary that will help you judge which way to interpret these. The help of experts is illuminating but remember that there are many false prophets and no individual has the monopoly on truth. Some of this guidance may lead you gently down the garden path but, after all, the difference of opinion simply reflects the reality of the markets. Any sensible market participant must exercise judgement on an array of conflicting information. The goal of studying Antilogic is the resolution of confusion and I hope that I will encourage you to look through the vapour to find outcomes that are to your personal benefit.

I

BELIEVING BECAUSE OF THE WAY THINGS ARE AND WHY WE THINK THE WAY WE DO

IN THE world of finance we are bombarded with information. There is an ever expanding media industry that tries to help us by publicizing the views of relevant politicians, regulators, economists, commentators and investors. We are presented with reports of regulatory action, analysis, forecasts, predictions and comment. Much of this is delivered with great certainty but the outcomes continue to surprise the market, although it is never a surprise to today's pundit whatever he may have said yesterday.

How is the individual to decide what to do? It helps to have an external guide to help form our beliefs. In this complex world people in general and investors in particular draw comfort from rules or conventions to guide their decisions. Sometimes these rules are directly determined in the guidance that they give. In other situations the influence is indirect with a respected person or institution pointing the way for the individual. Increasingly this guidance can stem from the tradition or prestige of an organization. But organizations are made up of individuals. These individuals can be insistent in pressing the validity of their advice and do not take kindly to competition or criticism.

One class of decision making support is to follow the sure fire rule especially if everyone else is doing the same. It is human nature to go along with the flow, justified on the basis that everyone else cannot be wrong. Being part of the crowd is certainly more comforting than standing alone, especially if taking that position attracts the attention of important critics. We all tend towards the consensus and the finance world is no different. This makes us feel more comfortable when our actions are in tune with the crowd and this finds its most obvious manifestation in our adherence to fashion. Economics is subject to fashion and that makes it easy for us to believe those theories that everyone else believes at the time.

Some analysts have noticed that some patterns in the investment world repeat themselves. They are fashions but they seem to follow a pattern so that the fashion cannot be seen as independent or spontaneous. Sometimes these are formalized for example as in the investment clock as the analyst attempts to predict the next stage of the investment pattern. Of course this encourages groups of investors to attempt to anticipate the fashion by switching their investments out of the current fashion and into the expected next fashion. This can become a self-fulfilling prophecy as bigger and bigger groups of investors try to get the advantage over the rest. This introduces a dynamic element to fashion that, because of its repeating nature, is known as rotating fashion.

The economic cycle is thought to follow a repeating pattern whereby certain sectors lead or lag economic growth up to the peak that leads into decline and ultimate recovery and repeats. All economic cycles are assumed to follow the same pattern and each investment class will have its consistent place in relation to the cycle. This stylized image suggests that investments follow a predictable pattern akin to the hours of day. Assuming that the day starts from the depressed position of the cycle the investor is encouraged to buy bonds and as the day progresses to buy yield stocks, then bank stocks and on to cyclicals, growth stocks, property and so forth. As the clock moves around to nine o'clock and on to midnight, the cycle is reaching and then going over the peak and the investor is recommended to take defensive positions or leave the market. Strangely enough the advocates of the investment clock tend to go quiet during this period. The theory is that the investor need only know the time by the investment clock to know what investment to make. This is reflected in the stock market and indeed is thought by some to precede the actual economic impact. Because investors are expecting this sort of cycle they are looking for signs that the time has come to move from the currently booming sector to the one that the pattern suggests will be the next. Thus for example, the resources sector may be popular with investors early in the cycle but will be suddenly deserted as investor sentiment now rotates towards the banking sector. By implication of the term, it is expected that further in the cycle the investor will desert the banks and via other intervening sectors will ultimately return to resources. The investment decision is thus determined not by the inherent worth of the stock or sector but by whose turn it is.

The dictates of fashion, cycle and rotation are too generic to suit those investors who like to find evidence of superior performance in particular shares or, more precisely, in the performance of the business. These business experts often have a favourite measure that will reliably inform as to the actual performance of the business. These magic measures are used to interpret or replace whole volumes of financial analysis. They may also be called rules of thumb. Each industry has its favourite but a few examples are cost income ratio and tier one adequacy level for banks, revenue growth and customer acquisition numbers for Internet stocks, etc. Despite the numeric objectivity claimed by their exponents, these measures are also very much subject to fashion as in the recession the favourite measures all relate to head count saving and rationalization benefits and in the boom relate to growth, innovation and customer acquisition. The drive of fashion is accelerated by the tendency for alert operators to optimize the measure rather than the business. A further problem arises when an exponent of a measure suitable for one industry applies it in another. The natural progression of magic numbers is that of the analyst who can use numbers to evaluate any situation so as to come up with the definitive numerical proof of any market price, although the explanation may subsequently be found to be inadequate.

There are even examples where the numbers go beyond confirming the action, they actually determine the action. This is the index impact. Share market indices have become so important in measuring investment performance that the funds will have to take their share just because the stock is in the index. If rocketing share price and global mergers lead to index participation above portfolio limits there can be technical problems solved by creating new indices with the built in excuses of correction to portfolio limits. The index effect is created by the business risk for fund managers who cannot risk being underweight in highly overpriced markets in case it becomes even more overpriced. Investors and particularly pension fund trustees would not admit to speculation but the desire for performance by trustees can lead to speculation through creating an employment risk for fund managers who do not speculate with their clients' funds in overpriced markets.

The index impact can become self-perpetuating as in the example of Newscorp. Traditionally the Australian institutions had not been followers of Newscorp, possibly because the bulk of its business is now outside Australia. However, the strength of the share price forced those same institutions to bring Newscorp up to index weighting at least. This forced the disposal of any other liquid stocks to make room, reducing their share of the index and increasing that of Newscorp still further. The sudden move to technology stocks created the same effect. The drive to follow the index, no matter what, is akin to a thunderstorm created by a rapidly rising column of air (Newscorp) balanced by an equally violent downward flow elsewhere (the rest). This phenomenon will continue until it stops. The only uncertainty is how violent will the process be and, as we know, it is very difficult to forecast the weather.

This concept of the share price having to go in a particular direction takes its generic form in the Weight of Money argument that states that so much investment in compulsory superannuation, American 401K and other savings plans means that the money has to be invested somewhere. As a result of best practice, portfolio advisors and regulation of the investment portfolios follow a consistent composition. The market for particular asset classes or shares has to go up even though the returns are low or uncertain. A similar concept is the Wall of Money that is periodically predicted to be about to escape from Japan. This is a two-stage metaphor as the image is of a wave made of money sweeping towards a particular investment class. Perhaps it is because investors are optimists but there does not seem to be a reverse direction associated with this concept. As we explore the ideas of Vapourcash further we will have reason to question the weight of a wall of money made of vapour? The bankers come close. They are sometimes more pessimistic (to be honest they are manic depressive alternating between euphoria and overwhelming gloom) and so routinely use the expression credit crunch to describe what happens in those periods when no credit (i.e. money) is available for even the strongest business case. There is a whole body of opinion and copious academic research based on the ability of the market to value future events and individual shares that should preclude mood swings emanating from different organizations. We will return to the impact of the market in Chapter IV.

Often we believe the way we do out of loyalty to the group. Supporting the cause is the somewhat tautological cornerstone of the business team objective. It gives the members something to believe in, to strive for or maybe just to follow. We believe in what we believe in. We are here, so we must believe in the cause. If we did not believe we would not be here. This inevitably leads to not only the language but also the behaviour of the religious or military group, the combination of the two, or the modern replacement, the sporting team. We find reference to chasing the Holy Grail, embarking on a crusade, the great march, a jihad. There are the great corporate competitive battles between one carbonated beverage and another, between different automobiles or brands of soap. The advantage of invoking slogans with religious or political connotations is that there is no need to be specific as to the cause or the objectives. It would be very bad form to question such a worthy campaign.

The easy to support idea finds its generic form in the self-evident truth. This is a very popular form of justification within corporations, as it requires only a little grammatical confusion and no pangs of conscience. So long as the reason appears satisfactory to oneself, particularly if you are important, then that is sufficient and there is no need to demonstrate any inherent truth in the idea itself.

A more aggressive variation is the no-brainer. This is currently a very popular expression suggesting a self-evident truth but is more overt in impugning the intellectual capacity of anyone who does not agree. When you hear the phrase you can be sure no brain has been used. The invocation of no-brainer can operate in a way akin to playing a trump in a card game. It is played to terminate a brain storming session at the company conference. No one has a card to beat the trump. The claim of no-brainer is strongly correlated to pronouncements from the Big Boss, in which case all brains have been temporarily disconnected. This is not necessarily at the wish of the Big Boss as it naturally arises where a cohesive team seeks to please. But it is difficult to tell the difference as it also arises with the dictatorial boss in which case it is wise to anticipate where the big intellect wants to go.

This situation can be conveniently reversed when things go wrong by using the slogan 'Who could have predicted it (the disaster) because nobody is perfect'. This implies that this outcome was too unpredictable for any sensible brain to have contemplated it. Supporting comments are 'would you have done better' with the follow up to any unwelcome retorts being 'it is easy with 100% hindsight'. At least this exchange is more consistent than the other common response, which is 'I told you so,' although not everyone can remember when this telling was done. It is bad enough to say it after the event but much worse to have said it before. Later we will pursue the possibility of covering all eventualities but we see here the basis of the aphorism 'success has many fathers but failure is an orphan'.

Irving L. Janis in *Victims of Groupthink* coined the term Groupthink to describe the strange outcome of coherent groups. He detected that some of the world's greatest political disasters had been provoked by the actions of groups that, on the face of it, displayed very positive organizational attributes. Blunders or errors of judgement are always possible but Janis' contribution was to discover that those positive attributes themselves were the cause. He found that members of cohesive groups develop informal objectives that value unanimity more highly than realistically appraising alternative courses of action. The protection of the very positive attributes of the clubby atmosphere and mutual reinforcement provides the perfect environment for the negative impact of error but also the possibility of negative manipulation as specifically identified by Janis with a parallel drawn with George Orwell's *1984*. The choice of the term Groupthink was intentionally chosen to resemble the *newspeak* vocabulary such as *doublethink* and *crimethink* with all the invidious implications.

This parallel applies particularly well in business, especially with the use of public relation techniques that come close to propaganda and management image making that is similar to the Big Brother personality cult highlighted by Orwell. The key theme is the capability of cohesive and well-intentioned groups to seriously blunder. Janis detected key decision-defects that contributed to the problems when the group or members failed to use their positive attributes to discover the best option. There is a tendency to limit discussion to only a few alternative courses of action and fail to check these out for non-obvious pitfalls. They also neglect to consider whether the courses of action initially rejected could be remedied by non-obvious gains previously overlooked or reducing seemingly prohibitive costs. Once determined on a course of action the group makes little effort to obtain information from experts and is selective in reacting to factual information and relevant judgement from others. Great interest is shown in facts and opinions that support their initially preferred policy. Facts and opinions that do not support their initially preferred policy tend to be ignored with the retort 'They would say that!' Little time is devoted to considering how the chosen policy might be hindered by inertia, sabotaged, or common accidents that happen to the best-laid plans and so they fail to work out contingency plans to cope with foreseeable setbacks. These possible impacts are often covered by Murphy's Law, which states that anything that can go wrong will go wrong. In the environment of Groupthink this Law holds no sway so no contingencies are considered.

A very common circumstance that illustrates the Groupthink effect is the brainstorming session held during a business conference. This is akin to

Groupthink in a pressure cooker. Months of strategic planning are replaced by lists written on the whiteboard during the last five minutes before the group must report back to the plenary session. Everyone wants to do their bit to finish the task before dinner and they all hope that Murphy's law will be suspended in this case.

Janis was not happy to accept 'nobody is perfect' as an all enveloping excuse for inexplicable disasters at competent organizations and looked for the reasons which he found in the psychology of groups.

> Nietzsche went so far as to say that madness is the exception in individuals but the rule in groups. A considerable amount of social science literature shows that in circumstances of extreme crises, group contagion occasionally gives rise to collective panic, violent acts of scapegoating, and other forms of what could be called group madness. Much more frequent, however are instances of mindless conformity and collective misjudgement of serious risks, which are collectively laughed off in a clubby atmosphere of relaxed conviviality. ... The group members know that no one among them is a superman, but they feel somehow the group is a supergroup, capable of surmounting all risks that stand in the way of carrying out any desired course of action: 'Nothing can stop us!' Athletic teams and military combat units often benefit from members' enthusiastic confidence in the power and luck of their group. But policy-making committees do not.[3]

He is rather uncharitable when he raises the unwelcome possibility that fiascos could be other than for technical reasons unforeseeable by the perpetrators. He even raises the dreaded words, stupidity and erroneous intelligence (I am not sure if a pun is intended here), information overload, fatigue, blinding prejudice, and ignorance. He goes on to conclude that decisions suffering from these defects have relatively little chance of success but I must take issue with this last conclusion. Many of business' greatest successes and the resulting heroes have been firmly based on the foundation of defect. More precisely, I should add that the link between success and hero is very weak. Indeed it may well be the inverse, as many a hero has gained credit for a success he or she did not create and many a hero has been created in spite of, or even because of, a fiasco.

Actually Janis waters down his earlier statement when he states that Groupthink is but one cause of a fiasco.

> Simply because the outcome of a group decision has turned out to be a fiasco, I do not assume that it must have been the result of Groupthink or even that it was the result of defective decision-making. Nor do I expect that every defective decision, whether arising from Groupthink or from other causes

will produce a fiasco. Defective decisions based on misinformation and poor judgement lead to successful outcomes. ... We must acknowledge that chance and stupidity of the competition can give a silk-purse ending to a command decision worth less than a sow's ear. Groupthink is conducive to errors in decision-making, and such errors increase the likelihood of a poor outcome. Often the result is a fiasco, but not always.[4]

This conclusion regarding Groupthink is very useful in illustrating the possibilities of Antilogic. He is telling us that there are many causes for fiascos and that fiascos can turn out well. It is to be expected that the badly done will turn out badly but it is Groupthink's contribution to warn us that in some circumstances that things turn out badly specifically because they were done well according to some criteria. This may have crucial implications for business because many of the positive attributes advocated in improving team and organizational effectiveness aim to create circumstances very similar to major symptoms identified in Groupthink. This is illustrated by the following series of positive phrases often heard in the team building situation. To each I have added the Groupthink characteristic revealed.

– 'We are winners'. An illusion of invulnerability, which creates excessive optimism and encourages taking extreme risks.
– 'They would say that wouldn't they?' Collective efforts to rationalize in order to discount warnings. An unquestioned belief in the group's inherent morality.
– 'We are the good guys. They are the enemy'. Stereotyped views of competing leaders as too evil to warrant genuine attempts to negotiate. (If they too are victims of Groupthink this belief may be warranted.)

Other common phrases also apply so that the Group maintain unanimity and discipline.

– 'We are all in this together'. Self-censorship of deviations from apparent group consensus.
– 'Are you with us or against us?' Direct pressure on any member who expresses strong arguments against any of the group's stereotypes, illusions or commitments.
– 'If any of you have a contrary view speak up now'. A shared illusion of unanimity.
– 'The Boss will be disappointed unless...!' The emergence of self-appointed mindguards.

For middle managers the law of the jungle applies. It is wise not to attract attention. Top managers are like the predators as they seek to impose their will on the organization, often supported by the new ideas brought by the management consultants.

The cohesiveness of the team in the Groupthink situation seems remarkable until we look at how prevalent it is in nature. Mutual support is inherent in the idea of the herd, flock and swarm. The individual co-operates in their appointed place to make the community great and clearly this is achieved without the benefit of language, personal computers or management consultants.

The individual middle manager on his own can never resist the new ideas and certainly would never challenge the predators, the lions, of the organization. However, adapting to the periodic new ideas is both inconvenient and risky. The individual might not know how, when and which direction to jump. Logically they follow the jungle defence and form into flocks, herds, swarms or schools of indistinguishable fellow participants. Any collective metaphor is good but the image of the herd of zebra is particularly appropriate. The life of the zebra is pleasant, comfortable and honourable. The zebra with his fellows lives on the Africa veldt under the warm sun, eating the plentiful grass and free to roam where their collective will takes them. The zebra can out-run or outfight most predators. From time to time the lion comes and roars his threat about a new paradigm or cultural change. For the zebra the choice is easy. He goes on eating the grass and frolicking under the sun. The cost of changing his behaviour is far too high compared to the minute chance that the lion will catch this particular zebra. After all the lion cannot eat more than one zebra at once and there are many zebras. The zebra has one further advantage in corporate life. When he is called upon to change from black to white no one can tell whether he has complied. Better still, when the zebras are together the lion cannot tell when one finishes and another begins.

Sometimes, the herd's productive energy is misdirected as in the lemmings' march. The troops loyally support the lemming leader as they rush to disaster or salvation. At least they will not be alone. The numbers supporting a well entrenched CEO do not prove the wisdom of his actions. We have to question whether problems arise because of misguided leaders who take their troops in the wrong direction or leaderless masses that look for someone or something that appears to fit the bill.

Another source of Antilogic is the power of the really big idea. We are vulnerable to ideas that promise great wealth or predict big trouble. To be effective as panics these forecast disasters have to be of gigantic proportions because of the need to get attention amongst all the other influences that are being canvassed every day. We try to build defences and so teach our children about the folly of Chicken Little who on reasonable evidence predicted that the sky was falling. Yet business has a remarkable capacity to be fearful of similar problems. Periodically the financial markets fall for some reason such as the millennium computer bug, derivatives, emerging market debt or other disasters. In the old days this used to be an irrational panic to prevent a new disaster that looks very like a disaster from the past that everybody missed. Now there is an element of misguided rational thought. Since corporation law has tightened up on the personal liabilities of directors they now seek to ensure that all bases are covered so that they can never be liable for having missed anything. A compliance program is initiated to solve the problem with special attention to identifying the management who would be to blame in any subsequent lawsuit. Many such programs will be undertaken so it is quite likely that the new disaster will arrive while everyone is busy with Chicken Little programs. The new disaster will lead to redoubled efforts.

Those who doubt that the Millennium bug was a Chicken Little program must ask two questions. Why is it that all previous major technology programs were always late and had such major glitches that they never worked perfectly first time yet Y2K was amazingly successful? And why were those less sophisticated countries enjoying a reasonable usage of computers but who undertook no Y2K preparations, so blessedly free of adverse consequences? It is easy to be wise after the event but it is also difficult to resist requests for unlimited resources on the basis that otherwise the sky will fall in.

Because the collective attention span is so difficult to capture for long enough to get a consensus it is important that the choice proffered is simple. Those that understand the drivers of public opinion realize that only limited choice should be offered. No alternative position should be given. The Antilogic is then created by the presence of those alternatives not considered. The absence of real choice simplifies the decision making process but still leaves the individual feeling responsible for making a decision and the worry that it still has to be the correct choice. It would be far more reassuring if there were other factors that would indicate who else might be trusted to make a decision on your behalf. This natural tendency to look for the easy way out, to find someone to decide on our behalf has led to an opportunity for those who would oblige.

This honour may fall to those great organizations that should know what they are doing. They are big and powerful. Often they have been around forever or at least looking as though they have been and should know more than any individual. The bigger they are the smarter they must be. Success is measured in size but there is a problem. Who is thinking on behalf of the giant corporation and what is their objective?

John Kenneth Galbraith has had an amazingly long and successful career. He has written several very perceptive and entertaining books about money and world financial affairs. He is a very keen observer of financial decision-making and its motivation. He is sceptical that size is the best credential for perception. He goes further. The sheer size of the organization is likely to have rewarded the conventional in their climb to the top and shielded them from the consequences of their decisions.

> In practice, the individual or individuals at the top of these institutions are often there because, as happens regularly in great organizations, theirs was mentally the most predictable and, in conse-quence, bureaucratically the least inimical of the contending talent. He, she, or they are then endowed with the authority that encourages acquiescence from their subordinates and applause from their acolytes and that excludes adverse opinion or criticism. They are thus admirably protected in what may be a serious commitment to error.[5]

If size is not the test of wisdom then perhaps it is something else. Is money the acid test of good decision-making? After all something must have been done well to come with the gratifying end result. The banks have the money and this could be a clue that they have the financial wisdom on which we can rely. Certainly their stock in trade is the giving of financial advice. This is not only in the course of the business where bankers and financial planners tell us how to organize our affairs but it goes further with bank economists predicting what will happen with markets and the economy. Bank CEOs go beyond prediction, being prepared to advise regulators and politicians as to what is good for the nation.

One possible basis to accept this advice is the deference due to lenders. This comes naturally for a combination of reasons. The handling and disposition of large sums of money puts the lender constantly in the position where his judgement is required in major transactions and over time the influence of the large sums begins to augment the individuals' mental capacities and reinforce the bankers' willingness to give advice. Of course this leads to a predictable level of deference from those who need the money so a mutually reinforcing cycle develops with no need for self scrutiny. Who would be there to rock the boat?

A second influence is our self-interested need to preserve business confidence no matter what advice the banker gives. If confidence is dented, investment is reduced and the recovery is delayed so accuracy is less important than support.

As the sums become larger the recipients quickly become reconciled to the wisdom of accepting the advice. Thus, the bankers are conditioned by years of supplicants hanging on their every word because of the periodic need to be looked on favourably when a loan is needed. It is a symmetrical situation in that both the banker and the supplicant are convinced of the wisdom of the advice. This effect does not only apply to bankers. It is caused by money. It makes no difference whose money it is. The very rich receive very similar attention although the money in question is theirs. The wealth aids both their ability and confidence. If you are rich you must be smart.

Unfortunately the corollary is also true. If you are no longer rich then you cannot have been so smart after all, thereby establishing that the presence or absence of money adjusts the level of intelligence. Fred Schwed saw it differently as a correlation between money and intelligence. If financial success came from superior intelligence then a subsequent absence of wealth must also imply a reduction of brainpower.

> When a speculator is riding the crest he does indeed give a convincing appearance of infallibility. Not only are all beholders impressed, but he cannot help being impressed with himself. The deference he receives from his associates, his rivals and the headwaiters of night clubs is a sincere and moving thing. But when he starts to toboggan down the other side of the hill, what becomes of the wisdom that was so evident a short time before? Who has gotten inside his skull and tampered with that fine brain?[6]

Fortunately the recession passes and new wealth emerges, probably in new hands. The link between money and intelligence implies that new intelligence must be at work. The presence of this new money brings with it a renewed willingness to perceive financial genius and accept again that a role of financial innovation will avoid the recurrence of past problems. This is likely to end in disappointment as economic recovery is like the cycle of the seasons. We have left winter and entered spring where everything is green and we see the flowers as though they are new and were never before present. This lack of awareness or forgetfulness is Antilogic because most of this innovation is really the same old financial structures presented in more favourable circumstances and possibly with a new twist. The same outcome can be expected as before. In due time winter comes again.

Money in the financial market fulfils the role of the sun in the seasons. Money from the banks and investors is needed to encourage the shoots of innovation and to ripen the golden crop of summer but by winter no warming fuel is to be found. This seasonal change in lending requires the banker to change his/her willingness to lend, and the nature of financial innovation and the strength of security demanded. Another way of achieving an identical level of innovation is to vary not only the strength of the security but also the degree of realism of the assets. The methods of the banks make it more likely that after the past financial disaster the security documentation is rock solid but the object of the security is a Vapour asset. A cycle can be seen at work here as well. Soon after the most recent financial crises the banks are not prepared to lend at all. As financial fear slowly subsides the bank lends only against excessive and very real security. Further into the cycle, provoked by competition, the bank relaxes its requirements for security. The documentation looks just as good but the security is now taken on Vapour assets. The emphasis moves during the cycle from lending against real cashflow, to Vapourcash flow until ultimately no security is required at all. The pronouncements of caution from the central banks will not be very helpful, as by definition these have to be non-controversial to preserve confidence.

Do not expect to be able to check the judgement of one banker by comparing it with another because they will all be the same. Keynes observed sixty years ago that sound bankers have a tendency to flock together. He found that they would rather be respectably wrong together than unconventionally correct so that no one can really blame them.

Finding a banker that agrees with you is also no test of soundness. Indeed in easy times you will always find a banker to agree with your proposals. After all the bankers you deal with are in the business of selling money especially since the recent trend of separating lending from risk management as explained by Alistair McAlpine a man with considerable experience with bankers.

> To those who start out in business and are unfamiliar with bankers, these people seem to take the role of referee. They look at your accounts and give what appears to be an impartial view as to the success or otherwise of your business. If they say you are successful, then you are flattered and pleased, thus making an easy and willing victim for those who would sell you money, for that is what bankers do when they make a loan. If they tell you that your business is worthless you are angry, depressed, and you visit yet more bankers until you succeed in borrowing – and if times are good, you will find someone to lend money to you, even for the most crack-brained idea.[7]

It might be supposed that banks have something to do with business finance and so are staffed with finance people. This is a mistake as banks are full of bankers, a very different breed.

> In both instances, the person who would borrow money for the company regards the banker as one who understands business. This is the most terrible of errors, for a banker is a man or woman who understands banking, a very different matter from understanding business in general and your business in particular. Bankers are interested in only two matters: first can your business service the interest that they charge on lending your money and second, if all goes wrong, will there be enough money left to repay their debt?[8]

Just following the money is a too simplistic and crudely mercenary approach for many in determining their financial and economic beliefs. It is much more satisfying to be conforming with social norms. It is much more comfortable to be doing the right thing. This encourages us to hold views that are consistent with those of our fellow citizens. When social views effect financial policy we find that social virtue is determined by the powerful in society. This is in turn based on wealth and so we have a satisfying symmetry. The wealthy classes have or had the money so it is only appropriate that they determine the reaction to any financial crises. They also have the means to make their message heard, a practical consequence of the view that money talks. You will hear little official comment about radical solutions or these new forms of money until after they have become well established. The rich have always been slow to accept the new forms of money until they personally experienced how it would add to their wealth or until they were inevitably replaced as the socially influential by the beneficiaries of the new wealth. Incidentally, this might help explain why you had not heard of Vapourcash and Anticash before picking up this book.

The business organization is a microcosm of society and reflects similar conservative tendencies. Indeed the one reflects the other, providing mutual support. Respectability influences the individual within an organization and this in turn influences the quality of the economic decision. The top management of large corporations are chosen by system and find dissent uncomfortable. If the individual stands out or disagrees it is likely that they will be sidelined or eliminated. In the conventional society of believers the doubter or risk taker is quickly ridiculed or silenced. But it is too severe if this suggests that there is no room for dissent or the off the wall idea. Many organizations encourage this behaviour as a symbol of their inclusiveness and creativity. Yet there are restrictions as to the scope of this tolerance. For example, a brilliant but inexperienced youth is permitted or even encouraged to come up with unconventional views. This becomes uncomfortable, but survivable, if these views cut into the comfort zone of the experienced. After all youth must learn by its mistakes. However, it is totally unacceptable to be unconventional and turn out to be correct. The problem with dissent is that it implies criticism of the existing situation, existing ideas and existing authority. Paradoxically even the more eminent the sources of dissent are unlikely to be accepted as it still represents a threat to the current men of authority.

The pressure to conform need not be crude or dramatic. It is not simply admiration of the affluent that prompts a conventional response but also the hope of an amiable lifestyle. Often subtle pressure is imposed on individuals to absorb them into the group or team. It is very harmful to a social and working relationship and damaging to prospects when the in-crowd make quiet comments along the lines that 'he may be bright enough but he is not co-operative'. or 'he is undoubtedly brilliant but is he sound', or 'the results are great but what about common sense'. There are conventions which by definition one's political foes are not good team players and of course all of this is far too sensitive to be included in the annual appraisal.

Another technique is to defuse criticism with pre-emptive general attacks by those in authority against those who might comment. This might emphasize how easy it is to criticize without responsibility, the value of hindsight and the need to crash through or crash, and similar macho comments. It is not actually that easy to criticize without a feeling of guilt especially if there is a feeling that lifting one's head above the parapet will result in it being knocked off. Should anyone dare to criticize, it is easy for the elite to challenge the motives of the critic. The critic can be branded as being a destructive force on the side of the current enemy or bogeyman. As a result there is considerable inertia before serious criticism begins.

The defence mechanism of the social elite or establishment becomes so strong that it becomes like a religion. Paradoxically most religions preach against the dangers of money. Nevertheless the establishment created by the moneyed shares many of the features of religion including of course the creed, the special language, rituals, ceremonies and special places of worship. The economic religious functionaries closely guard all these aspects. The bankers and brokers make up the primary ranks of monetary priests with the economists providing the theology. The architecture of banks is supposedly intended to inspire the trust and awe of the depositors in the immutable strength of the institution but it is more than a fortuitous additional benefit that this awe is also accorded to the banking officers. The financial organs of the state in the form of central banks, government instrumentalities and courts also benefit to an exaggerated level from the support of splendid architecture, impenetrable language and carefully orchestrated ritual. The strength of this combination can be seen in the hullabaloo when Dr. Greenspan does or does not adjust interest rates. We can almost smell the incense propagated by his acolytes during the publication of innumerable vital economic indicators.

Those who make their living by forecasting, teaching and talking about money like to encourage the belief that they possess more than an passing acquaintance with black arts and the occult. These religious and magical parallels explain the widespread continuing acceptance of the general financial wisdom that prevailed prior to periods of crisis. The congregation guided by the same priests closes ranks after any crisis. They are happy in this solidarity, gaining comfort from having made the mistake together and seeing no reason why they personally should have the error exposed. Other reasons must be found.

> There will also be scrutiny of the previously much-praised financial instruments and practices – paper money; implausible securities issues; insider trading; market rigging; more recently, program and index trading – that have facilitated and financed the speculation. There will be talk of regulation and reform. What will not be discussed is the speculation itself or the aberrant optimism that lay behind it. Nothing is more remarkable than this: in the aftermath of speculation the reality will be all but ignored. There are two reasons for this. In the first place, many people and institutions have been involved, and whereas it is acceptable to attribute error, gullibility, and excess to a single individual or even to a particular corporation, it is not deemed fitting to attribute them to a whole community and

certainly not to the whole financial community. Widespread naiveté, even stupidity, is manifest; mention of this, however, runs drastically counter to the earlier-noted presumption that intelligence is intimately associated with money. The financial community must be assumed to be intellectually above such extravagance of error.[9]

We see from Galbraith that the word stupidity is too dreadful to be used about financial ruin. The intelligence had been there when we had been rich. It is bad enough that we have had to suffer from the money running away leading to present loss of intelligence without having to reappraise past intelligence. It is likely that the actual outcome was a random consequence of what we did. After all we only said we knew what we were doing.

When things have gone wrong there must be somebody to blame as the theology of the current financial religion cannot be at fault. A sin has been committed such as the carrying of excessive debt. Somebody must have sinned. Mistakes could only have arisen in our fine organization if there is a sinner in our midst whose actions have undermined the rest of the team. Somebody must have caused the disaster. This is the scapegoat that will atone for the sins of the establishment. Every group has one and some religions insist that one be present. In Dutch the same concept is called zondebok, being literally *sin goat*. The high priest sent the goat out into the wilderness carrying the sins of the tribe. So it is in business today.

Finding the scapegoat is not a problem, just round up the usual suspects. This should not be taken to excess. If all the usual suspects become scapegoats and are sent out into the wilderness they will no longer be around to be usual suspects. How would we then round up the usual suspects if there were none? The answer, as in the movie *Casablanca*, is to let most of them escape or be released for lack of evidence in which case no damage will be done. This is acceptable in the situation when the appearance of retribution is more important than the wish for actual punishment.

This list of suspects varies from firm to firm but there is a familiar pattern of people to blame. The bean counters are generally near the top and their numbers are generally unbelievably flawed. The Human Resources department is another favourite as are lazy salesmen, unnecessary government regulation except against the pesky foreign producers who dump their product here and so on. This is sufficient for public relations but when it becomes serious some named individuals in the firm must be blamed. The scapegoat need not always be an individual or organization. It can be a concept. The consultants tend to prefer this as it is harder to pin down a concept and there is less blood and unpleasantness if no individual is fingered.

In some cultures, the search for the scapegoat takes on much more serious connotations in that a victim must be found to purify the rest of the organization. If the sinner confessed his sin, the tribe was obliged to forgive him and welcome him back into the fold. Denial of the sin was taken as pride and prime facie evidence of guilt to be pursued without mercy. Confession does not seem to be working in business today. Through multiculturalism or modern pragmatism we have re-engineered the process to eliminate the forgiveness stage. This new harshness regards guilt as guilt and repentance is after all an admission of guilt. If the scapegoats confessed and were forgiven who would we have to blame and where would we find our cost savings.

After the big financial crises it will be particularly easy to find scape-goats, as the financial crash will have brought personal crashes as well. The loss of money implies loss of genius and also loss of defensive capability that, together with our macabre delight in seeing the once mighty suddenly fallen, provides many candidates.

As with religion, the wealth induced faith will have its saints, heretics and martyrs. We need not dwell on the saints because they can be found amongst the super wealthy. There will be plenty of heretics as there are many more aspiring to wealth than have it. Many will find it politic to keep their doubts to themselves and seek personal advantage in following the current dogma. Some speak out and we will try to resolve whether they speak Antilogic. Success or failure provides only a partial clue. We have seen in this chapter that pronouncements by the financial establishment are quite likely to be Antilogic but it is not necessarily so. Probability dictates that sometimes the establishment gets it right.

Those in power will defend their position and resist those perceived to be a threat. Of course ideas different to their own will be seen as a threat and they will react accordingly. Sometimes Mr. Big will want to be harsh so as to encourage the others. At other times he may have been personally involved and it will be necessary to declare a success. This may be the dynamic situation where we have the disaster that elevates Mr. Big and that will subsequently have to be seen in a new light. All of these situations may lead to show trials. These are not pleasant and dangerous for the career although often both prosecution and defendant are drawn from the ranks of consultants. There is also a specialist class of fall guy who may even be at the very highly paid CEO level.

With this background there are always going to be martyrs. Many people may suffer as a result of Antilogic but to be an Antilogic martyr one must have publicly identified the Antilogic before the decision that leads to a fiasco and then to be the most obvious scapegoat after the fiasco. Janis studied the Bay of Pigs fiasco in detail and identified a clear Antilogic martyr.

> The outsider was acting Secretary of State Chester Bowles... Bowles behaved in the prescribed way and confined his protestations to a State Department memorandum addressed to Secretary of State Rusk which was not communicated to the President. Chester Bowles was the first man in the new administration to be fired by President Kennedy. Some of Bowles' friends had told the press that he had opposed the Cuban venture and had been right in his forecasts about the outcome. Evidently this news annoyed the President greatly. This may have contributed to the President's solution to the problem of what to do about the inept leadership of the inefficient State Department bureaucracy. He decided to shift Bowles out of his position as second-in-command, instead of replacing Rusk, whom he liked personally and wanted to keep as a central member of his team. 'I can't do that to Rusk,' Kennedy later said when somebody suggested shifting Rusk to the United Nations. 'He is such a nice man'.[10]

It is safer to be sound than right. Those who are in authority determine who and what is sound. They do not take kindly to challenge. This sets the scene for the next chapter in which we apply this general principle to business and look more closely at how decisions are made and rewarded.

II

BELIEVING THE CORPORATION

THIS CHAPTER is about believing the pronouncements of important corporations. These organizations have considerable prestige, perhaps because of the large amounts of money they represent. This influence rubs off on the people that make up the management team and the non-executive directors who are the Greek chorus of corporate life. We discover how the organization works, its politics and the influences on the management team including the CEO credibility cycle and the win-win options game. We find that often there is a great business leader, the Stalin in the boardroom that tells us what to believe. We believe the great leader because we must.

The corporation is the organization of choice of the western democracies for the conduct of economic activity. They are the show exhibits of the free enterprise system and dominate international trade and global financial markets. The great corporations are the producers of the most sophisticated products even when government might be the customer as for infrastructure and instruments of war. This is hardly surprising given the accumulation by corporations of capital and intellectual resources far beyond the capability of the individual or partnership.

Despite the current ascendancy of the corporation, opinions as to its efficacy are mixed. Corporations are not always popular with everyone. Several authorities question the role the corporation plays in society and attribute many of society's deficiencies to the lack of corporate accountability. Saul uses a negative term corporatism, which he applies to any interest group whether specialist, professional, public or private, profit-oriented or not that share the characteristic that the primary relationship of individual members is to the organization and not to society at large. The loss of democracy is justified by the implied promise of better efficiency. He regards the modern corporation as the direct descendant of the medieval craft guild.

Antony Jay began his career in a government owned media corporation, which might explain both his view of the nature of the organization and his ability to so perceptively describe its functioning. From this basis he reviewed the company structure and its inhabitants in *Corporation Man*. In *Management and Machiavelli* he also draws out historic precedent with his image on the grander scale of the medieval kingdom with all its political intrigue.

> The power politics of the company itself we soon realize is no different from any other organization, whether church, university, army or club. It contains, like any human society, the elements of monarchy, aristocracy, nobility and democracy. ... Antony Jay[11] compares the modern corporation with the medieval kingdom. It is headed by a king, (or president or managing director) who is surrounded by his courtiers and advisers (directors and specialists) and who seeks to maintain his authority over his provinces, some near some far (divisions and subsidiaries), each immediately ruled by a baron (or plant manager) who may be either docile or turbulent and whose own authority (over his factory) may be effective or weak ... The competition for power is between the king, the courtiers and the barons.

The medieval court seems to me to be the more appropriate setting for the corporate life. The image of the craft guild quaint though it is does not conjure up an image of time wasting. Medieval craftsman without craft would not have lasted long. The life and death intrigues of the indulgent court seem a much more appropriate setting for endless meetings targeted against rivals rather than actually doing something. The kingdom at least had the resources to absorb the rivalries and jealousy.

The idea that the staff of the corporation is intrinsically less committed to the outcome than the individual is far from new. It was the subject of comment from the great and original Adam Smith more than two centuries ago where he expected directors to show less anxious vigilance for other peoples' money than partners in a private company would show for theirs.

Then came the excesses of the industrial revolution and the careers of the great industrial entrepreneurs. The twentieth century brought the growth of corporation and in reaction, the growth and subsequent reduction of government regulation. As we move into a new century the problem is loss of reality or substance stemming from the lack of ownership and the responsibility that goes with it.

Our modern economic doctrine still draws from Adam Smith the requirement that the management of the corporation maximize profits, yet these are for the benefit of owners rather than for themselves. This rather altruistic presumption provides an unstable basis to the theory of the firm. It is odd in that management has the power over the firm whereas the owners are notably without power. Indeed management is specifically engaged to have power and carry forth the execution of the business. Yet the expectation is that management will forgo its own interest in the selfless pursuit of profit maximization for shareholders.

If this immutable doctrine about making money were religious rather than economic there would be another doctrine directing money to society rather than to the individual. But the theory of the firm directs the rewards of enterprise not to society but to the shareholder. The connections between the actions of the manager and maximization of profit have several links and loose ones at that. At various times society has concluded that these links were too loose, resulting in corporate governance regimes to impose on business those disciplines that the theory tells us should happen automatically. Not surprisingly, this has led to frequent tensions between those who want an unfettered market and those who seek regulation.

What is management really trying to do amongst all this confusion? It could be the simple biological urge for survival but we can quickly dismiss the common self-serving exhortation of management to provide for its continuity by training successors. This emphasizes survival of the organization although these actions are often concentrated on dominant managers who recruit acolytes in their own image with the purpose of ensuring their own survival rather than permitting their departure. This is an example of a common form of corporate Antilogic. Do as I say, not what I do.

The desire for survival alone is not sufficient to explain management's actions. It must also be related to the concept of satisficing, which is doing just enough to get by comfortably. Economic theory often depends on the concept of maximizing, perhaps because the maths is simpler. Yet management behaviour suggests that the objective is to do just enough. Amiable survival can become the prime consideration of the current custodians of the corporation. Robert Townsend does not beat about the bush in his humorous best-seller *Up the Organization*. He was a successful chief executive and he knew what he was talking about when he set out the actual priorities of the corporation starting with the care and feeding of the chief executive, his entourage, and the board of directors (mostly his friends, put by him to ensure the tranquillity of his reign) and ranging through management, employees, to customers and well down the list to the shareholders. This attitude demonstrates the limit on the level of profit management needs to seek. Profitability is a means to an end with most managers, particularly in the higher echelon wishing to enjoy what they are doing. Profitability need only to be sufficient to deal with shareholder's needs and to ensure the survival of the organization. Once that is achieved the management group can enjoy themselves. They achieve this by ensuring that those other interest groups get enough to avoid a fuss. What is left over is for growth, interesting projects and play money devoted to the management group itself.

The controlling manager group retain power so long as earnings are sufficient to pay the regular dividends to shareholders and to provide reinvestment. This profit proviso need not be very onerous. In many successful corporations survival is not realistically in question although it is frequently mentioned to keep everyone on their toes. This occurs even when the ownership position is secure. One example is a consumer goods multinational that was take-over proof because of a complex ownership structure. Teams of accountants diligently ensured that all shareholder-reporting requirements were correctly met. But who acted on the reports they produced? No new share equity has ever been raised during the career of any current employee. So, for whom was the company managed? Initially it seemed to be managed in the interests of all management but for some reason the holders of power retreated further into the citadel. Life became tougher for management in general and they began to suffer the same rigours as elsewhere. After a time, internal pressures intensified, presumably as a result of external competition, benchmarking or some other Holy Grail. The power-group retreated further and the pressure to perform reached the general cadre of senior managers. Businesses were sold, structures downsized and the heroes of past battles were put out to pasture. Cost cutting exercises caused the regimental dinners to be cancelled and the old victories to be forgotten.

Considerable attention is indeed given by the corporation to the commitment, loyalty and morale of the business group to the extent of demanding participation of the individual to the exclusion of other activities. However, for the individual continued inclusion in this demanding club is far from secure. As corporate downsizing and take-overs have become more common a new paradox has emerged with company men clinging more closely to the idea of belonging in the face of declining security. They conspire with their employers in the pursuit of bonding with organizations that are more likely than ever before to dispense with their services. But there is only so much worrying the individual can do. Better to participate enthusiastically in the belief that the group that parties together is less likely to cast individuals aside. No one can be sure of the outcome but in the meantime it is best to enjoy the party and certainly try not to look like anyone who is drifting away from the group.

Simple survival for the individual is not enough. Contentment comes when just enough is done to achieve survival in comfort. The individual can take steps to improve their own contentment in a process that reduces aggravation by accepting the established action. Toning down individual thought reduces effort and makes it easier to accept the errors of private organizations. The contentment quotient is improved further by reducing the effort necessary to achieve a satisfactory outcome. Better still the avoidance of thought reduces the risk of taking decisions that might prove to be unpopular and so also aids survival. We have seen how the company pursues profit satisficing. The individuals pursue self-satisficing with the optimum position often involving going along for the ride and accepting whatever strange things might be going on. Galbraith called this process the pursuit of contentment.

> For most, mental effort is something that is exceptionally pleasant to avoid. From this comes the nature of all great organization: those serving it have a powerful commitment to established belief and thus to established action. This regularly rewards those who surrender independent thought to organizational policy. Their surrender in turn serves personal acceptance and social harmony ... The organizational man is happy with what exists. As this mood controls his private life, so it controls his public attitude.[12]

The net result he identifies as misjudgements, eccentricities, error, inanity and delegation are all variants of Antilogic. What is very significant is the rather fierce way he identifies corporations as particularly prone to these outcomes as though he regards the corporation as the prime source of Antilogic in society.

> Nothing so breeds acquiescence in or indifference to social shortcomings as daily exposure to the misjudgements, eccentricities and inanities of private organization. With the rise of the great corporation there comes a contented accommodation to the larger errors of public life and notably those with no immediate effect on the one who observes them.[13]

It is wise for the manager to avoid attention and decisions. Taking decisions attracts both attention and risk. If action really is required this should be delegated. The more successful the manager is the greater are the risks he runs and so there is a tendency for less action and less thought the higher the manager rises unless he is prepared to make very large mistakes.

In previous generations the personality of the company was very much that of the proprietor and his family. They invested in the trade that they knew and probably in the community where they lived. This led to the tendency for most of them to make the best of what they did and be content to earn a return that permitted them to live well and their business to grow. They were not so much driven by profit maximization. They just needed enough profit in what was a more positive form of community satisficing. But times change and such an approach is no longer safe. The emergence of the major corporation, of financial engineering and globalization has led to large business lions that like to feed on small business zebras. Now stretching the metaphor in a rather unpleasant way the small business begins to suspect that it would be rather more pleasant to be bought out by the lion than to be eaten. Small business owners begin to believe that life would be more comfortable as an employee of large company than as a small company entrepreneur. Rather than the theory of the economy being driven by the entrepreneur seeking to establish new business we may find that the statistics would suggest entrepreneurs rushing to become managers. In several countries there has been a trend towards industry consolidators racing to use recently established share market listings to buy up small business and professional practices. As part of the process the selling entrepreneur hopes to receive the capital sum that represents the market worth of his business. Once on board as an employee, either as a career recruit or as our acquired entrepreneur, the manager becomes a cog in the corporate machine.

He discovers that the role of manager and employee does not have as exciting an image as that of the entrepreneur or speculator. Just as the urban dweller dreams wistfully of the life of the cowboy or beachcomber, the employee cultivates a dashing image. The difference between image and reality confronts the manager with a paradox. The workings of the corporation require inactivity yet his image requires immediate results. Corporate success may come from the application of the law of large numbers to a single participant among many in an essentially neutral system. If the individuals avoid standing out they retain the chance that they are the survivors who one day reach the top in a sort of corporate mortality table.

The solution is simple in concept; find apparent results without risky commitment. Easier said than done as it is not always possible to avoid action. Internal rivalry may force activity and there is always the unforeseen outcomes of dithering. Those who do take action in the drive for speedy results provide another basic example of Antilogic that so often begins the downward spiral in a company's fortunes. The initial smallish problem creates an embarrassment that has to be covered up and replaced with profits from elsewhere. New aggressive risks are taken with unfortunate consequences leading to a cycle of staff replacements (the usual suspects, not necessarily the culprits), new policies, forgotten history, new losses, new staff, etc. until stability eventually re-emerges probably with a new owner. Because of inherently high gearing, the banking industry is particularly prone this type of risk. Similar effects are also common in business with commodity exposures or risky new product decisions and so we may infer general applicability. This may provide a clue to the broad cycles that apply to the fortunes of top management and especially chief executives as they initially soar and subsequently decline in esteem.

If actual decisions must be made there is a fundamental protection for top management. The more senior the decision-maker the more likely the decision will be wrong but the less likely the decision-maker will suffer adverse personal consequences. This is the benefit gained from the combination of effects of financial genius. Those involved with large sums must be smart. Consider how this works in the typical borrowing transaction. The person who requests a very large loan must be positively influenced by the very large sum involved and so will tend to be seen as a financial genius. The bank officer with authority to approve such loans will have constant involvement with large sums and so will also have been greatly influenced in this case by the rub off effect. With a financial genius proposing a loan and a greater genius approving it is no wonder that such transactions can be speedily waved through. The seniority of the people involved will ensure that the strict rules required for small transactions will not be applied and no junior experts will challenge the decision. This example was from the banking industry but applies to any large financial decision. If the error is large enough the perpetrator can be promoted all the way to the CEO's chair.

No matter how they get to the position, all Chief Executives begin with a positive balance in their CEO credibility account. This is a notional account that reflects the balance of public regard for the CEO and functions very much like a bank account. The precise starting balance depends not only on the CEOs' own characteristics but also on the profile of their predecessor's account and the state of the business. A typical new CEO begins with a balance of, say, 100 units. A unit has no absolute value but has a relative value over time and in comparison between CEOs. Boards, journalists, analysts and investors are all very interested in the relative balance. The board must react if the relative balance becomes too low. The typical credibility account has a life of approximately three years and is constantly declining, analogous to a glider that must lose altitude unless the pilot can find a new source of lift.

In the first year he can do no wrong because of good-guy momentum and this may temporarily offset the decline. All new business leaders are given the benefit of the doubt for a period, even the most unlikely appointment. This can reach the extent that the new man is accepted because, when appointed, the illustrious predecessor looked as unlikely as this man does now. All CEOs are given a honeymoon period because the market wants a new approach, new thinking or a new broom. This is the period when he can do no wrong and all he says is brilliant. It seems that the tides of fortune are flowing in his direction but in reality when things are going your way all explanations are seen as brilliant new insights. When things are going poorly the same explanations will be regarded as folly. Never the less for a while at least, the Gods smile on the new CEO. In the second year, depending on performance, the good-guy momentum slackens and the inherent decline takes over. In the third year the CEO can do no right and this, together with the ongoing decline, exhausts the balance in the credibility account.

The job of leading any business has the same basic feature. The basic truth for CEOs is the same wherever they are. This is not very obvious to the incoming CEO excited and buoyed up by the honour and prestige of his new appointment. It therefore behoves the outgoing CEO to prepare the successor for what to expect by leaving instructions. The departing CEO had no advice for his successor other than to give him three envelopes with the instruction to open each in turn if things became really tough. At first everything was fine but after a period trouble started and the new CEO became the subject of criticism. Our hero opened the first envelope, which contained a message that read 'Blame the old CEO'. Our hero followed the instruction and life became easier. After a further period the situation deteriorated and the now experienced CEO opened the second envelope and found that it contained the message 'Blame the economy'. Again our now battle hardened and experienced CEO took the advice and life improved. After a further period of challenging conditions our veteran CEO opened the third envelope and read the final message 'Prepare three envelopes'.

Ultimately, the non-executive directors act to replace the CEO. However, the new CEO is given only a credibility balance of 75 due to the nervousness of the board in the face of the investors looking for quick results. This lower balance is exhausted more quickly. The process may be repeated once or twice more with each new CEO receiving a smaller and smaller balance. After this the Chairman and board are replaced and the next CEO is given a credibility balance of 200 plus options and the cycle repeats. Why does he get more than the original CEO? After the disaster the replacement board will over react and find the most spectacular candidate possible and so ratchet up both expectations and reward. Just as our glider pilot can find himself swept up in a weather change so can the post disaster CEO benefit from the work of his predecessors and cycles in the economy.

The choice of the successor CEO is a natural occasion when Antilogic comes to the fore. The board must now fulfil one of its main reasons for existence by choosing the new CEO. They had probably hoped for happier times when the illustrious long serving CEO would choose his own successor. We have seen how even the unlikely successor can be accepted if he follows a successful CEO but when a CEO has to be replaced it is more than likely that the board will chose the well prepared likely appointment. This will be applauded by the market but probably turn out to be an inappropriate choice. If the board wants to have a choice of likely candidates the process can be very wasteful. It is the result of a process apparently designed to make the wrong selection due to the difficulty of an illustrious leader identifying a potential supplanter from amongst his subordinates.

A good leader has his own vision of where the enterprise should be going and how it should get there, and his idea of a successor is the man most likely to keep going in the same direction. Obviously this man is probably his closest associate, his number two, the man who has supported him most ably and loyally throughout his career. But the mere fact of having been a loyal number two is prima facie disqualification from becoming number one. It suggests someone who is better suited to following than leading, someone whose qualities are complementary to those of the leader instead of identical. A leader will have his own vision, and his own ideas, and they are unlikely to coincide exactly with those of his predecessor; consequently he may have antagonized the outgoing leader, or at least questioned his ideas, put up alternatives of his own, and generally created a slight chill in the atmosphere. It therefore takes a very wise man indeed to realize that this thorn in his flesh may make a better successor than the apple of his eye.[14]

Farmers would recognize this as the problem of the old bull and the young bull. However this situation of the outgoing CEO choosing his successor will be the exception rather than the rule as few can choose either their time of going or their successor as the credibility cycle reveals that the typical CEO has his lowest credibility precisely at the moment that he is to be replaced.

Once he or she is safely in the seat it is prudent for an incoming CEO to take down the decorations accumulated during his predecessor's reign. Incoming CEOs are notably Spartan and fundamental in their tastes and keen to eschew the excesses of the past. This process is called window undressing. It is also known as clearing the deck. It would be bad form to take down too early the decorations of an illustrious predecessor who is still in the neighbourhood. This could be seen as hasty and ungrateful and regarded as premature window undressing. The precise timing is dependent on how illustrious was the predecessor and whether he had overstayed his welcome.

With the growth of the media has come a whole new process by which corporations seek to ensure that their interests are portrayed in a favourable manner. This may involve influencing government policy, or investors or customers. A complex process is initiated depending on the audience to be influenced. Much of the process is indirect in that the message is issued to journalists, especially financial journalists and to broking and financial analysts in the hope that they will favourably influence the public or investors. To facilitate this process the corporation establishes a team variously known as Public Affairs, Public Relations, and Investor Relations whose function is to service the needs of the opinion formers. These people are also known as spin-doctors and flacks and draw their expertise from the media and advertising industries rather than from finance, investment or the industry of the corporation. The external distinction between company and CEO very easily becomes blurred so that the principle task of this process is often to describe the great beauty and quality of the Emperor's new clothes. This is just the same as the children's fairy tale but with a modern media twist. The dominant CEO can deny the journalist access to stories until such time as the CEO's influence declines and past scores can be settled. For a period this leads to the journalist seeing the world through CEO coloured spectacles. The role of the analyst and financial journalist is to determine whether the Emperor is wearing the new clothes today or not. Their ability to fulfil this role follows a distinct cycle not unrelated to the CEO credibility cycle. Indeed it may be one of the causal factors. The analyst or journalist is unlikely to discover that a new CEO is wearing new clothes but with experience may spot that an old CEO is trying to get away with new clothes.

It is not important for the Emperor to have new clothes; he only needed to appear to have them. With a little sleight of hand there is no need for dishonesty. Being caught out in a lie is very counterproductive as is the inflexibility of always being truthful. The cunning use of the truth can be used with impunity while retaining adherence to the ultimate truth of the end objective.

After practising long enough to appear what you are not, it seems natural for CEOs to develop sufficiently to become the reality of their image. Fantasy and reality have a tendency to blur in a sort of self-fulfilling prophecy. This evolution follows a pattern that again looks suspiciously like the credibility cycle so that we may postulate that the rate of transition between reality and image and vice versa determines the duration of the credibility cycle. Courage is good but a little public relations help just as well. What they say need not be true but it is easy and most effective if the image is not far from the truth. This may coincide with what the audience wants to hear or already believes and become the perceived truth.

With all this public relations help it actually takes quite a while to discover where the great leader is marching. Much is made of the power, wisdom and leadership of the Great Man. No one questions the reality of this until some bright spark realizes that the great leader is never seen without his minders, speechwriters and spokesmen. Later they realize that they have not actually seen him in the flesh for a long time. Just like the Wizard of Oz this Great Leader may be an illusion.

There are considerable dangers in using ex-journalists as public relations consultants to put across the CEO's story. The current journalists do not like it. It seems to undermine the purity of their profession and reminds them of the retirement from the press that will be their lot as well. As a consequence they are keen to point out the shortcomings of the spin-doctor's work, accelerating the credibility decline.

Consultants are the other source of support for the CEO. They function like mercenaries in the employ of a monarch to ensure domination of his kingdom. They bring few surprises. They say, never to ask a consultant before you know his answer and a good consultant will never answer until he knows what you want.

After a while the CEO credibility cycle became apparent to many observers and finally to the CEOs themselves. Not unreasonably they found it prudent to seek some protection in the form of employment packages that include the predetermined severance packages known as golden parachutes. The prevalence of the golden parachute has begun to attract adverse comment because of the apparent cost to the company. Cost is not the end of the story as there is also benefit for the company. There is a group of CEOs who by good luck or good mismanagement succeed in failing in a succession of high profile positions. The employment of such a CEO is calculated to encourage a take-over with attendant premium and the generation of real shareholder value. The triggering of change of control clauses provides the CEO with a welcome change from the golden routine. Some CEOs embrace this golden technique as a counter to the iron discipline of the CEO credibility account.

The rapidly moving CEO demands immediate results. The quality of the results is of secondary importance. The speed of their movements may come through their own realization of the limits in their management capabilities. This interpretation implies that the CEO knows his shortcomings whereas the various boards did not. The phenomenon of the rapid impact CEO is so pervasive that this explanation has to be unlikely. Possibly the boards have chosen to ignore the shortcomings but it is much more likely that the Manager is unaware or unable to admit to this shortcoming whereas the board recognize both their own role of inactivity and the contribution of incompetence to the ultimate release of value.

The board is supposed to know about the capabilities of the CEO. It is their main responsibility as expected in corporate governance. Corporate governance is broadly defined as the way companies govern themselves with a little help from the government in the form of corporations' law and regulators. Managers are supposedly paid to manage the business in the interests of the shareholders. The board is appointed to see that management carries out its job with their leader the Chairman given the onerous task of replacing the CEO when the time comes. Annual general meetings and so forth set the stage for this drama to unfold. I will now consider these distinct governance categories and see how well it has been working out in practice.

Starting with the managers we immediately encounter a problem. The managers don't just want to manage but they want to own as well. Their rewards have begun to look like those of owners except that the rewards go up even when profit does not. The reality of this self-interest was put in stark relief by the simplistic speech on the topic of options for the incumbent CEO made by a small shareholder at the annual meeting of a major corporation. His comments were along the lines that the CEO was a fine leader who was already working all the hours available with great results and so patently giving him more options was a waste of the shareholders money as he could not conceivably do better.

Share ownership schemes and executive options have taken rewards beyond payment for service to payment as capitalists towards actual ownership of the company without the risk. This started as a legal way to save tax on extra income and was encouraged by some mutual funds to provide an incentive similar in character to ownership. Over time the tax situation and incentive needs have changed but the ownership benefits remain.

For the CEO the granting of options is a win-win situation. He must be attracted in the first instance with an internationally competitive package irrespective of the chance that he will move internationally or whether an international rival is realistically likely to move to this location. The convention must be honoured. Of course, sometimes there are some international transfers but this is subject to fashion and comes at a particular point in the credibility cycle when a clean new start is required. Then the convention is to pay more than the previously disclosed comparable international remuneration in order to attract the right person. This provides the necessary periodic upward adjustment in CEO salaries as all the other local CEOs are brought into line due to the comparative survey.

The CEO will also be given the options justified by a comparative survey that delivers about the same as the other CEOs. Because our particular business is not doing as well, it will be necessary to issue a lot of cheap options to provide the necessary incentive, perhaps increased because of the perceived risk. Although the options are issued in the expectation of an improvement in the share price the conservative accounting assumes no success and no increase in value and so there is assumed to be no cost to the shareholders. It would be churlish to begrudge those few extra shares later and international investors positively want CEOs and management to be rewarded in the same way as shareholders. When it comes to the retirement of a popular champion there is a divergence of rewards between CEO and shareholder. It is still common to give a retiring CEO new options in his retirement years because of the wisdom of his decisions having an ongoing beneficial effect whereas shareholders cease to receive dividends or capital gain after they sell their shares.

Once he has actually received his options our CEO is now in a win-

win-win situation. If the share-price goes up he is rich and everyone is happy. Perhaps his actions even caused the price to go up. If the share-price does not go up and he is a fine chap regarded by the board as doing a good job they will have to issue further options at a lower strike price to restore his incentive. If he is not popular the board will terminate him but compensate him as if the options are valuable (despite having been accounted at nil cost) in order that he goes quietly. There is a going rate for this as well so that, success or not, the rewards for CEOs continue to be ratchetted up. The shareholders might not be so happy but the working of the credibility cycle tends to have them look forward to the performance of the new CEO.

The real owners are the shareholders but do they take an actual interest in the company? Are they stock speculators or faceless mutual funds who treat their holding as simply a negotiable instrument? It is likely that management and the shareholders will disagree about these questions. However, there is widespread agreement that the formal forum for reporting to the shareholders, the annual general meeting, is an historic relic of limited modern use. The central fallacy is that an enormous company often with more than 100,000 shareholders is controlled by the shareholders at the annual general meeting or that the board has the ability to control such an extensive organization. The AGM is an elaborate exercise in popular illusion with the element of democracy so reduced as to be merely vestigial.

The widespread condemnation of AGMs is reinforced by the participants themselves who see it as a historic showpiece often abused by interest groups who treat it as opportunity to gain attention for their causes. Labour, consumer, environmental and landowner groups frequently interrupt meetings in an increasingly persistent manner. In Japan organized crime made meeting disruption a profitable sideline. It is conceded that the AGM is a meeting that is to be endured and at which the minimum possible business is to be conducted, questions are to be stonewalled and where possible directors are silent.

The shareholders own the company but they are numerous with individual votes counting for little. The set piece meetings are dominated by small shareholders who lack the understanding or information to effectively interrogate the board. Institutional shareholders normally do not take part other than providing their proxy to the Chairman. As a result the board continues to control the outcome of the meeting even if shareholder activists are able to gain a majority of shareholders present. This is part of the philosophy of institutions supporting incumbent management and only showing their displeasure by selling their shares. Naturally, after selling they no longer have any interest in the affairs of the business. This convention provides a line of least resistance for management who respond to shareholder criticism with the suggestion that if they do not like the way the company is run they should sell their shares. After which of course they would no longer have any reason to comment. This approach is encouraged by the psychology of fund managers who have no interest in continued public exposure of their investment let alone disappointment in an unsuccessful company. The net effect is that the general meeting only has relevance in the aftermath of financial catastrophe and is seldom influential in correcting ordinary mismanagement.

Ostensibly the board represents the shareholders yet they generally only vote on issues and election lists provided by management and often no choice is possible. This allows self-perpetuation by the board who are in fact appointed by themselves and by each other as a network sometimes with support from other institutions concerned with finance.

The effective power of corporate governance lies elsewhere. It is suggested that the real power is wielded at the board meeting. Although the board may hold the power over the shareholders the management often holds the board. Townsend is not very flattering about the directors with the idea of non-boards.

> Most big companies have turned their boards of directors into non-boards. The chief executive has put his back seat drivers to sleep. This achievement is understood to be admired. In the years that I've spent on various boards I've never heard a single suggestion from a director (made as a director at a board meeting) that produced any result at all. While ostensibly the seat of all power and responsibility, directors are usually the friends of the chief executive put there to keep him safely in office. They meet once a month, gaze at the financial window dressing (never at the operating figures by which managers run the business), listen to the chief and his team talk superficially about the state of the operations, ask a couple of dutiful questions, make token suggestions (courteously recorded and subsequently ignored), and adjourn until next month.[15]

A more sympathetic view is that board inactivity comes from the sheer difficulty of carrying out the real role of non-executive directors of guiding company affairs and the selection of chief executives. The non-executive directors are burdened by their lack of knowledge of the detail of the company's affairs and must rely on management for the crucial information necessary to fulfil their responsibilities. They are forced of necessity to concentrate on compliance issues. Management has all the detail but is often unable to judge the company's performance objectively because they were too close to the issues at stake.

It is hard to distinguish the difference between a board that is regarded as good because the results are good and the board that ensures that the results are good. Directors are going to be flattered by success whether it exists or not. The accounts will show the profit in the best light. If the value of the shares rises life is sweet. The commentators write flattering pieces about the company and the directors bask in the association. They are welcome all over town and new offers flood in with the hope that they may achieve the same result in other places. The board meetings are very pleasant. But if the share prices dips the adoring crowds begin to thin. Little by little the commentators begin to question what is happening and after a period of expressing confidence in the management the directors begin to ask more questions and hope that they are the right ones. The meetings become much less fun but the public image must be maintained. Generally the directors continue to serve. It is sometimes suggested that this loyalty is due to the money involved in fees. Maybe there is an element of financial self-interest affecting the directors and their attitude to fees but this is to overstate their personal financial interest in the outcome, as this is relatively modest. The outcome is there but the motivation is a more complex mixture of influences. First and foremost their role is a continuation of their own business career and now it is their turn to do to others as they have already received. It is prudent and justifiable to act in a manner similar to the other comparable organizations. It gives a very easy satisficing choice and it is much more comfortable to do the same as everyone else rather than to risk the loss of prestige associated with a board seat at a well known company. This gives a dynamic that drives the interrelation between board, chairman and CEO that is most obvious in the area of remuneration but influences all areas of decision making. For remuneration the impact is accentuated by the combination of herding where the boards of each corporation compare themselves with the others and slipstreaming as each takes a successive advantage over the other.

The role of the directors extends to participation in networks between boards. There is a group of individuals subject to that influence who know how to play the game and identify the venerable and subtle rules of the public role that the board plays. The prospect pronouncements that are as opaque as a Delphic oracle and the ritualistic characteristics, especially in the set piece shareholder meetings, give a clue that the origins of the board lie with a Greek drama. In the typical Greek tragedy the chorus is comprised of twelve elders, still a popular number today. The chorus presents the voice of moral conservatism, traditionalism and a reluctance to challenge the present way of thinking. This conservatism is most probably a function of their age. They are a group of sound but elderly businessmen with few exceptions. In this sense I mean sound to be seen but not heard! The chorus must stay inactive, as it is the role of the characters to respond to the circumstances. So we see the directors remain completely silent at the AGM despite all sorts of provocation from the floor.

The chorus could not respond other than their continued expressions of foreboding (which must be their concern about personal liability) yet they do nothing to either confirm their fears or to act in such a way as to negate them. This idea of foreboding is part of the role of creating atmosphere for corporate governance to reinforce the impression that the interest of shareholders is being taken very seriously indeed. The creation of atmosphere is linked to the role as historian (corporate memory) and poet (corporate image). Sound also indicates an ability to act in the expected way.

By definition non-executives are required not to be involved in the executive decisions of the company. This is probably the explanation why a survey by an international executive search firm revealed that 75% of all non-executive directors of Australian listed companies are present or former chief executives of other listed companies. Most chief executives are generalists by background and specialists in their particular industries. They will have concentrated on general management for many years before being invited to non-executive roles. For conflict of interest reasons they cannot be appointed to the boards of competitor companies in their specialist industry and current corporate governance practice frowns on appointment as non-executive directors in the same company where they had been executives. Consequently 75% of non-executive directors bring neither specialist skills nor industry knowledge to the boards on which they serve. This is not a practical impediment, as non-executive directors are required not to do anything, hence the title. The principle criterion for acceptance of a non-executive board invitation is the suitability of the monthly board meeting day. Once on board the board they join the Chairman in supporting unquestioningly the actions of the CEO until, at a moment determined by the Chairman, they will join him in not supporting the CEO.

In due time this will lead to the removal of the old CEO and the selection of a new CEO. The intervening period may provide the board, which has trained by not involving themselves in the affairs of the company, with the opportunity to take over the day to day direction of the firm and the chance to relive their former days of executive glory. Loyal service as a non-active director is likely to be rewarded in due course with promotion to Chairman with the responsibility to determine when the CEO is no longer to be supported. This progression is not automatic as certain prerequisites also apply. Non-executive directors should not only be non-active, they should be sound. In this case we mean sound like a barrel, do the right thing and do not leak.

A recent development has been an increasing number of female non-executive directors. This is a welcome strengthening of board talent as generally these women have reached the previously mandatory level of experience at a much earlier age and without the necessity of having had the previously mandatory chief executive role. This may be the positive effect of fishing in a smaller jean pool. We may expect that, if current seniority criteria for the appointment are maintained, within ten years most company chairmen will be women.

Despite the ability of management to control their boards there still remains the irksome compliance duties and for the CEO the ever present danger of the credibility cycle. Some therefore hanker for a further solution, really the definitive solution, to the problem of shareholders control and corporate governance. That is to eliminate the shareholder. The managers go out and raise the funds to buy out the shareholders. Periodically there are conditions when the management is optimistic and the shareholders pessimistic so it proves possible for a management committed to the success of 'their' enterprise to bid for and buy the company. This is when there are waves of management buyouts (MBO) and leveraged buyouts (LBO). Each corporate strategy swing gives the potential that some part of the corporation might become available to its management. There are problems when this happens, not least the position of the board deciding between the position of management and that of the shareholders. Knowing what they know, management would never want to buy what the shareholders would want to sell! There is also the conceptual difficulty that the funding must be serviced by the same business. At least for the CEO it eliminates the board and shareholders before the CEO credibility cycle takes its course.

There are plenty of CEOs who subscribe to the Alfred Chandler philosophy that the modern business enterprise became a viable institution only after the 'visible' hand of management proved to be far more efficient than the 'invisible' hand of the market. They set out to provide that visible hand and some have succeeded. These leaders share all the human characteristics, good and bad, of politicians and, sadly, sometimes of dictators. Business leaders generally begin their reign with humility and enthusiasm. Their confidence grows with experience but over time there is a tendency towards expecting acquiescence and sometimes towards hubris.

We have seen that the evolving nature of corporations has led to a loss of effective control by the owners, the shareholders. Power has migrated towards the managers supposedly held in check by the non-executive directors. Although much of the trappings of the entrepreneur are lovingly embraced, the organizations have become more bureaucratic and political in nature. Successive waves of management consultants have introduced the culture and terminology of the sporting field and of the battlefield. Much play is made of leadership, loyalty and team spirit. Generally, the tendency for this to become a personality cult is held in check by the natural working of the CEO credibility cycle. Sometimes by force of personality or lucky chance a CEO succeeds in outlasting his board and re-balancing its loyalty in his favour. Key to their success is an ability to hang onto power to give enough time to change the organization in their image through control of personnel.

Once the constraints of the cycle have been loosened it is likely that the CEO will survive for a dramatically longer term. He or she becomes the respected industry leader and a phenomenon. This enhanced status together with the respect it brings can lead to remarkable results and with the loss of the self constraining nature of the cycle these may be more extreme, both positive and negative.

The chief executive naturally will seek to get the best out of his cohorts. Sometimes that may be outright manipulation to rubberstamp his own ill conceived proposals. Even in benign circumstances where the group are not sycophants there are inadvertent dangers that prevent a group member from expressing doubts when the others in the group appear to have reached a consensus.

This puts a premium on being the first to express an opinion although it is wiser to guess, or better still know, what the leader's opinion will be. It is not loyal to make a mistake and guess wrongly. Loyalty also means that once a consensus is reached truth must be consistent with that decision.

In his own mind (President) Johnson regarded his in-group of policy advisers as a family and its leading dissident member as an irresponsible son who was sabotaging the family's interests. Underlying this revealing image seems to be two implicit assumptions that epitomize Groupthink: 'We are a good group, so any deceitful acts we perpetrate are fully justified. Anyone in the group who is unwilling to distort the truth to help us is disloyal'.[16]

The consensus group of course defines help according to the rules of Groupthink. Janis outlines three concepts that achieve this.

Construct a set of objectives that the leader is intending to achieve 'presuming always that he acts in a rational manner'.[17]

This proviso is very unrealistic. The second concept emphasizes those factors that limit rationality of decision making. These could be limits to the ability to obtain the necessary information, limits to the ability to process that information and a tendency to find a course of action that will satisfy the most minimal of goals (a satisficing strategy). This is more like the typical organization. The more information there is the more satisficing takes place. Then as the third concept we have office politics.

A variant is a matter of 'muddling through'. Policy-makers take one little step one after another and gradually change the old policy into a new one, all the while making compromises that keep every politically powerful group that enters the bargaining reasonably satisfied or at least not dissatisfied enough to obstruct or sabotage the new trend.

This will tend to diffuse dissent, as it is often not worth the personal risk to indulge in sabotage because the process of incremental change will also pass. The less technical description is to call it the salami technique. Each slice individually is not worth making a fuss.

Sometimes the leader is a person of great tenacity both in insisting that the new trends take hold and in ensuring that he sticks around long enough to outlast the doubters. He insists that the team plays the way he wants. He may be so keen on being a team player that he takes it upon himself to be manager, coach, captain and leading goal scorer. No detail is left to chance but often it is clear that the new techniques are for the others to follow and not for the boss himself. One such example is ''Neutron' Jack Welch of General Electric, one of the most admired managers of all time.

Welch certainly saw himself as a liberator, inspiring others to realize their responsibility and talents: his key slogan was 'Control your destiny or someone else will'. But everyone knew who was really in control. He had chosen his own men to push through his reforms and weed out 'resistors'. He replaced the old wedding cake corporate structure with a 'cartwheel', with the thirteen spokes of the business units all radiating from his own office. There was now much less scope for opposition and balancing forces: he had replaced a republic with a monarchy.[18]

There are many more examples of business leaders gaining such domination over their organizations as to begin acting as monarchs or dictators. Their careers have led to colourful reporting of both the heights and depths of achievement. Sometimes the story ends in tears, which gives the journalists a further story opportunity as they explain how they had seen it coming and the rest of us should have known. Each period and each country have their famous names with Tiny Rowland, Robert Maxwell, Howard Hughes, the Hunts, Alan Bond, and Al Dunlap amongst the standouts. Other CEOs show the same tendencies but have been able to avoid the financial disasters that often provoke a rethinking of a chief executive's contribution.

In the world of corporate regulation, transparent reporting and the efficiency of the market, these situations of CEO domination should not happen as often as they do but there are factors that help them. Firstly, we like the idea of the big boss. We encourage them in their displays of importance. This is an important business. Our leader must be suitably impressive so that we can bask in the reflected glory as employees or feel justified in our investment.

Not only should they look grand. When the times are difficult it is reassuring to have a leader who looks commanding. This applies even in the best-governed companies. Special challenges require special measures. The media, staff and investors all look for strength. They want charismatic leadership. The problem is that once in place the special challenges leader naturally entrenches his position and it is not so easy to change the formula or get them out again reflecting a universal human characteristic. Its prevalence changes over time and varies between countries depending on the impact of shareholder activism, and corporate regulation in moderating the credibility cycle. One would expect the more open the reporting of corporate activity the more rapid the working of the credibility cycle would be yet Sampson claims the greatest difficulty with autocrats escaping the credibility discipline occurs in the most open of markets, Britain and America.

The biggest companies in America, Europe and Asia all have problems with controlling autocrats, within their widely varied versions of capitalism. The Japanese claim to organize retirements and successions better than the West through their system of consensus, but they also find it harder to dislodge dominating bosses ... 'They are absolute corporate kings'. The German chairmen are becoming harder to dislodge, in spite of their supervisory boards and the industrial failures of the 1990s. 'The chairman always begins to think he owns the company', said one Anglo-German sociologist. ... Even the French are becoming more worried about their traditionally over-centralized power. 'The French caste system based on a mandarinate gives huge power to presidents: it's really based on monarchic principles', said Octave Gelinier. But British and American companies face the greatest difficulties in controlling their autocrats.[19]

It might be imagined that the mounting criticism would be a clear enough message for the big boss. This is not the case because those aggressive characteristics that won the position also serve to reinforce their own self-esteem with in-built defences. As they work their way through the credibility cycle the level of applause will subside and gradually be replaced with criticism. This will have little impact as it is to be expected!

The danger with autocrats and the charismatic leaders appointed to meet special challenges is the misdirected energy and uncertain motives. Commanding action has to be taken and no dissension or even debate can be tolerated. It is the classic environment for Antilogic. This may lead to trouble no matter how well meaning the group or benign its intentions. This is the negative side of Groupthink, which ascribes the finest motives to those actions deemed to be in the interests of the group. Loyalty demands sticking to the policies of the group even when there are unintended adverse consequences or policy is working badly. The outcome might disturb the members' conscience but this is not allowed to overrule their loyalty to the group. Janis calls this soft-headed thinking, leading to hard-hearted action.

> Paradoxically, soft-headed groups are likely to be extremely hard-hearted towards out-groups and enemies. In dealing with a rival ... policy makers comprising an amiable group find it relatively easy to authorize dehumanizing solutions ... An affable group is unlikely to pursue the difficult and controversial issues that arise when alternatives to a harsh ... solution come up for discussion. Nor are the members inclined to raise ethical issues that imply that this 'fine group of ours, with its humanitarianism and its high-minded principles might be capable of adopting a course of action that is inhumane and immoral'[20]

Many of the current management techniques aimed at establishing a vision, mission statement, team-building, cultural change, compliance program or whatever are designed to create affable groups. Group cohesiveness is likely to increase hard-heartedness relative to other sources of faulty decisions. The same tendency can lead to the cover-up. The reasoning goes as follows. Because our fine group performs to the highest standards any adverse publicity must be for the wrong motivation and gratuitously damaging. Therefore, to prevent unjustified criticism and needless concern to the public/investors we will prevent disclosure of problems. The non-disclosure of problems at Mitsubishi Motor Corporation and Snow Dairy in Japan are recent examples.

The origins of the hard-headedness adopted by the autocrat are clear to see in the following quote about a much loved political leader who applied forceful leadership to achieve what were generally seen as worthy aims.

> In the professional study of leadership, style is the man. The school that thinks leadership is a collection of *macho* qualities in which not thinking too deeply, being thick skinned and *can do* without too many scruples or much delicacy, as well as relying on well-placed mates, are taken to be all that you need. It doesn't matter how complicated the world becomes, these are the old leadership verities; divide the world into the leaders and led; play by the book when you must, otherwise do what you have to; claim to be tough unswerving, always and everywhere positive; and treat those who object as less than men, emotional, impractical and possibly subversive – though the odd sop, the gain-after-the pain doesn't go astray when it can't be avoided. … There's an element of the gangs and games of 11 year old boys in all *macho*-type leadership … Every *macho* leader knows, if he's pressed, that his … authority is derived from some reference to force.[21]

So, there we have it. The most respectable and benign groups are particularly prone to Antilogic and this Antilogic can take a sinister turn against those that do not share the in status. This applies to individuals, corporations, nations and other groupings. This is particularly obvious in politics with history littered with the most unfortunate examples but it is also endemic in the world of finance. The clubby world of business and the ceaseless requirement for soundness from its participants appear almost predestined to be the laboratory for Groupthink. It also helps to explain why so many corporate disasters are accompanied with such adverse consequences for participants and bystanders alike.

This is no doubt a shock for those that would participate at senior levels in such an environment. It was clear that actual and aspiring chief executives would resort to savage action to protect their position and so ensure the future prospects of the corporation. This could be foreseen and avoided by choice of organization or by willingness to pledge allegiance, without mistake, to the leader. But Groupthink has revealed that participation in a cohesive and supportive group is no guarantee of a successful outcome. Far from it as the more cohesive the group the more likely that softthinking will lead to hard-hearted action and this means victims.

Not everyone thinks that this is a bad thing. The Great Leaders believe that it is natural and probably inevitable. Remember, they expect criticism and are ready with the response; 'no pain, no gain', 'you can't make an omelette without scrambling eggs', 'when the going gets tough the tough get going'. It is for them to do what is necessary to survive and prosper. This may mean tough decisions and hard yards and if this means the components of the group must change then so be it. One change may lead to another and before we know it there are special rules for the Great Leader. Whatever they do becomes what is necessary for the group to survive and prosper. When they begin hearing voices then watch out for trouble. Corporate history is full of colourful examples but in order to avoid favouritism the following quotes are about one particularly uncivilized political leader. These quotes relate to extreme political outcomes but provide troubling parallels with business practice.

Stalin was given a business nickname, the Boss. He had a firm grip on public relations and personnel, especially where his grasp of succession planning had the victim run faster and faster to avoid causing disappointment. Despite the promotion to the most senior levels the victim could not resist personal ambition and for the good of the team will need to be removed. The end comes as a surprise in contrast to the less effective modern technique of transferring the individual into a non-existent role.

> Much would be written later about the Boss's sadism, as seen in the inevitable promotion of a victim before liquidation. In fact, he simply wanted his prey to work harder and to be unaware that the end was near. Above all, he promoted them at the last minute so that people could see how much he loved them, and how they had betrayed his trust.[22]

With globalization or whatever other competitive threat there will be need for frequent changes of strategy and attendant changes of conviction.

> For the Party's sake you can and must at 24 hours' notice change all your convictions and force yourself to believe that white is black.[23]

In the rough and tough of business it is recognized that our caring and upright leader will not and should not be associated with some of the essential actions that have to be taken. This may mean he is thought to be unaware of unpleasant activities assisted by the growth of in-depth language where prohibitions mean the opposite.

The whole gathering of course realized that there was no conspiracy. But they also knew the in-depth language. They had been told that the party must have a conspiracy. It was essential for success in the struggle with world imperialism and the schismatic Trotsky. In conclusion, a secret circular from Yagoda was read. The People's Commissar warned them that the use of illegal methods of interrogation such as threats and torture would not be tolerated. In 'in depth language' this meant that such methods were necessary because the accused must be ruthlessly 'broken'.[24]

The ultimate justification for the contrast between the language and action of control is the belief that the corporation must be protected and the leader is above the principles so as to ensure that protection is achieved.

For the Party's sake! When the former seminarist Stalin called the Party the Order of Sword Bearers he had just that in mind: the sacred nature of the Party. Trotsky expressed the same thought in his dictum 'the Party is always right'. Like the church their Party remained pure even if those who served it erred. For like the church, the Party was founded on scripture, in this case the sacred Marxist texts, which would never allow the Party to err, or sinful individual members to change its sacred nature. Hence the principle 'everything for the Party' which allowed them to betray themselves and humble themselves before Stalin – the head of the Sacred Party.

The whole process of control demanded by the big Boss depends on the unquestioning loyalty of assistants who are perversely reassured when in due time they are also the victims of the process. It is a question of simple arithmetic that this must be the case.

Bad though the image of Stalin is C.S. Lewis found a still greater evil that all Company Men would recognize.

I live in the Managerial Age, in a world of 'Admin'. The greatest evil is not now done in those sordid 'dens of Crime' that Dickens loved to paint. It is not done even in the concentration camps and labour camps. In those we see its final result. But it is conceived and ordered (moved, seconded, carried and minuted) in clean, carpeted, warmed and well-lighted offices, by quiet men with white collars and cut fingernails and smooth shaven cheeks who do not need to raise their voices. Hence, naturally enough, my symbol for Hell is something like the bureaucracy of a police state or the offices of a thoroughly nasty business concern.[25]

Lewis does not explain what makes a business concern thoroughly nasty. Is it a very efficient firm that inevitably becomes nasty or is an inefficient firm that inadvertently becomes nasty? The combination of Groupthink and Antilogic suggests that it is the affable groups applying the most modern techniques that through unintended consequences stumble into trouble.

III

GUIDED BY THE MARKET

WE ARE told by the theorists that the perfect answer is revealed by the invisible hand so it is no use fighting against fate. We can let the market do the thinking for us. Not everyone agrees.

There is an extensive body of economic literature devoted to the analysis and understanding of financial markets. Often this emphasizes the working of the invisible hand or the ability of the market to process all known information about a commodity, share or currency to establish the appropriate price. There is an ongoing and lively debate as to whether the market is as well informed and rational as the theory expects. This chapter explores the lore of the market with a change of emphasis from who's who to what's what.

Opinions about the role of the market are very sharply divided. But as they say, it is a difference of opinion that makes a horse race. The investors scrutinize the messages that the market gives but they do not all draw the same conclusion. Just as some believe in the dominant influence of management others believe the impartial process of the market will reveal and correct all. The efficient market advocates believe that it is the influence of the market that determines the success or otherwise of the corporation and the CEO. They contend that, although corporate history might be of passing interest, it is of minor significance in understanding financial activity. We should not treat this personally and ascribe blame or praise. The rise and fall of companies and individuals are inevitable and do not relate specifically to decisions taken. The markets will tell us why there are winners and losers.

There are many champions both for the supporters and for the sceptics about the power of the market. The problem is that the supporters use complicated arguments and mathematics but to get the debate going I start with a very simplified summary of market theory. This argues that market prices of all sorts move in a random walk. The idea is that the market prices incorporate all information without systematic bias. Relevant information includes the value of the firm and this is not influenced by either capital structure or dividends because investors could make their own arrangements to replicate the corporate activity. There are a lot of empirical studies to support these ideas including comparisons to random stock selection and buy-and-hold strategies.

The first problem arises from agreeing as to who calls the shots. One school would have it that it is always people that determine price. Yet the others contend that is the market itself that brings objectivity because, after all, the market never lies. This line of reasoning would indicate the 20% fall of the market on the 18th October 1987 suggests that the value of the US economy fell by this amount from one day to the next. Surprisingly enough it turned out that it was worth the original amount again a little later. This means that the market must be rational, whatever it does. There may be many opinions but value is what the market will accept. The strange thing is the market also determines the value of things that we do not sell. We are now trained to value the things we still own and do not sell on the basis of what someone else got for theirs.

Saul is very concerned as to the consequences to society because of the store that many put on the efficiency of the market. It enables them to justify all outcomes as a result of the market and removes any incentive to try and change the outcome.

> Our belief in salvation through the market is very much in the utopian tradition. The economists and managers are the servants of god. Like the medieval scholastics, their only job is to uncover the divine plan. They could never create or stop it. At most they might aspire to small alterations.[26]

The market has become the excuse. It represents a dictatorship stronger than some notorious totalitarian regimes. Stronger still, he fears that the market has become a deity for some.

> We are enthralled by a new all powerful clockmaker god – the market place and his archangel technology. Trade is the marketplace's miraculous cure for all that ails us and globalization is the Eden or paradise into which the just shall be welcomed on Judgement Day. As always with ideologies, the Day of Judgement is imminent and terrifying. I would suggest that Marxism, fascism and the marketplace strongly resemble each other. They are all corporatist, managerial and hooked on technology as their own particular golden calf.[27]

There is another group not at all convinced by the evidence supporting the market. They believe that the studies were too remote and general and that there is evidence of non-random price behaviour of market prices (such as the general tendency for price reversal between trades relatively concentrated at particular prices). They make this the basis of a business.

Peter Bernstein, another market practitioner and a thoughtful author about markets, capital and risk, takes a middle road distinguishing efficiency from the rational and accurate.

> An efficient market is not necessarily a rational market, nor is the information it reflects always accurate. Investors in their enthusiasm, or in their collective gloom, sometimes agree among themselves that certain stocks are somehow worth more or less than their intrinsic values. Although reality will ultimately assert itself, an efficient market is one in which no single investor has much chance, beyond luck, of consistently outguessing all the other participants.[28]

He also points out that the claims of efficiency cannot be confirmed.

> Farma starts off by admitting that the statement that efficient market prices 'fully reflect' available information is so general that it cannot be tested empirically. As an alternative, he suggests that an efficient market exists when trading systems based on available information fail to produce profits in excess of the market's overall rate of return.[29]

> Before we throw in the sponge and abandon the field to the Samuelson team we should recognize that their basic assumption is vulnerable. Stocks will be priced at what they are worth only when a sizeable number of investors, with big sums at play, know how to value stocks correctly. If that assumption fails to hold, the market is noise, a game of Snap, a casino.[30]

Here, he echoes the games image drawn by Keynes, himself a successful investor experienced in the ups and downs of the market.

> This battle of wits to anticipate the basis of conventional valuation a few months hence ... does not even require gulls amongst the public to feed the maws of the professional; it can be played by the professionals amongst themselves. Nor is it necessary that anyone should keep his simple faith in the conventional basis of valuation having any long-term validity. For it is, so to speak, a game of Snap, of Old Maid, of Musical Chairs – a pastime in which he is the victor who says Snap neither too soon nor too late, who passes the Old Maid to his neighbour before the game is over, who secures a chair for himself when the music stops. These games can be played with zest

and enjoyment, though all the players know that it is the Old Maid which is circulating, or that when the music stops some of the players, will find themselves unseated.[31]

Keynes also called this idea of anticipating the other investor 'beat the gun investing'. This leads to third order investment decisions, i.e. investing on the basis of predicting how the market will react to the markets reaction to an actual profit outcome. He has another admirer in 'Adam Smith' that is the nom de plume of another successful investor.

> In support of the sceptics we can only look again at the premise, that the market is reasonably 'efficient,' that it is a market where numbers of rational, profit maximizing investors are competing. It may just be that investors – even cold, austere, professional money managers – are not rational, or are not 100% rational. It may be that they would rather have some profit and a feeling of company than a maximum profit and a feeling of anxiety. The investor in the random-walk model is suspiciously *Homo economicus,* and we did wander among some thought that Homo is not *economicus.* There is nothing more disastrous, said Lord Keynes than a rational investment policy in an irrational world.[32]

This picks up our theme of irrational versus rational having distinguished efficiency from rational and he moves on to logic. It is but one more step to Antilogic.

> But the market does not follow logic, it follows some mysterious tide of mass psychology. Thus earnings projections get marked up and down as the prices go up and down, just because Wall Streeters hate the insecurity of anarchy. If the stock is going down, the earnings must be falling apart. If it is going up, the earnings must be better than we thought. Somebody must know something we don't know.[33]

Overall it seems that the consensus is that the market works well except when is does not. It is good news indeed for those analysts that there may be a question that the market is less than perfect. If it was perfect how could they justify their jobs and the modest salary they receive? Of course it is a fine line they must walk between redundancy in a perfect market and illegality in an imperfect market. There have been some that suggest that they have come to close to insider trading with those exclusive briefings much loved by the investors who pay the bills.

Think of those poor analysts on tenterhooks to process every new snippet of information faster and better than another hundred colleagues down the street, or even in the same organization. What could be more boring than relying on the analysis of the company prospects according to the same models that were taught to all the other analysts at the various finance courses. With the efficiency of the market and the onward march of computing power all the models must inevitably come to the same answer. And why should the investor pay for the generally available answer? There must be something more. There is gambling, as stated by Keynes in the General Theory.

> The game of professional investment is intolerably boring and overexacting to anyone who is exempt from the gambling instinct; whilst he who has it must pay to this propensity the appropriate toll.[34]

The secret of a transparent and honest gambling game is the ability to receive predictable odds and that in turn presupposes the ability to calculate the actual odds. The regulators have made the market tamper proof yet we find that punters cannot even calculate the odds at any point of time and they keep on changing.

> Let us heed, a moment, Mr. Gerald Loeb, long-standing champion tape-reader and author of *The Battle for Investment Survival*. 'There is no such thing as a final answer to security values. A dozen experts will arrive at 12 different conclusions. It often happens that a few moments later each would alter his verdict if given a chance to reconsider because of a changed condition. Market values are fixed only in part by balance sheets and income statements; much more by the hopes and fears of humanity; by greed, ambition, acts of God, invention, financial stress and strain, weather, discovery, fashion and numerous other causes impossible to be listed without omission'.[35]

Not surprisingly the punters come to different decisions and this suggests a lack of any logical bond with contradictory ideas occurring simultaneously. This increases the task of the efficient market that somehow must generate a rational outcome out of inputs lacking logic that emanate from the investing crowd suggestible to images and themes. The simultaneous presence of contradictory ideas must give considerable scope for Antilogic to flourish within the market.

Clearly the workings of the market do not easily fall into the definition of a self-evident truth. There is a big difference between what is going on and what people are saying is going on. The market predicting techniques might not work but a lot of people are trying to make a living from their application.

If the market were truly efficient there would be no opportunities for value investing. The market would always reveal what an investment was worth. Let us begin with a practical story of the impact of a windfall in the efficient market. You might call this the perfect market in the street. One version of a story that illustrates how this works tells of two professors who subscribed to the perfect market theory walking along a pavement, in this case between the stock exchange and the office. One professor sees a $US50 note lying on the pavement and darts forward to pick it up. His colleague restrained him with the words. 'Don't be a fool. If that was really there, someone would have picked it up already'.

Burton G. Malkiel in a *Random Walk Down Wall Street* uses the same story with a slightly different and intriguing conclusion. The professors are not alone. They are accompanied by two students sceptical of Wall Street professionals and learned professors and they pick up the money. It is not clear why the good professors needed to be accompanied by two students in the first place as this creates the problem of how the two pragmatic students were able to pick up and share the single $US10 bill. Perhaps Malkiel wants us to think about how they might share a multiple mirage although there is probably no limit to the number of times a mirage may be enjoyed. It is also easy to inflate a mirage from $US10 to $US50.

The idea of taking their mirage bill and having it changed so that each student may receive half brings to mind the story of the careless counterfeiters. These skilled craftsmen made use of the most modern printing equipment to make the perfect counterfeit notes. These notes were perfect in almost all respects and so the counterfeiters produced them in large numbers and packed them in boxes prior to taking them to market. As the boxes were being sealed one of the counterfeiters says to the other 'These notes look perfect but are they really supposed to be denominated for £18?' Too much time and cost had gone into the project to scrap the notes now so it was decided to travel to Ireland where the locals would not notice the difference and would change the counterfeit notes for legal tender! After much excitement and danger our heroes arrive in the far west of Ireland where one enters a bank to test changing a few of the notes. 'To be sure Sir, how would you be liking the change? In sixes or nines?' The moral for our random walk students is that there may well be those who will change the currency for them but might not change it from vapour to real.

The charming story of the random walk professor was created to illustrate the problem created by the impact of news on the working of the market. This affects investors and reporting companies alike. A company announces a bumper profit and the share price goes down. Good news is suddenly bad news. Similarly, bad news can just as well be good news, as when a rise of interest rates by the Federal Reserve was met with relief by the market because having done it, it no longer had to do it. Share markets jumped in sympathy. Sometimes the Federal Reserve raises interest rates in response to increased corporate profits. Good news profits thus leading to a fall in share prices because of the expectation of the Federal Reserve raising interest rates. A particularly dramatic response was the price fall following the absence of Y2K computer chaos despite previous weeks of a bug worry induced price slump.

This type of market response often comes as an unpleasant surprise for company executives as they proudly announce record profits. Much effort is put into preparing the market for the bonanza that is to come but the price often goes in the opposite direction. Sometimes it works in reverse, as the market becomes over enthusiastic despite the efforts of the company to restrain its expectations. Clearly, the efficient market sometimes ignores the information it is given.

I have encountered several occasions when our company came with results that comfortably exceeded any published analysts estimates yet when the results were released the share price fell with the media comment that 'the results failed to meet expectations'. Just whose expectations were they? Perhaps the market is subtler than we think. The response could simply be that the market was disappointed that the company had failed to exceed their expectations by as much as they had expected. This explanation is plausible but does not accord with the efficient market theory as it implies the market has the ability to aim off from the analysts' forecasts in which case it would not be surprised with the actual result and no price adjustment would be necessary. This can therefore only be an incidental explanation and we must look further for a structural explanation.

This is the finite profit to perpetuity theory. The market always looks forward, and so, is interested in past results only as far as it is an indication of what is coming. There is only a finite amount of time between now and the end of time and there is only so much profit an organization can earn in the time remaining. Therefore, it stands to reason that if actual profits are higher than expected, then the market will see that there is less to be earned in the future, and will mark the share price down accordingly. The more you earn today the less you are worth for the future. The unexpected higher profit today must mean lower share prices tomorrow.

The recent experience of several Internet and technology stocks that have achieved very high market capitalization without either profit or positive cash flow has provided the opportunity to test the corollary. This is the finite profit to perpetuity in cyberspace theorem. It is based in turn on the standard dividend growth model for valuing stocks (the formula for a growing perpetuity) where price equals the next dividend divided by the sum of discount rate less the rate of growth. If all the hype around the Internet is in fact correct and these companies can really grow at double-digit rates, growth could actually be *greater* than the discount rate resulting in the formula computing a large negative value for the stock. But if the companies are not making profits, they cannot pay dividends and if they continue to require capital to grow and if the additional investment does not remain as capital invested, but is consumed in expenses, then each capital injection is equivalent to a reverse dividend. We then find that we have both a negative number for dividend growth, and a negative value for discount rate less growth. Dividing one negative by another negative of course is a positive number and the dividend growth model works after all. The more a company loses today the higher is its potential for the future.

In considering the value of an investment we must not only consider estimated future earnings but also the probability that the earnings will eventuate as predicted. This is the variability of earnings or risk. Theory tells us that the higher the risk, the higher the return the rational investor will demand in compensation. This is the risk/reward trade off that is the basis of the capital asset pricing model (CAPM) central to finance management courses. Beta is the designation for the measure of risk. The CAPM model expects that risky investments with a high beta will have high returns whereas dull safe stocks with low betas need only provide a correspondingly low return.

In Australia, industrial stocks have performed better than the more risky and volatile resource stocks for which that country is famous and which made up more than half the market capitalization in 1980. The outperformance was more than 8% per annum compound for the last twenty years. Several possible explanations have been advanced for non-compliance with the accepted theory.

One of the explanations advanced in the defence of CAPM is that the variance is not statistically significant. The possible further retort is that this is an isolated result, an outlier. Without knowing all of the observations I cannot be sure but this looks like a non-trivial discrepancy to me.

Another explanation is that a forward revenue or profit estimate by necessity must be uncertain. Not all estimates turn out to be valid. The defenders of CAPM calculations claim that they were as valid as possible when made but unfortunately reality changed subsequently. That the estimates turn out to be optimistic does not necessarily turn out to the disadvantage of the estimator, a result not expected from the efficient market. Actually it is not so surprising that estimators tend to be optimistic but it is surprising that the market does not adjust for this tendency. A study has shown that not only is there a tendency towards optimism but also that there is no market punishment for getting the estimate wrong. For example investors do not notice the optimism of broking analysts working for the firm underwriting share issues. Although the investors react with disappointment the share price remains higher relative to shares evaluated by conservative forecasters.

The lack of a definitive valuation method supported by overwhelming statistical proof leaves the door open for the many different sharepicking methodologies that make the financial markets such interesting if not necessarily rewarding places. There are many systems broadly called charting based on share trading patterns. There are probably just as many books written that claim that the chartist systems do not work. There are many others that advocate their own particular method for becoming rich presumably motivated by altruism, as the authors would clearly not need the money. We need not follow the nuances of all these systems but be alert to the three broad categories of method into which they fall. I have already touched on value and will now look at momentum and then psychology. The combination of these factors is believed by some to fool the efficient market. Sadly my review does not lead to any sure-fire investment tips

The advocates of momentum buying are convinced that the market is going further in the direction it is going, which is normally up. If not they will be expecting the direction to soon change and today is a cheap buying opportunity. We expect this despite the random walk assumption. We look at a price trend and decide that it will continue just because it is there. In good times it seems wise to buy today before the shares become more expensive tomorrow. This is due to the inherent value of the investment and particularly the need to get on to it before the other fellow.

If we expect the market price to continue upwards we are provided with a frame of reference for all stocks within the total market. Each stock can be evaluated as being cheap or expensive relative to the others. This provides the basis for slipstreaming. My stock is priced at a discount to yours and so yours is priced at a premium to mine. If your premium becomes too large my price will increase to close the gap. If the premium becomes too small your price will rise to open it up again. The stocks perform like a team of racing cyclists. In this metaphor they are riders of racing bicycles not followers of economic cycles. One strong cyclist (or stock) sets the pace by sprinting out in front of the pack. Eventually he weakens or needs a rest and drifts back into the pack and a new champion takes his turn. Some are stronger than others and the lead changes although from time to time a rider falls behind the pack and is not seen again. Unlike the Tour de France the sharemarket has no finishing line and the share-riders must pedal (or peddle if you prefer) forever.

There must be a psychological motivation as well as our ideas of value that determines when we buy. If we were influenced mainly by value we would buy shares when share prices were cheap. This is not the case. Share market volumes are at their peaks when prices are the highest, i.e. when value is at its lowest. When prices slump the buyers go away and volumes also slump. Thus, bull markets are much more popular than bear markets. One reason is that we are influenced by price in much the same way as when we buy consumer or luxury goods. If the price is high the quality must be good, whereas we must be cautious about those cheap bargains.

The evidence of the market volumes that the majority of investors can only buy when the stock has become expensive is a considerable impediment to profitable investment. The investor now has to have the patience of Job to wait until the next upturn to exit profitably. We may question whether the investor who has difficulty in timing their purchase will be successful in timing their exit. Further evidence to support this contention comes from the structural influence of portfolio advisers who prepare lists of the most successful fund managers and encourage investors to transfer funds from the currently unsuccessful managers to the champions of the period just past. This reinforces the tendency to buy high, sell low. For many years *Investors Chronicle* magazine calculated the comparison of two hypothetical portfolios. One was based on always buying last year's winner. At the end of each year the remaining balance was transferred to the best performing fund in each portfolio category for that year. The comparison was to follow the same process but this time with the worst performing funds of the previous year. Over the years, choosing last year's dog of a fund outstripped last year's winner fund by a considerable margin.

This bias is often not apparent to the investor because we all have a tendency to distort our memory of what we really thought before we actually made an investing decision. Of course we have no memory at all of all those things we should have bought but never got around too or did not even consider. When we have taken decisions that did not work out perfectly at first we have the tendency to try to make it good by attempting to retrieve those particular prices despite ever changing circumstances.

This all supposes that we have a reason to validate how our decisions turned out. This temptation can be brushed aside with the knowledge that everyone agreed with our decision beforehand and anyway everyone else was caught in the downturn as well.

The combination of momentum, the reinforcing signal of price, and feeling of consensus can really start to generate very powerful effects especially as many in the industry are rewarded by the growth in volume and price. The idea of the efficient market suggests a smooth iterative process that balances the competing forces to bring the optimum outcome in a sort of self-damping mechanism. Tvede instead brings the image of a powerful engine where interconnecting forces accelerate and exaggerate the effect like interconnecting turbochargers. Rising prices bring the interest of the financial community, the media and then the general public. There has to be a reason for this they think, there is no smoke without fire. New players without any previous interest in the market jump on to the bandwagon. Significantly Tvede's machine has many more forces than the risk/reward balance at the individual investment level. In his engine, disasters are always possible. If the pressures are out of balance or some part of the mechanism breaks, wild fluctuations may result. And this already assumes the machine began operation in good working order. Is this an explanation of booms and busts as the turbocharger overrevs or bursts?

In some cultures where bargaining is ingrained in the everyday routine the combination with the goodthing philosophy causes a particularly powerful feedback loop. A change in the dynamics of a goodthing could be the reason for the 1997 financial meltdown in Asia. In a culture of bargaining and Asian negotiating, the buyer always knows that he has paid too much and can never be satisfied with what he gets. This must be true otherwise the other party would never sell. For the last couple of decades, this basic instability has been overridden by a pervasive Western culture of investing in a goodthing. It is well known that the more you spend on a goodthing the better off you are. This is not specifically a geographic influence as classic examples of goodthings that are deemed to have the power to automatically transform the prospects of any corporation are advertising, research and 'our number one asset is our people'.

It is also well known that when you change the label of a badthing to a goodthing the benefit is doubled, for example in the beneficial effect derived by changing the description of bookkeepers to sales routine assistants, costs become investments and so forth.

Investing in Asia clearly became a goodthing until a combination of circumstances suddenly made it a badthing. The cataclysmic effect of the swing for goodthing to badthing introduced enough countervailing pressure to the Asian culture so that people selling now always got too little for what they were selling.

Times change. Popular investment themes fall out of fashion. Goodthings become badthings and sometimes very quickly. For the investor this means that there has to be a strategy of exit to cover the eventualities when stable enjoyment of expected value is no longer possible. The problem is that we are better buyers than we are sellers. This is a shame because you only make money selling and not from buying. It is easier to start off with high hopes about something that is new than it is to crystallize whatever disappointment disposal may bring. This is held back by inertia and so evolves slowly until a different kind of psychology applies that can also develop violent characteristics. The pressure builds. After various stages of disorder the market begins to display the psychology of the mob, the psychology of panic by which the market goes down because it goes down.

Speculation develops when people buy assets expecting the prices to rise because of new theory or insight. The chances are that the rush to take action serves to confirm their expectation, or of the erroneous expectation of getting out before it is too late.

One test of the efficient market is to observe whether the financing actions of corporations are consistent with that theory. We can look to see whether their decisions with regard to corporate structure and share offerings take account the market's ability to correctly value their activities. The evidence would suggest that many corporations, or at least their investment bankers, remain unconvinced of the ability of the market to accurately assess their value especially when the share price is lower than convenient. This distortion is attributed to the perfect market being fooled by industry combinations within a conglomerate and geographic spread within a multinational. Antilogic solutions have been provided for both problems.

There have been fashions as to corporate structure and so over the years we can find examples going in both directions. Business seeks to expand by acquisition and at various times there are trends to not only obtain growth but also spread risk and gain a portfolio advantage. Sometimes it is called forming a conglomerate. The financial engineers were able to prove considerable financial synergies by putting disparate businesses together. After a period the advantages of cheaper finance and superior management are no longer reflected in the share price. Revenues slow and it proves difficult to manage the diverse range of business. The CEO credibility cycle begins to bite and the new man reverses the policy away from diversification and is keen to stick to the knitting so a process of divestment begins to achieve the benefits of focus. Finance policies are also transformed from the pursuit of growth to a burning ambition to reduce gearing.

The rating agencies take contrasting positions on diversification with one marking down the specialist for putting all its eggs in one basket and being exposed to the risk of a downturn in its main business. Curiously the other main rating agency is worried by the risks of the overly complex business with lack of focus.

Sometimes the conglomerate is broken up while it stays together! This is achieved by the technique of alphabet stocks. This is a process by which investment banks earn a fee for giving shareholders a new share for a specific part of the business they already own. Typically after five years and under a new CEO, investment banks earn a fee when the company buys back from its shareholders that part of the specific business that it no longer owns.

There is a current trend to create new structural alphabet stocks by joining previously independent corporations together by contract to form dual listed companies. Royal Dutch Shell pioneered this supposedly new invention in 1907 followed by Unilever in 1929. After nearly a century the efficient market is unsure whether these structures are simple or complex, separate or homogeneous and more or less risky relative to a conventional structure. There is a variation employing what are called stapled stocks. This concept is akin to the bundled pack in the supermarket. The various attributes are combined in an indivisible way so that it is hard to know if you paid for the steak knives or not. Adding to the confusion is the role of the sharemarket listing committees awarding points for technical difficulty and artistic merit.

Dual listing and stapled stocks are often used to solve the problem of combining corporations that have investors and operations in different domiciles. There is nothing new about globalization although there is a vogue in using it to justify corporate activity, especially relating to change of domicile. The problem of the corporations share price will have been attributed to either its investors or the business being in the wrong country. This has led to lot of confusion. Sometimes the idea is simply to change the home exchange. Many multinationals have multiple listings to tap the various stock markets around the world thus providing investors with choice and convenience. It also brings publicity for the company concerned. Despite these efforts almost all volume is normally still transacted on the home exchange. Periodically some multinationals seek a share price boost, from changing the domicile of the home exchange from amongst the locations where the company is already listed. The perfect market is supposedly confused by these actions.

Sometimes the idea is more complicated as the investment bankers seek to carve out just that titbit that will tempt a particular sort of investor. This is called a partial float. The opposite is achieved some years later by successfully buying back the minorities. Could this be called the partial-sink? Both actions are designed to add to shareholder wealth and, presumably, doing both will add double.

A change of the corporate structure can give the chance to liberate value and not just in the form of adviser fees and executive options. This can permit robbing the reserves created in the past or the reserves accumulated for the future as in the case of demutualization.

Similar issues arise with the share market flotation of the Australian Share Market (ASX) itself. We are uncertain how one can logically float on oneself but it happened. The financial arithmetic is also complex. The sole revenue of the ASX was brokerage levied on the participating brokers who were the owners of the exchange. In the new world the floatation of the ASX has made the brokers rich through the increased value of the shares. This is due to ASX increasing the charges to the brokers which makes them poor or perhaps the individual brokers have become rich whereas their corporate employers who have to bear the increased future costs have become poor. Many farmers' co-operatives have or are going through the process of corporatization and flotation. Again shares are given to the owners who instantly are worth more as a result. Reuters had a similar background being owned by the newspapers as a co-operative source of information. Where are those newspapers today? MasterCard and Visa are two credit cards co-operatives that now do the same thing. They are owned by the banks but are not expected to earn a profit. Their apparent purpose is to compete with each other and their owners.

Funding restraints are often given as a reason why governments around the world are so keen to privatize activities that have been in public ownership for generations and so float the public asset. If the government cannot find the funds for these activities, who can?

The common theme that runs through these many examples of changing corporate structure is complexity that demands large professional fees and a highly paid management capable of managing the change or at least sitting in the seat while it happens because that is when you win the door prizes.

IV

BELIEVING THE WORDS

THE PROVIDERS of information go beyond the reporting of facts, to the relaying of opinion, to the provision of entertainment and worse. This may be a legitimate effort to add value but it may also be the result of a conscious effort of those with an interest to create a favourable outcome. The net result is that the information sources may report as facts, items that are opinions, intentions and predictions. These do not always turn out as expected.

Interpreting information from our colleagues, the markets or the media is never easy especially if no information is provided which is often the case as the simplest method for justifying a situation is to dispense with explanations. If you already know the answer why waste time fiddling around with so-called analysis and evidence? Let's get on with things. Time is money. Go straight to the heart of the matter. Just jump to the conclusion. Shoot from the hip.

Sometimes this is not enough. If it is necessary to do any analysis in order to reach a conclusion then only to look at part of the picture. This greatly improves efficiency as you can move to the desired outcome that much faster if there is less to consider. This is known as the KISS principle for *Keep It Simple Stupid*. This is easier for some although some purists believe that simple solutions exist only in the minds of cowboys, fools and investment bankers.

The rest of us are smart but the world is oh so complex. It is not our fault that it is so hard. We need help from all manner of information providers and it turns out that they provide much more than facts. The result is a lot of confusion although heaven forbid that anyone would be misled. Words are confused with the action they describe (where there is a lot of talk but nothing happens), action confused with objectives (where a lot happens but there is no progress to achieve predetermined objectives), alternating strategies and mistaken direction (where there is action and objectives but there is confusion about matching the two; as financial techniques become more complex this type of confusion is more common). There is also a sinister tendency to deliberately go in the wrong direction, to justify errors to this tendency and finally distortion (through interaction of feed back loops). Each category represents a type of Antilogic.

At the senior management ranks it is easy to confuse words with action. With several layers of organization between the decision makers and customer or production worker or research scientist there is little opportunity to directly participate in activity. For most large corporations or bureaucracies management equals doing. The days are filled with strategy formation, planning, meetings, coordination and motivation. With the growth of technology, e-mail, Lotus notes or video may replace face-to-face committee meetings. Irrespective of the medium, the basis of persuading colleagues to move forward is talk. Once the message is transmitted the task can be ticked off as completed. The forward and copy buttons on the e-mail have automated the process by which everyone is informed and responsibility assigned or transferred. But talking is not doing although the growth of public relations has made it more difficult to detect the difference. So good is the process of creating announcements that it is easy to confuse announcement with achievement. Articulating competitive advantage is seen as the same as capturing it. With the veracious appetite from the analysts for new information there is always scope for the new announcement and this squeezes out the need to report against previous announcements. In order to come with a convincing presentation of intentions there has to be a minimum level of decision making. But deciding is not doing. It is just talking with emphasis.

Business has long used the set piece meeting as the forum for the demonstration of support for the leadership and their direction. More than sixty years ago P.G. Woodhouse described such a situation when his charming but impecunious young hero must prove his worth to his sweetheart by getting a job. He succeeds triumphantly by becoming employed in the film industry as a *nodder*. The head of the studio holds set piece meetings surrounded by his staff. At his right hand are those with speaking parts, further down the table are the *yes men* and at the foot of the table are the nodders who nod in vigorous affirmation of the ideas of Mr. Big.

Much of the leadership language of business relates to aphorisms or even parables that help to put across simply the message to employees and shareholders. They have also had an important role in decisions made in large meetings. The recent trend towards employee empowerment, cultural change and other leadership techniques has greatly increased the importance of the adroit public use of proverbs as more participants now have a role with speaking parts. The *self evident truth* and the *no-brainer* are important techniques in this situation and depend on the general willingness of the audience to automatically accept and identify with the point being made. This is most easily achieved if the concept has been learned at mother's knee, as often is the case with proverbs. Because Chief Executives generally have extensive experience before assuming the role, they have a wide vocabulary of such expressions. Their leadership team will also be well equipped allowing them to participate fully in management discussions where each appropriate aphorism can be countered by its antidote, an equally appropriate aphorism advocating the opposite position, e.g. look after the pennies and the pounds will look after themselves – penny wise, pound foolish. In some organizations hours of innocent pleasure can be passed in aphorism debates.

Globalism and the Internet have greatly added to the extent and cultural diversity of the available proverb pool so it is possible to repeat the process several times and indeed this would be both necessary and good form to permit each speaking participant in a set piece meeting to make their contribution. If the available proverbs exceeds the number of participants or time available it is likely that the decision will be deferred. However, in those organizations where set piece meetings tend towards becoming show trials it is likely that the available proverbs will spontaneously become lopsided in favour of the party line. Given the balanced nature of the proverb pool this is a good litmus test to the openness of the leadership team. In organizations with strong willed leaders the aphorism of the day needs to be discovered to avoid embarrassing mistakes.

The trend towards vocational education has unfortunately reduced the study of language with many managers only having an imperfect understanding of the true meaning of proverbs and so they are especially prone to confuse the direction of the advice or to confuse different proverbs involving the same subject. Consequently it is quite common for answering proverbs to be less than perfect counters and over successive rounds it is possible that the two sides completely reverse their positions through the imperfect use of incremental response. This is especially so in a collaborative team working situation where direct contradiction is seen as unsupportive.

Much of leadership is about encouraging the team in the face of uncertainty and fear. Sometimes the chosen strategy may have risk or unpleasant consequences for members of the team. It is essential to have a range of exhortations that will encourage the team to go forth and do its duty. This frequently involves sporting and military images so that the image of business struggle quickly goes beyond excellence to competition and beyond to battle. Quotes from Churchill are particularly popular not only because of the quality of the language but their suitability in the face of impending disaster. The choice of image and quote appear designed to emphasize the inevitability of unpleasantness and the virtue contained in its conquest.

If there is progress beyond talk the chances are that the basis of the decision will not be sound and failure will bring retribution for those deemed responsible and bystanders. If by some chance the decision is successful there will be plenty of others to claim the credit. The asymmetry of business rewards is apparent to management that recognizes the danger of making a decision, especially if there is a risk that it will be carried out. It is far wiser to avoid this risk despite the general corporate requirement to be both busy and decisive.

Small problems are subject to the disaster/credibility trade off. In most established bureaucracies the going rate is at least five *hoorays* to make up for one *Oh dear*. Therefore the avoidance of mistake is valued much more than the creation of success, however defined. The trade off is too extreme for most managers so in order to reduce the chance of an *Oh dear* they are prepared to forego the risk of even an inadvertent *hooray*. The belief is that a success is all very well but it is likely to be followed sooner or later by an *Oh dear*.

There is a very big exception to this disaster/credibility rule. This is rewarding the real disaster. Business is similar to politics and the military in this regard. A very big disaster is often rewarded by promotion. This demonstrates leadership and allows the disaster to be declared a success. It is not wise to bet too early in the career on the disaster route to promotion. Generally a fair degree of seniority is already required to have sufficient influence to generate a worthwhile disaster. The disaster route has the advantage that few will take the risk of claiming responsibility.

One solution to personal risk is the no-business meeting where business leaders gravely consider many possibilities but take no action. A common variation of this concept is to affirm the non-existence of the problem, especially after thorough discussion, so that nothing needs to be done. The other strategy is that of taking multiple solutions. At least one of them must be correct and with luck they will all cancel out again avoiding the need for action.

Modern management techniques have introduced new disciplines for determining strategy and setting plans with profit targets and budgets.

Unfortunately investors and analysts have been to the same courses so now demand the companies use these techniques and announce their methods and targets. Generations of business leaders have resisted announcing specific targets on the grounds of commercial confidentiality so as to avoid giving encouragement to competitors. Little by little they have been forced to give ground to flexibly respond to changing market conditions. It is now deemed prudent to continually set targets thus plotting a path to a future objective. Sometimes the CEO finds the progress inadequate and will encourage the team with inspiring speeches. When new targets become essential, drawing a line in the sand emphasizes this importance. In a rapidly changing environment you must move with the times and not bury your head in the sand so it becomes a flexible line in sand.

While getting the actual results is hard enough, planning is an additional burden. Planning is a process by which a lot of effort is taken to study the economic environment, the market, consumer preferences, competitive activities, new product plans and cost profiles. All this is put into a computer model and made to show the desired increase over the last year. This can be greatly simplified by adopting asymmetric planning where revenue increases are included without costs. Sometimes costs are included without revenues but only to restrain profits from growing over target. Formal profit planning estimates often include the future upturn. This is intended as a positive when described as the J curve but is negatively described as the hockey stick by the sporting aficionados. By the time it reaches the investor relation presentations it has become the dynamically deferred upturn, just turning the corner or the light at the end of the tunnel.

When business has difficulty in achieving its business objectives there is a tendency to devote more resources to planning so as to avoid repetition of the short fall. This leads to greater detail planning, greater intrusion into the business of the operations, more frequent reporting, and the imposition of stringent budgetary and project approval processes. As the planning process obtains more data it provides opportunities to seek optimization of resources, exploitation of cross group synergies and other techniques that imply that no part of the plan can be finalized before the results of the rest are known. The more sophisticated the planning process the slower it goes and the more likely that the few surviving operational managers revert to informal planning processes outside the planning circus. It is quite common for a developed (three ring) planning circus to be planning for all of the year. In some highly developed examples the planning process takes longer than the period of the plan and so is not ready to provide guidance for that period. It is sometimes claimed that the planning circus is imposed on the business by the head office. The enthusiasm by which the planning process is generally embraced contradicts this because when you are planning you are not doing. This has distinct advantages in optimizing the disaster credibility trade off.

Revenue on its own is not sufficient to ensure bottom line success. Volume should not be at the expense of margin and here inflation proofed margins come to the Planner's rescue. There is no need to estimate prices separately. We can assume that over the life of the project/product we will achieve inflation-proofed margins. This is because the competitors are rational, the industry needs to recover its investment or this is the way it has always been. Industry protection by exchange rate follows the same pattern. Our project need not contemplate unpalatable exchange rates as these would imply the demise of industry in our land and the government won't let that happen. If the starting position is a little tight we can expect that prices will rise because present levels do not give the industry suffi-cient returns to ensure re-investment.

A wise old chairman once spotted the correlation between planning effort and subsequent profit. Each year the businesses were equipped with an economic forecast of growth and prices and told to generate the profit increases. Each year the plans were to target but the actual fell short. The problem was solved at a stroke when the chairman scrapped the economic forecasts. He banned assumed economic growth and still demanded the profit increase. Management, denied the easy arithmetic profit growth assumed from economic growth, inflation proofed margins and assumed efficiency improvements (that never materialized in prac-tice), was forced to find profit some other way.

A key element of the planning process is to prepare the ground for the allocation of resources and for justification of major capital projects. When large investments must be made in capital works or new brands or acquisi-tions we would hope that the standard of debate would be at its highest. Sadly the relationship is the bigger the investment the wilder the argu-ments. This tendency is the parallel of a similar law that the more senior the officer deciding the lower the level of analysis employed. The cry goes up that we don't need all this bureaucracy for such vital projects.

Major projects bring their own collection of supporting arguments.

- This is a strategic investment
- This affords us a window of opportunity to expand
- This is a technical success
- Bargain prices can be obtained on unexpectedly available equipment needed for the as yet unapproved project

- Think how much we will gain in economies of scale if we just make the factory twice as big as we need just now.
- Think what we will loss if we don't spend.
- The world ends this Friday unless the project is approved and the proposal will be available for your signature at six o'clock Friday evening.
- Every one else has signed. We only need the formality of your signature for the records.
- This is for essential but unallocated infrastructure. By definition if it is essential we must have it. If we must have the infrastructure it is a waste of time justifying the investment by seeking a return. Because it is essential the more of it we have the better. Because it is essential it will only confuse the budgets by including it there in the reports of actual expenditure but it would be helpful to include an estimate in the plans.
- This is one of the CEO's cherished projects.

These arguments make it possible that we will gain approval for proposals that are not entirely thought out. Not to worry! The absence of initial analysis defers a lot of the anxiety about projects for ignorance is bliss until one day it is revealed that the project is off the rails and overspent. What is to be done? Two solutions will be suggested. One will suggest that as we've invested a million dollars it's time to pull the plug. Apparently word has not been received that the costs have been sunk? The second will suggest that as we've invested a million dollars we've got to keep going. Apparently word has not been received that the costs have been sunk.

When a project is in big trouble, declare a success and say no more. If the project is in really big trouble declare a major success and promote those responsible. After all, think how much worse it would have been if we hadn't ... There are also losses that are not really losses because they represent transactions that were undertaken for a good purpose. Losses may become investments.

Our plans must make due allowance of resources. Businessmen love extra, just in case. This may be extra capital or extra capacity or extra stock. If they ever achieve this nirvana they become used to it and seek only to add to the hoard. This influence is well described by the story of the country taxi. The tired business traveller arrives after a dusty train trip and is pleased to spot a single taxi waiting in the rank outside the station. 'Take me to the best hotel in town' the intrepid travel asks of the Cabbie. 'Sorry Sir that can't be done. The regulations require that there always be a taxi in front of the station'.

Iron stock is the inventory equivalent of the country taxi. Enough stock is held in excess of normal requirements to cover unexpected demand fluctuation until new production or bought in product can bring the inventory level back to normal. The business gets so used to having the extra that it tends to anticipate the fluctuations so that the iron stock is never touched.

During the planning mode it is tempting to stretch the linkages on paper. The deadlines are put back, the costing assumptions are relaxed and so forth. This is the concept of having the cake and eating it too. This comes in many guises but all with the common theme that conscious action is taken to permit a greater capability of choice. For example it could be the simplification of the product range to assist production but all the old variations continued as one offs for good customers. Or the budget for specified activities being eliminated but the activities continued.

The idea of flexibility in the guise of constant update can also be applied to strategy. It at first you don't succeed then try try try again. This facility to create multiple approaches that are only loosely connected to the actual progress of the business has reached the virtual category in the recent wave of dot.com start-ups where there were plans but no business. In practice the lack of disappointment with the non-existent business meant that it was rather easy to find money to commence.

Fortunately there many mutually exclusive alternative strategies that can be explored indefinitely and even pursued. The timing of the changes owes something to fashion but is also linked to the CEO credibility cycle. Clearly political rivals must follow opposite strategies but the nature and timing of change in the event of a smooth CEO succession or during the reign of a commanding CEO is subtler. In both situations consistency must be demonstrated, in the first case to the illustrious predecessor, and in the second to the triumphs from earlier in the reign, but as the credibility cycle rolls on a flexible response is demanded. This is a dangerous period for bystanders, as previous heresies suddenly become current dogma. The politically correct ideology has changed. Timing is everything.

The most regular phenomenon is the tendency to alternate on the decision to centralize or decentralize. This leads to the Accordion Theory. Many factors come into play when a new CEO decides about organizational structure. The location and size of the head office is directly coupled to the decision whether to centralize or decentralize. Naturally the conclusion is likely to be the opposite of his predecessor and there are many reasons for this. The head office or its absence is a goodthing subject to fashion. It is also the location of undesirable costs. It is also the likely location of disloyal political rivals. A change in the configuration of the head office provides the opportunity to save or appear to save costs and to reward or punish the barons of the organization. The centralized organization is similar to the accordion in the closed position. The great musician extends the instrument and is greatly pleased by the pleasant sound of savings falling out. The notes that this instrument plays are of currency and not music although there is the expression that the sound of money is music to my ears. Encouraged by this happy result he reverses the direction and closes the instrument and again rewarded by the pleasant sound of savings. Those decentralized departments that had picked up the work of the centre without increased resources now find their budgets cut to match the return of functions in the latest optimization and coordination exercise. The process can be repeated so long as there is scope in the credibility cycle. The sound of the savings will mask the cries of the victims and the movement of costs and records around the organization will always result in proof of great success. The effect is accentuated if the location is changed each iteration. The cost of moving is high but the numbers who actually move is low. The new headquarters, despite the brochure emphasizing work lifestyle balance, are always just a bit too small to take everybody from the old location. The head-office move is a feature of US business as there are more possible locations.

The alternation can move in other dimensions. The pairing of vertical/ horizontal integration and also of upstream/downstream (a particular favourite of the mining and energy sector) gives a double opportunity of the synergy and business certainty of the integrated business and the specialization and flexibility of the focussed business. Globalization and local champion is a further alternating pair. Positioning here depends on whether the corporation, or more particularly its leader, sees itself as an acquirer or as the victim. Naturally in the fast moving market this choice has to be quickly and frequently made.

Brands also go in cycles as alternating brand managers either extend or focus the brand franchise. Once brands are established there is a drive to increase revenues by extending the brand to new products and categories thus giving a low entry price and economies of marketing costs. After revenues stagnate the remedy is to eliminate peripheral products from the brand family and the main products are given more clout.

Acquisitions are one of the greatest paradoxes of business strategy. Most acquisitions fail and yet some of the biggest, most successful and enduring corporations owe much of their present success to astute acquisitions or mergers in the past. There are many academic studies that confirm that the batting average for acquisitions is not very high with the added conclusion that mergers within some industries had the best chance of success. The competition lawyers would say that this was because of the anti competitive nature of such combinations. Success was at the expense of the consumer. Another conclusion would be that there is more chance of a successful merger if the parties know what they are doing which is to be hoped within their own industry.

There is another paradox relating to mergers. Advocates are so convinced that they will do better at running someone else's business that they are prepared to pay a takeover premium of about thirty percent for the right to take control. This is quite a handicap to take into the competitive battle. The saving grace is that it is more than likely the competition is doing it too. Warren Buffett used a children's fairy tale to explain this effect. As a great investor Warren must have another technique to ensure that he does not make the same mistake.

> Many managers were over-exposed in impressionable childhood years to the story in which the imprisoned, enchanted prince is released from the toad's body by a kiss from the beautiful princess. Consequently, they are certain that the managerial kiss will do wonders for the profitability of the target company. Such optimism is essential. Absent that rosy view, why else should the shareholders of company A want to own an interest in B at a takeover cost that is two times the market price they'd pay if they made direct purchases on their own? In other words, investors can always buy toads at the going price for toads. If investors instead bankroll princesses who wish to pay double for the right to kiss the toad, those kisses better pack some real dynamite. We've observed many kisses, but very few miracles. Nevertheless, many managerial princesses remain supremely confident about the future potency of their kisses, even after their back-yards are knee-deep in unresponsive toads.[36]

The toad kissers are succumbing to the oldest delusion of management of believing that the grass is greener on the other side. Business strategists have a tendency to confuse the industry in which their company is active augmented by a lack of knowledge of actual conditions in an unfamiliar territory. This can lead to companies simultaneously seeking to enter each other's industry both with the idea of exploiting higher margins or what ever. It is not that they believe acquisitions are easy, as they have read of the problems. It is just that in this case there are particular advantages such as automatic synergies that will bring additional revenue from an over-lapping product range or from economies of scale from rationalizing the production overlaps. This is not how it works out.

It is a shame that economies of scale are so seldom achieved in mergers as they would have also been a big help in justifying new machines where the expected cost benefit will be so great that our competition will melt away. The strangest synergy is to acquire a company that is a supplier to or distributor of products for the acquirer. In effect an inflated multiple is being paid to buy your own business.

This is to underestimate the imperative of the CEO to pull off the spectacular merger. The credibility cycle is at work here too. When our hero takes over the mess from his tired out old predecessor he has a lot of time to sift through plans and properties of the company. Not for him the rash move into an overpriced acquisition. He puts in train new organic plans with ambitious growth targets to reverse the previous share loss. The untapped potential of those famous old brands is finally going to be harnessed in the interests of shareholder value. The reality of globalization and the adjacent competitive imperative are discovered after the first full year of disappointing organic progress. The acquisition begins to look not so bad after all. An acquisition strategy is drawn up and once it is announced it becomes important for credibility to carry it through.

That this is claimed to be the oldest delusion is the hint to another possible motivation for acquisitions that goes beyond mere ego. It is a primeval drive for survival. The Stone Age warrior sought to gain more than just victory in battle with the transfer of strength from the victim to himself. This was the basis of cannibalistic rituals in which the victor would eat specific body parts of the vanquished. Naturally this practice has been discouraged on health grounds (not least for the victim) but the instinct remains. If you see that your competitor is doing something good, eat him so that you may be strong. It is also a good way of settling old industry scores.

Now that cannibalism is no longer the done thing, a change of control is not so bad for the victim with the appropriate contract. Not everybody has such protection and so the impression has built up that it is not so good to be at the receiving end of an acquisition. The first approach will cause an outcry with threatened management allying themselves with unions and government that they have never previously met. Consequently it is very common for aggressors to say merger when they mean acquisition. The fun starts when the implementation begins. Did you mean it when you said this was a merger and not an acquisition? Thus the acquired management can begin to reassert their position. The tensions mount. The swift campaign to harvest the synergies begins to slow and then bog down in the corporate version of The Battle of the Somme. The happiest managers are those who pulled the rip cords on the golden parachutes and departed the scene.

At a particular moment it becomes impossible to only talk strategy and further reset budgets. Now the budget finally has to be set perhaps because the year has already passed. Anyway, once the final (no longer resettable) target has been passed without meeting the pre-set level a success may be declared by selectively revising the interpretation of the original target. As in all history, the particular role of individuals becomes blurred so as to confuse heroes and villains. Retrospective analysis can only be conducted by the incumbent of the day. This is one indication of the tendency towards revised history or revisionist history.

There is a changing fashion of words or actions that are willingly adopted or have to be adopted by all participants in the corporate environment. You must know the current politically correct word or action. Support of the current theme is a token of support for the current organization, a willingness to change with the times and to be a team player. Any hesitation, let alone refusal to participate or opposition on grounds of relevance, damage to the business, etc. is immediately categorized as intransigence. The individual is either in or out without any reference to the validity of the politically correct activity. However, it is understood that it is only vital to say the right thing. Action is not required and depending on in-depth language might actually be discouraged. The leader will speak against unpalatable actions but the lack of subsequent action reveals implicit support. This is in contrast to key interests of the leader which are rigorously enforced. In-depth language emerges when the currently popular politically correct activity conflicts with some other strongly held objective or the personal aspirations of influential management.

In the politically correct environment it is very difficult to know which way the wind is blowing. Sometimes we are required to do what we are told. Sometimes, with in-depth language we are required to not do what we are told and finally there is the unspoken truth that lies in the hidden words. George Orwell in *1984* created a whole language to accommodate the mental gymnastics required for survival in this political environment. In such an environment it is not safe to be alive. Uncertainty is the reason that many fall back on the comforting anonymity of the management herd where fate is determined by probability.

After a while talking without action is insufficient, especially if reward is linked to outcome. If there is no alternative to action the next best solution is to pursue action that can only have favourable outcomes because any unfavourable outcomes are deemed not to exist or occur elsewhere. When unfavourable outcomes have to be sheeted home others can carry the blame.

The time split of reality gives the best chance of reward. The here and now real reward of a bonus can safely be enjoyed when the possible unfavourable consequences can only occur in an uncertain future and hopefully not while the individual is still around. This effect is structural because of the tendency of making predictions, incurring expenses or investment before the anticipated enjoyment of a successful outcome. The combination of optimism and enthusiasm for one's own project together with the need to compete against other projects makes it natural that projects look particularly attractive before they start and so tend not to live up to expectations. The prudent individual will encourage the receipt of reward before the uncertain outcome is known. This is even more valid when considering the risk that when the success does come the rewards may be purloined by someone else. What could be more reasonable than to anticipate the reward now and let the future look after itself? Traditionally this reward has been in the form of promotion before implementation is complete but early declaration of success can bring financial reward as well.

We all like certainty even though the personal consequence of uncertainty need not be bad for the individual. At the dramatic level of the CEO in suitable industries it is possible to surf on a wave from promised solution to promised solution. Salespeople and traders can enjoy similar effects in suitable industries such as volatile financial markets. Traders must take risks to make profits. Those that are successful are regarded as undoubtedly being very skilful and in great demand so earn high rewards. If they are unsuccessful they are paid to go away and are paid to start somewhere else. The interrelation between financial markets also helps, for example between interest rates and foreign currency exchange rates. One market is hedged against the other leading to a tendency for the interest desks to do well in one period and the foreign exchange desks to do poorly and for the situation to reverse in the next period. Nothing has been achieved overall but half the dealers have to have done well and are rewarded appropriately.

The passage of time and lack of memory helps us to survive the consequences of the previous disasters and expect future success. This is no doubt linked to the personal experience of the key participants and if associated with activities in the financial markets the brain is dulled by greed. It would be quite wrong to suggest that all memory has been suppressed. It is still there but selective. Within the corporation the corporate memory is often paraded as a talisman to guide the decision-makers at crucial moments. It has a status akin to the battle honours of the regiment that are paraded at great occasions until they become so tattered by use over generations that they are laid up as icons at the regimental chapel. The parallels go further in that the battle honours of the regiment are often won through great valour on the part of the soldiers as they struggled on the battlefield to redeem the blunders created by the high command. Many fall in such battles. Although the corporate memory is revered as though it were the ashes of a previous Great Leader it could be more appropriately treated as the symbol of the Unknown Manager lost in corporate battle. As it is, the senior officer present guards the corporate memory as is appropriate for this important source of wisdom. The corporate memory has an important role in revisionist history and is a source of considerable power for the regime. It is also a source of considerable danger for other veterans of the same corporate skirmishes if they do not have the correct recollections. Stalin and others cleared away the old soldiers to ensure that there was no possibility of errors of memory.

Having progressed through the stage of talking without doing, we can now look at the doing to see if it gets us to our objectives. I take as a given that we have an objective because if you have no destination then any road is good. To get going we need a decision. This can require decisiveness. Some businesses think they are decisive because they make so many decisions. What they decide this morning is reversed this afternoon. This might be thought to be associated with lack of discipline with the different factions milling around. In fact this is likely to lead to no decisions being taken. Often Great Men feel the need to show strength in front of their team. Great Leaders must lead and so when asked for decisions they will give decisions without having been given all of the background or informed of the influences involved. The entourage of the Great Leader knows that he must decide and so if a particular individual seeks to gain his favoured outcome he will ensure that only information favourable to his cause will reach the leader. Believers of the contrary position will do exactly the same at another moment. The Great Leader cannot play favourites within his entourage so the contradictory decisions are safely given but at different moments. This leads to the sort of manoeuvres captured in the children's ditty.

Oh, the brave old Duke of York,
He had ten thousand men. (after downsizing eight thousand);
He marched them up to the top of the hill,
And then he marched them down again.
And when they were up, they were up,
And when they were down, they were down,
And when they were only halfway up,
They were neither up nor down.

Another way of looking at this is as an analogy of the CEO leading his corporation in the face of sharemarket indifference. The danger is that in this global environment the marching about might get in the way of a bigger international force described in the alternative ditty.

The King of France, the King of France,
With forty thousand men,
Oh, they all went up the hill, and so-
They all came down again.

Change is fine as long as you say that you are staying on the original line. This environment of movement gives the Great Leader the flexibility to achieve consistency. There is something to be said for this flexibility as it avoids the spectacle of elastic management which is the opposite extreme. This occurs where there is a tendency for established management to become somewhat set in their ways. This may be correlated with age but may also relate to the stability of the organization. New CEOs who want to change the way things are done apply pressure to the existing management directly or through a process of corporate values or cultural change. Naturally management will want to assist and at least show willing when the new boss is looking. So their action moves or stretches in the approved direction. However, if the boss stops looking and the pressure is relaxed they will snap back to the old ways just like an elastic band snaps back when released.

The CEO may display the same characteristics as new management techniques clash with his own habits but it is not likely that the rest of management will find it politic to notice unless it becomes the more dramatic form of elastic management known as horizontal bungee jumping. In their efforts to please, the new converts to cultural change programs are likely to adopt the new faith with crusaders' zeal and throw themselves into positions more extreme than called for. However, their beliefs are still anchored in the past and if the supporting momentum is lost they will rocket back to the original position or beyond. This demonstrates much movement but no upward progress.

When action is finally unavoidable it may be headed in the wrong direction. This is a very common and is often implicated in financial disasters and in what is subsequently described as corporate fraud. It is a particularly interesting and subtle form of Antilogic in that it is very difficult to determine at the time whether the error of direction was inadvertent, a difference of opinion or the basis of a fraud. It is even more difficult to determine when the history gets to be written, as it is the last man standing who says what happened. For those disasters that do not end in happy promotion there must be somebody to blame. It is rather limp just to disclose a blunder. It is a much more satisfactory finale if the motives of the scapegoat can be impugned by attributing fraud. Thus a blunder becomes a fraud.

The stated cause of many speculative disasters is buying instead of selling or vice versa. Who knows if it is being wise after the event or a misunderstanding by subsequent management? Many speculative frauds have been attributed by the perpetrator as having started as innocent mistakes that led to losses that he tried to cover up or trade out. The advance of technology has made this confusion even more exciting. Not only might the dealer confuse the direction, he may simply push the wrong computer button and so sell instead of buy. The game can be so simply begun. The dealer involved in a major fraud at the Chilean government owned copper company claimed this as the reason why he began down a path to disaster. The small inadvertent loss had to be traded away and it was downhill from there. Of course if there really was fraud the perpetrator when challenged will claim mistake.

Similar problems can arise with the decision to hedge or not to hedge a commodity, interest rate or currency exposure. It is easy to mistake the direction especially when acting on the sporadic intervention of distant leaders and any hedging can introduce risks that were not previously present. Who is to say which way the market is going to move or whether the planned exposure ultimately eventuates? But often the problem is just so confusing that the market player gets things back to front.

The inability to reliably distinguish direction finds its way through to the reading of balance sheets with confusion between long and short positions. This applies to industrial companies for their raw material positions and also for financial positions such as foreign exchange and interest rate positions. The problem does not just lie with the balance sheet but is fundamental to bookkeeping. We all have trouble knowing the right way round between credit and debit despite the descriptive labels.

Credit starts the problem with the wide ranging and qualitative meanings used not just for accounting but the process of creating credit for lending and the general description of good standing. Its power, magic and ultimately confusion come from the idea that a thought creates wealth for the word stems from *creditus* the Latin for *believed*. If it is believed then it must be real. Debit should be more straightforward. Its origin is from the Latin *debitum* meaning something owed. The problem is to know who owes what to whom and who is to be believed. Of course each language has its own word and connotations for the same concepts. In German, the word for debt is *schuld* the same as guilt revealing an attitude to debt as an obligation or burden. We find this concept back in English as the debt burden.

The main culprits for the confusion are the banks who with typical insensitivity send statements to millions of customers quoting debit and credit from the banks' point of view. The general public has been trained to believe that their money at the bank is shown as a credit (a liability) when in fact it is an asset for them.

The accountants have not made it any easier to understand. The hope was that if you did not understand the label you could at least recognize on which side of the ledger the entry would lie. Unfortunately, just like for road rules the British and the Americans chose different sides for the same thing. Even within the same side of the accounting entry the language provides further confusion. On the debit side we must distinguish between those things of use, the assets and the burdens, the expenses. On the credit side we find perplexing language as we try to distinguish liabilities, that are obligations to others and the more satisfying equity. It is satisfying because it belongs to the proprietors and it sounds better because the word stems from the Latin *aequitas* meaning equality or justice. Just what is to be equal is never explained but this could be the reason why many accountants see it as just that they cause liabilities to become equity.

This brings us to the dreaded derivatives. Because of some recent high profile difficulties such as the Orange County case, Barings, Gibson Greeting Cards and Proctor and Gamble derivatives have gained notoriety as if they were the creation of the devil. In fact derivatives are simply contractual rights based on another straightforward transaction. Initially they were devised as a means of reducing risk although brave spirits recognized the power of this capability to change direction and increase risk. This notoriety seems to lead to a programmed response for many operators and observers to confuse both the purpose of calls and puts and also to confuse their direction. Adding to the difficulty is the difference of impact between writing calls or options from the purchase or sale of the same option.

Confusing cause and effect is as though the causal molecules are going the wrong way through the problem. It is like we are all sitting in a train but no one cares which way it goes as long as we get movement. Business is like that. We have action plans with carefully programmed goals and responsibilities. These must be diligently ticked off but no one cares if we arrive at the destination.

It is not necessary to head off in the opposite direction to generate directional Antilogic but it helps. The exact opposite is easy to miss. Every thing is in the right place, the train is on the track, and the paperwork looks to be in place. All is in order except the train or the transaction moves off in the opposite direction. If conducted with confidence most observers will not recognize or comment on the error. Inadvertence is quite likely to be exercised with the great confidence that accompanies ignorance. In some individuals, uncertainty is compensated by considerable external confidence. The more uncertain they are, the more they feel the need to get their way. Thus confidence in execution is no clue as to correctness of direction.

Many decisions are of this nature and require a single choice. Buy-sell, stop-go, black-white, red-green, put-call, short-long, debit-credit. But of course, many other decisions allow considerable discretion and there are many opinions as to the correct way to go. A conventional wisdom may build up as to what is the normal way or a normal pattern. It then becomes obvious and noteworthy if the activity no longer conforms to this conventional wisdom. Questions are asked. Explanations must be given. Opinions are formed and debate ensures. Much less activity ensures if the observer receives a message that suggests that there has been no change when in fact reality has altered. By some means the message has been distorted either by the recipient or the transmitter. Clearly the distortion must still be a message that is quite close to the original unless the recipient is overcome with wishful thinking or some other impediment. For whatever reason there are frequent situations when the understanding of the financial situation is distorted from reality. This may derive from phenomena that distorts how journalists and their audience process market information

There are several good psychological reasons why individuals will react in particular ways when confronted by particular circumstances and how their perception of the actual situation may be distorted These are general characteristics of the population so I am only singling out the journalist because of the impact it may have on attitudes of the market. We tend to adopt the same attitudes as those with whom we associate, so analysts and journalists tend to read the output of their fellows and tend to adopt the same views. We often use the behaviour of others as our source of information about a difficult subject. If this means following the smartest people or the majority in the financial markets it is almost inevitably wrong.

None of us likes being wrong. When the evidence shows that our assumptions were wrong we try and avoid such information. This may lead to journalists and analysts ignoring information that conflicts with current market price trends. We misinterpret information we receive so it seems to confirm our actions. Journalists and analysts are committed in the market through their previous writings just as investors are committed through their investment decisions. We try to look only to information that seems to confirm our behaviours and attitudes. Analysts and journalists may use selective exposure to protect themselves against unpleasant realities compared to their previous writing and misinterpret information so as to confirm their attitudes.

For all these reasons those who have already written about the market may have reason to believe that it is still true even in the face of contradictory evidence. This is especially the case with the rising market that creates the framework through which the economic information is interpreted. It is exacerbated by the tendency to avoid turning points and so predict a continuation of the framework situation.

The application of psychology to analysts and journalists as well as the investors themselves suggests the possibility of mutually reinforcing feedback loops, a form of opinion supercharging that at each stage amplifies and reinforces the distortion. The investors seek out information that supports their opinions. The journalists need to find comment to provide news items and commentary about this news. The analysts not only have to come up with ideas to support the sale or purchase of shares but also to generate a public profile to demonstrate that they are experts whose predictions are worth following. They therefore cultivate the journalists. Increasingly the investment institutions and especially the trustees need to demonstrate that their investment decisions are appropriately judged against prevailing public opinion. Consequently the investor, the analyst, the journalist and the trustee all have a comment interest in repeating the opinion of the other. The only problem is that these joint opinions, these words may not accord with reality but no one has an interest in pointing it out.

V

BELIEVING THE NUMBERS: THE CONTRIBUTION OF THE ACCOUNTANTS

THE REPORTING of actual results to the financial markets have been prepared by accountants. So the reality that the market receives is that as perceived by those particular accountants. There are many opinions and many different solutions for the problems of presenting the financial affairs of any company. Confronted with choice and their own sense of professionalism it is only natural that the practitioners would continue their search until they found the right answer. When shopping for accounting opinions if you at first do not succeed try, try and try again.

In this chapter we will dip into quite a few of the techniques that the accountants employ to tell the market what we are told it already knows. Some of the same techniques are used as management accounting within the business to tell the managers themselves what is going on. The accountants take their perception of reality and consider what it will reveal and how it will be received.

It really should not make any difference what the accountants report as the perfect market is supposed to know what is going on. But we are very interested in what the accountants have to say and feel misled if we do not agree with their pronouncements. There are those who say you can test the realism of the accounting by using the old maxim that cash is fact but profit is opinion. Follow the accounts to the cash and you would find reality, except that this depends on your definition of cash. By the end of this book we might conclude that cash is opinion and that profit is fact. This is already becoming metaphysical and it gets worse. There are others who say that the accounts themselves are the reality and before double entry bookkeeping there could be no capitalism.

> One cannot even imagine capitalism without double-entry bookkeeping: they are as intimately related as form and content. There is a legitimate

doubt whether capitalism created double-entry as a tool in its realization or whether double-entry bred capitalization out of its inner spirit.[37]

This is heady stuff and not what is fashionable to expect when considering the work of the bean counters. It as though the numbers shown in the accounts are reality itself. This would be fine except this reality can also show a considerable variability as noted by Fred Schwed.

> One can't say that figures lie but figures as used in financial arguments, seem to have the bad habit of expressing a small part of the truth forcibly and neglecting the other part, as do some people we know.[38]

This requires a nicety of judgment both as to what accounting reveals and what it conceals. The regulators around the world are busy ensuring that any variability is controlled, at least within each country. Generally Accepted Accounting Standards (GAAP), Securities Exchange Commission (SEC), Australian Stock Exchange (ASX), Australian Securities and Investment Commission (ASIC) and others insist on reporting requirements that are highly technical and driven by corporations law. How is the efficient market to get its information and what is the impact of accounts and market reporting on investors? Apparently the accounts are not important for the big investors who get their information direct from the horse's mouth in direct briefings.

> For whom are they prepared? The management know it anyway but have an incentive to make it look good. The Boards only need it for compliance and avoidance of personal liability. The public meetings, e.g. AGM, are for the small shareholders but they represent an infinitesimal proportion of the shares. These small shareholders present have a limited grasp and ask questions close to their experience. They do not get serious answers. Institutions do not attend unless invited to support management. They do not ask questions but vote with their feet by selling out if dissatisfied. Institutions expect to get their briefing in private meetings with management. These inside meetings are now seen as shameful by SEC and are being attacked by ASIC.[39]

Those who do not accept it as being an objective science tend to regard it as an art form and are quick to attach the label creative accounting to accounts they distrust. So widespread has the belief about the flexibility of creative accounting become that the well-informed market assumes that it exists and becomes very concerned if the creativity is insufficient to meet expectations.

It explains the overreaction by the market to a minor failure by a company to meet results predictions. The market has expectations as to the capacity of window dressing (an important end result of creative accounting) to absorb minor result hiccups. Chief Executives are often upset by the tendency for the share market to overreact to small profit shortfall against market expectations. The market however has learned that the considerable flexibility provided by accounting assistance has meant that an inability to meet an expectation can only mean that all hollow logs have been exhausted.

Some financial analysts have spotted the interrelation between weakening accounting quality and inevitable missed earnings forecasts. The subsequent over-reaction of the market provides a basis for investment opportunities. Companies cannot afford to come clean in this era of consolidation. They wish to retain optimum strategic flexibility and do not advertise when they will show bad results. We have come to the stage of totally reversing the role of accounting from use as the basis for investing to using what it does not explain as the investment basis. Analysis of discrepancies now seeks to determine management's state of mind and from that the state of the business.

Most of what we seek to unravel, put aside or simply understand is not fiction but that described as window dressing. Window dressing is the presentation of the most favourable aspect of something, especially when unpleasant facts are concealed. In business it was largely confined to the work of accountants in ensuring that the financial reports are as attractive as they can be. This process requires taste and artistic flair. A recent trend has been for the engagement of other disciplines to help the accountants in the process of window dressing. The employment of public relations and media people to assist in investor relations has extended the exercise well beyond the financial statements themselves so that it has much in common with a Christmas pageant.

There is also window undressing, the sudden revelation that the previous accounting situation in the last days of the former CEO was shocking in the extreme. A cyclical pattern in accounting changes is to be observed. Incoming CEOs tend to be accounting zealots who uniformly detect a certain laxness in the policies of their predecessors. A newly rigorous accounting regime is implemented with temporarily depressing effects on the bottom line. The incoming regime will take away all pretty packaging and show the investors, for the time being, how bad things have become. As he settles into his regime the CEO needs to make good on his promises of ever improving results and the accountants stand ready to serve.

Subsequent periods reflect a satisfactory if not spectacular improvement in profits although in the interests of more accurately reflecting the business's true performance it proves necessary to relax certain accounting principles relating to intangibles, capitalization of expenses, etc. This upwards trend of profit continues for a few periods until a new strategy is unveiled that seeks to dramatically change strategic direction or lower cost with such an impact that the associated costs are treated as abnormal and so removed from all comparatives except the total of shareholders' funds. An inevitable crisis of conscience follows in the following year compelling management to include the abnormals in all historic comparisons.

Acquisitions provide a useful alternative to abnormals providing the opportunity for the creation of intangibles, a dramatic statement of new strategy, a major restructuring provision, a change in accounting policy and a new basis for comparisons. If enough momentum can be created with the acquisition it can be possible to reappraise the provisions made at the time of acquisition to the benefit of ongoing results. Repeat process. The same effect without the acquisition is called *take a bath accounting* where you throw in all the problems including the kitchen sink.

Actually there is more to it than that. Adverse events require the special treatment of asymmetric explanation. If the event comes unexpectedly in the future it is a problem but with a prior explanation it is no longer a problem when it arrives because 'I told you it was coming'. The news is therefore already in the market and the effect gradually becomes a positive when it is corralled as an abnormal and decisive action is taken to address the issue including upgrading the computer systems, dismissing the usual suspects, engaging consultants and forming a compliance committee.

After the incident is past it becomes a strong positive because everything else now looks good in comparison. The special magic of the abnormal is that this process can still take place without even having to have the transitory problem of the initial negative because it is in this special category designated as being different. This permits the continued declarations of record profits and publication of charts that demonstrate an upward march of favoured positive measures. The description has had to be changed over the years from *exceptional* through *extraordinary* to *abnormal* and will undoubtedly change again in the future with *unusual* a strong tip. Particularly adept exponents of the abnormal are able to make the announcement itself a positive event with Churchillian declarations of resolve to tackle the issues of the industry head-on, to grasp the nettle, to bite the bullet and other images of worthy pain to be followed in due course by the pleasures of the uplands pastures and the elysian fields. The process is apparently so pleasurable that some organizations repeat the process time after time although the workings of the CEO credibility cycle strictly limits the number of times the normal CEO practitioner can employ the abnormal technique before he exhausts the balance in his credibility account.

The precise solutions vary by industry and change over time as they are overused and become passé, often with the assistance of the regulators. Some generic techniques survive in one form or another. The asymmetric matching of costs with revenues (or not) provides the greatest opportunity, simply due to the scale of the activity. Revenues are simple. They are brought forward or even anticipated because they are virtually certain. Costs are complex and a view must be taken as to whether they need to be taken this year, whether they are really an investment, or whether they fall into some special cost category. Costs may be treated as abnormal but this is not frequently possible and only at specific times in the CEO credibility cycle. At other times other categorization is necessary. This might be as a restructuring provision or other special one off costs. These preferably will have positive connotations so that although they have been prudently booked as costs the implication is that they are for a goodthing that will provide lasting benefit. Great care is taken to ensure that future generations of management share in the benefits of today's computer programs and other initiatives by adding the investment to the balance sheet.

One-off costs or losses are likely to be abnormal and worthy of separation from the results because management intends to strive mightily to prevent their repetition. One-off profits reflect future aspirations and are likely to be retained in the results. Therefore it is likely that the one-off benefits will be included via the price-earnings multiple in the share-price. In the event of a trade-sale or acquisition negotiations the management will be convinced of the validity of such an approach.

If times have indeed been good the hollow logs are replenished. This gives scope for new costs to be offset against previously accumulated provisions. It is particularly useful to be able to offset disposal deficits against previously accumulated revaluation reserves.

Today's analysts are now very interested in all aspects of cost control. So is the typical CEO but the internal workings of the accounting system may make it a mystery to him as well. Companies who find they have an increased level of cost despite these cost saving activities try to optimize the cost allocation methods with a new allocation each period. During this period the tendency is towards taking one-time gains in preference to long-term revenue, both in the sense of business pursued and how business is accounted as this will tend to justify the costs.

A common claim prior to introducing a big savings target is that costs are going to be reduced by working smarter than before. This is a warning for danger coming. The Big Boss will want to participate in the budget process to ensure he gets the necessary improvement in numbers the market demands. This involves planning with the ruler. The same process is also known as planning by the ruler. The boss runs his eye along the row of numbers revealed above the ruler and changes any that are above the determined approval level (i.e. same as last year, 10% down, etc.). The cut is not popular and there will at first be no savings. The haircut is the answer when there are no obvious candidates for savings. It is the saving of choice in some organizations because of its equity. Everybody is given their opportunity to do their bit for the cause, shoulder to the wheel and all those good things. The Big Boss sets a target for cost saving or profit increase. This is shared out to the lesser leaders with a full sense of democracy as everyone is invited to make an equivalent contribution to the cause irrespective of any other circumstances within their operation. The expectation is that saving 10% on all costs will save 10% from total costs. Where the cost increase is due to the inclusion of a previously blessed pet project the rest of the items in that category have to be reduced to avoid the total appearing above the ruler.

Recognized defence tactics are the accounting change and the generous relinquishing of activities to colleagues. The original departmental budget is retained albeit reduced by the statutory 10% despite the transfer of activity. All stoutly resist any new initiatives, no matter how deserving, because of the ruler effect on the rest of their budget. When the glare of publicity fades the special pleading begins.

The easiest way to save costs is to create a class of migrating costs. These are costs that are saved by transferring them to the other department. There is no need to feel guilty about passing costs onto colleagues as they will pass them on in due course and have already passed other costs to you. In any event this process has no adverse personal consequence in many organizations because of the wise precaution of never accepting costs transferred from other departments. With many planning systems based on the aggregation of the individual cost centres a very satisfactory cost position is achieved. The market approval of the subsequent promotion of proven cost savers is only marginally tarnished by subsequent accounting adjustments.

The question of transfer pricing has recently caught the attention of the taxation authorities as a means by which multinational corporations are thought to move costs and hence profits from jurisdiction to jurisdiction. Although this might happen internationally, the greatest artistry occurs within the corporation as each particular area seeks to ensure that their results are presented in the best possible manner. The basic rule is that transfer prices to other units are high whereas transfer prices of products or services into a unit must be low. Often there is no necessity for the price to be the same for the sender as the recipient.

Astute investors do not regard publicly trumpeted cost cutting exercises as necessarily a good sign. A good understanding of costs does not suddenly require a spurt of activity from one day to the next. The manager should understand his costs and be ready. A prudent manager seeing a sudden interest in costs by the Big Boss will husband his resources so as to have a surplus to disgorge at the appropriate time.

More sophisticated managers confronted with the cost saving message (or revenue enhancement for that matter) passed down from on high are well aware of the prospect of slippage as they in turn pass the message down the levels of the organization. To guard against possible embarrassment with their boss they increase the target for the next level by the estimated rate of slippage plus a bit for good measure. This happens at each level so that the original arbitrary ten percent cut by the Big boss can become an edict to save more than the total existing level of cost at the lowest level of the organization.

There are two refinements of the top down ruler approach. The first is the collaborative whiteboard supported brain storming. The management team invited to receive the ten percent cost cut by the Big Boss, go off site for a weekend. Without the distraction of information from anyone who knows anything about the numbers they will after a period of passing the parcel deliver up a number of suggestions of unnecessary activities in colleagues' departments. On balance, the ruler approach is better because only one person doesn't know what he is doing whereas the whiteboard brainstorm involves a lot of people not knowing what they are doing. The saving grace of the whiteboard is that no one remembers who is to do what so little damage is actually done.

The second modern method is to introduce science in the form of activity based costing. By this method the linkages between costs and output are traced through the linkages of activity in the production process. In the days when most business made widgets and it was possible to trace costs to the various widget machines and widget makers this method had some merit. Today with the growth of service industries and a more ephemeral product using generally shared costs, the activity linkages have become little more than each particular accountant's view of the appropriate allocation key. Change your opinion and a new model can be run.

Each of these techniques abhors delay. Each eschews paralysis by analysis. Quick results are to be achieved by going after those simple savings that even Blind Freddy can see. Quite why we have all been so slothful to tolerate this obvious waste over all these years is not so clear but there is the normal list of suspects here too, bureaucracy, bookkeepers, belt and braces, paperwork and tea ladies. All must go. This is the low hanging fruit ripe for the plucking. Strangely enough this often turns out to be still just out of reach.

The extent of the necessary savings can be determined by best practice exercises that require expensive consultants and extensive foreign travel. The problem of suitability in applying these good ideas becomes particularly fraught if a number of practices are put together in hybrid best practice combinations. This is when best practice becomes worst case as mutually exclusive solutions are cobbled together.

Head count savings fall into the Holy Grail category. Labour is the largest cost item after raw materials in most manufacturing operations. In service companies it is often the largest cost item. This has led to crusades to reduce labour costs by eliminating headcount, i.e. no numbers, no cost. This is easier said than done because it is difficult to do tomorrow what you did today without the people who did the doing. Yet the number reduction must be achieved. Varied solutions are pursued; make fewer people work longer unpaid hours, engage replacement workers in other unmeasured categories such as temporaries, outsource the work, eliminate maintenance and development activities (also known as cutting the fat), give up the activity and as a last resort improve efficiency. Much use is also made of the abnormal or restructuring provision to achieve headcount savings thus giving a double benefit of demonstrating progress to the target without sacrificing any real profit. The heads who are cut are not necessarily disadvantaged by this process as they are often the recipients of the abnormal restructuring provision and are likely to retain their old jobs with enhanced terms as a knowledgeable employee of the firm that provides the contractor or outsourced service.

In the old days it was easy enough to simply say that the just about to be completed program was a success as you moved your attention to the new program. Recently the incidence of post implementation audits has greatly intensified and it has become necessary to employ some of the latest techniques now considered. Savings to perpetuity are claimed especially when alternating pairs exist as in product formulation. Linear programming models provide a fruitful area during periodic cost savings exercises as the savings of all the alternatives may be added. Updating the linear programming results will indicate that for example bean oil could profitably be substituted for palm oil in the margarine formula. At another moment that conclusion is reversed. Management keen to ensure no slippage against savings targets will record all the savings, double savings if possible. The automobile assembly plant had the benefit of highly professional work-study engineers and value engineers. The work-study engineers claimed major savings by introducing a special material that improved the speed of car body finishing. The value engineer also found savings by introducing a much cheaper specification of the material that slowed the finishing. With management keen to prove the success of their programs it is quite common that an audit of cost savings programs is carried on for more than a few years which will report cumulative savings in excess of total costs.

An obvious first approach to any efficiency campaign is adding positive labels and removing negatives. The more you have of a desirable function the better the company will be. Some parts of the organization feel that they are just not appreciated for the contribution they make. The Sales Department makes a lot of noise but is not treated nearly well enough. Not only does the Sales Department lead the company but without them the company could not exist because they bring in the revenue. Without sales it would be like a car without an engine. Apparently it is satisfactory to have a powerful engine without worrying about the wheels or brakes applied by the other disciplines.

A favourite of the Sales Department is the push for a simplified administration. The unnecessary complexity of the company administration prompted the frustrated salesman to propose that the administration be scrapped and replaced by two sacks hung on the factory gate. One was for the customers to come and put the payment for the goods sold and another sack for the suppliers to come and take only what was necessary to settle their invoices. Fortunately the administrator saw the folly of the proposed system. Because there were two sacks an administrator would still be required to move the money from one sack to the other, so he proposed an improvement. This would be one sack only with the added advantage that what was left at the end of the month would be the profit.

The Research and Development scientists also feel neglected despite their role in inventing the products. Without them the Sales Department would have nothing to sell. Irritated by continual carping from his colleagues the Research Director set out to prove the high return earned from the discoveries of his Research and Development programs. He diligently added up all the costs of the Department for the last several years. He then added up the total gross contribution made over the same period by products invented by Research and Development. A broad smile emerged as he found that the contribution was about half of the costs. 'Great' he said, 'A fifty percent payback'. The smile vanished when his colleague suggested that they try the fifty percent payback game with their own money. 'You give me two dollars and I pay you 50% back. Good, now lets do that again'.

Asymmetric balance dates within a group help to facilitate the asymmetric explanation of adverse events within large groups by eliminating the precise moment when the event is recognized in the accounts. Careful choice ensures that when viewed from the main accounts the event has not yet happened and so is not yet recognized and then in the subsequent years accounts have already happened and has been explained in the previous accounts of the subsidiary. Further refinements can be achieved by grouping unprofitable activities where they will not be included with the 'real' business that must be shown to shareholders or investors. This may be in the form of a special category that is shown but does not register because it is intended for discontinuing a loss making or unfashionable business. This process can be repeated until there are no businesses left with the market applauding the absence of negative cash flows, that is until they start to look for growth prospects in which case negative cash flows are again acceptable.

Banks have a variation that can reach major proportions when activities are sorted between the good bank which will continue, and the bad bank that was someone else's fault and is being wound up. Banks also have a pass the parcel technique where otherwise unprofitable lending transactions are passed around a club in a cooperative manner. It was prevalent in mortgage banking in the US and Holland in the early 1980s. If we all pass on property to each other at higher and higher valuations everyone is happy until the money runs out. If you are a bank the money need not run out for a long time and the economy may recover in time to save us all.

There are many other transactions that *sort of do not really belong to us* because they are the responsibility of someone else. These are the off balance sheet activities. Some activities disappear into the limbo land of belonging to nobody. These are the de-consolidated activities much loved in the past in Japan with the helpful assistance of foreign banks. Such constructions designed to park losses were never illegal but were subsequently deemed not to have been appropriate. It was the disappearance of documents designed to make losses disappear that proved to be the most unacceptable feature.

There is even more scope when the there is only a loose company grouping with no consolidated picture at all or one based only on equity accounting principles. This is where the interest in an another entity is recorded as the proportion of the results to which the share holding would entitle the owning company whether or not this is ever transferred in the form of dividends or other cash flow. Remarkable things take place when there are reciprocal equity holdings in listed companies and these are accounted for in the equity method. If the share price of one company goes up the value of the equity accounted stake held by the other company also goes up. Because the first company also holds a stake in the second company its equity also accounts for the rise and so justifies it original rise in price, which in turn leads to a further price rise and the process repeats itself. This form of feedback link can give a massive turbo charging effect. The Adelaide Steam Ship Group in Australia was powered by this effect through the 1980s and was able to gain control of several substantial listed companies by means of reciprocal holdings of only part of the shares with the rest still listed separately. All was well while the share prices were going up but the same powerful arithmetic worked just as effectively in the down-draft following the 1987 crash.

Perhaps there is a coriolis effect at work here? The upward spiral of positive equity accounting results with reverse on the down. The suspicion is that it works in the opposite direction in the Southern Hemisphere just as water going down the plug hole also spirals in the opposite direction. This image would not be a comfort to those investors who saw their investment disappear down the drain and care little whether it spirals left or right.

In the their enthusiasm to remedy the short comings of historic valuations the accountants have pushed the corporations to value their assets according to the mark to market method. This forces the use of the one value that we know the economy cannot achieve. At least with historic cost accounting we know that the asset was actually bought at the price recorded. Implicit in the mark to market valuation is the assumption that no one actually tries to sell at the market price. If more than a few do sell, the price must fall. This may imply that nobody actually bought at that price.

The difference between the aggregate of all these mark to market valuations for the particular class of marketable asset and a realistic realizable value is pure Vapourcash and one of the most prevalent causes. Calculations based on this assumption such as market capitalization or investment value are subject to major swings caused by the Vapourcash created in the valuation process. The extent of the excessive creation of Vapourcash becomes very obvious in the situation approaching bankruptcy. The debtor tries to liquidate the holding, or worse still the bank tries and suddenly the Vapourcash condenses as the market valuation plunges.

Goodwill is one of the greatest paradoxes of modern accounting. It is another of those accounting words where its technical meaning is now at odds with its literal meaning. The general commercial meaning of goodwill is simple enough being an intangible, saleable asset arising from the reputation of a business and its relations with its customers, distinct from the value of its stock, etc. Clearly it is saleable because we just bought it and it is intangible and it does bridge the value gap between what we paid and what we received but that is about the end of the simplicity. From then on no one can agree on anything. The rules vary from country to country, from time to time and from case to case. Some do not believe in its existence and so it should not be recognized in the accounts at all. Others believe it is of permanent worth and should be capitalized for all time. Of course there are others who believe a bit of both. As a result the arguments have become acrimonious and heated. There is very little general goodwill, i.e. friendly disposition, benevolence or favour to be seen around accounting goodwill.

Goodwill plays the role of the Cheshire Cat for the accountants. The Cheshire cat originally appeared in *Alice in Wonderland* by Lewis Carroll and has the disconcerting habit of gradually fading away until only his smile remains and would also start with the smile and reappear. When goodwill is put on the balance sheet as an intangible asset and it is gradually written off over an arbitrary period so the asset gradually fades away until only the smile remains. Bankers are not very sure about goodwill and have been known to refer to it as fresh air on the balance sheet. The banking regulators are sure that they do not trust goodwill and insist that the value of goodwill is deducted from the value of the Tier 1 regulatory capital. This declining deduction from amortization leads to the gradual reappearance of Tier 1 capital as Cheshire capital (or the Cheshiring of capital).

The main reason for the debate about goodwill is that it is one of these cyclical accounting concepts. It is very desirable at certain times and inconvenient at others and so it is necessary to tailor the Antilogic to flexibly respond to the circumstances. At the moment of making an acquisition goodwill is a goodthing because it serves to help explain all those strategic advantages that come from paying too much for the acquisition. It justifies the price. The ideal solution was to follow the recently discontinued British method of writing off goodwill that permitted its presence at the presentation announcing the acquisition and then it disappeared.

But when explaining the future profit projections continuing goodwill is a problem if it has to be amortized, as it will reduce the reported profits. Inclusion on the balance sheet will further depress the return on equity. Some subtlety is necessary to get a good outcome in these circumstances. Most practitioners argue for the permanent value of the purchase and challenge the need for amortization. By this method they retain maximum profit and accept the inclusion in capital. More advanced practitioners argue that because goodwill is an intangible it is a non-cash transaction and so cannot have a real impact of profits and switch the main emphasis in reporting to cash earnings and tangible assets. Goodwill simply disappears. This approach has some elegance as it confirms that the acquisition was settled in Vapourcash.

The debate has even more vehemence in the US, as it has been possible to avoid the intricacies of goodwill altogether by deeming it not to exist. This outcome is achieved by the *pooling of interest* method that has a magic of its own. The meaning of pooling is captured in the name. Two businesses come together. They pool their interest and no question of value arises in the accounts of the companies irrespective of the value transfer between the owners. The accounts are simply combined. Pooling is under threat and the potential loss of magic is regretted. Pooling provided an interesting echo of hydraulic economics. The pooling of interest method is flawed for two crucial reasons. Firstly it is unusual in that one company does not acquire another. Further it would be even more unusual that the two companies combined to become one without being either being improved or diminished. Secondly, the pooling of interests method generally and no doubt coincidentally produces higher reported net income after combination. This is because historic cost of assets and liabilities are carried over into the combined enterprise and no inconvenient goodwill appears. This higher level of net income is supposedly achieved simply because stock was exchanged but it was exchanged at fair values and not at the historic values retained in the books.

The alternative called purchase accounting does recognize value differences and creates goodwill but is not so great either. It is inconsistent with one part at historic cost and one part market. The excess of purchase price over fair value is assumed to be a wasting asset no matter what may actually occur. Who can say that either method is correct? Maybe the average is acceptable.

The accounting profession in Australia cannot agree as to the correct answer. The Australian Accounting Standards Board (AASB) was asked to adjudicate on the recognition of goodwill in internal reorganizations. The ability of the company to chose which method became known as the magic pudding because of the ability to create goodwill at will by adopting revaluation during the reorganization. The AASB had several split votes and finally approved the standard on a split three to two vote. All was reversed when the Australian Federal Senate refused to approve the standard in the first political intervention in Australian accounting history.

Intangible assets are not only created with acquisitions. Some industries have discovered that a large part of their value comes not from physical assets but the ongoing revenue streams that emanate from their loyal customers and are thought to be due to the strength of the brand names that they own. This may be in the form of product brand names but is very commonly used in the media industries where value is ascribed to newspaper mastheads or television licences. The methodology computes what a participant should earn in this industry and any surplus must be due to the intangible asset in question and the capital sum equivalent to the surplus is capitalized on the balance sheet as the intangible. It is a sort of back-fill calculation that gives the answer necessary for normalcy. This gives a wonderful feeling of symmetry because in future periods the return is now an average so the value must be correct. Here lies the basis of future difficulty because a superior share price requires a superior performance but this method by definition reduces profitability to an average. The solution can be found in growth from acquisition. Organic growth would be good as well but that is harder to achieve. The booking of intangibles of this sort can lead to very curious results when the business turns bad, e.g. formerly blue chip companies teetering on the verge of bankruptcy despite a balance sheet that attributed very high brand values to loss making businesses.

The criticism levelled at accounting for intangibles is that they recognize something that might not exist. This may be so but it will tend to net out against other things relating to employee costs such as pension plans that do exist but are not included. The Human Resource department is always convinced that there is no cost impact associated with pension benefits and will always be prepared to negotiate pension concessions rather than be associated with a wage concession during their time in office. The pension plan is the widow's cruse of the company as supposedly surplus cash can be taken without detriment to the benefits. The surplus also grows because half of the scheme members were retrenched in the last downsizing.

Employee options are the other great employee benefit to have the same characteristic with the added benefit that the cost is not borne by the company. The shareholders will no doubt welcome the issuing of additional shares to their loyal employees, as this will assist in future liquidity. In some industries currently unprofitable because of their explosive growth, most of senior management remuneration is coming in the form of executive options. The advantage is that it does not depress present profitability such that it is but so many options are issued that it is unlikely that the world is big enough to accommodate the company that can absorb that many shares.

Insurance is another expenditure that falls in the non-cost category. Don't worry about the fire, theft or loss. It is covered by the insurance. This attitude is even more of a worry for companies following the current fashion for captive in-house insurance companies. The common thread is the time delay in incurring the liability and having to bear the cost that gives plenty of time to vacate the scene of the crime. The insurance company does not mind. They will ultimately adjust their premium.

If you are left a little queasy by the valuation of intangibles and absent liabilities we can always resort to the fair value method. After all that must be fair, but when and to whom? Attitudes can and do vary from very enthusiastic to pessimism as to the assets being there at all. This is not just the difference between buyer and seller but the attitude of the same individual or organization at different times. The arithmetic of finance and management tends to be comparative standards, i.e. relative to itself rather than objective standards. So, this year is better than last year or banks are cheap relative to resources or vice versa. Investors gamble on the historic relationship reasserting itself. A bad year can help as this gives scope for improvement because the more you lose the better the subsequent return. This provides not only the favourable comparison but also reduces net assets, capital, equity, and shareholders funds so permitting all ratios that use these measures as the denominator to display a future improvement.

Part of the problem of understanding the accountants is the tendency for pairs of terminology to swap in different circumstances. Familiar terminology can be taken for granted and change with time. Even without the current trend to invent hybrid capital instruments debt and equity have always had a disconcerting tendency to change place with each other in particular circumstances. Banks often think that they are lenders only to find that they have ended up with equity in all sense except the return that they receive. There are many examples where business has been conducted on the basis of debt dressed up as equity especially when banks are involved. Sometimes it is easy to confuse debit as credit. Often business-men do not know if they are coming or going. So why should bookkeeping entries be treated any differently? There are also assets that become liabil-ities. This applies not only to white elephants. As well as those assets that disappoint there are those that are known to be less attractive in the future, e.g. those requiring remediation, etc.

A very positive transformation comes from treating costs as invest-ments. By changing the classification the expenditure is not only changed from being accounted in the profit and loss to the balance sheet but the time period is changed from now to sometime in the future. Rather than being a drag and a cost this expenditure gives the prospect of future returns. Some industries follow this technique as a matter of course such as mining companies that capitalize exploration expenses and the interest cost incurred during the development of mining projects. This new asset would then be amortized at the rate at which the ore reserves are mined. As can be imagined the economic size of resource changes with the price of the mineral so this process of amortization can be flexible or should I say responsive to market realities. With a falling price, a rate of production may fall to such a low level that mine life becomes infinite and the required level of amortization falls to zero. The miners have their own special technique for responding to shareholder calls for higher returns and cash-flow. This is called high grading where improved extraction efficiency can suddenly improve profits. This is very useful for incoming CEOs.

The miners are not alone. The Internet revolution has brought a new twist to the old theme of the capitalization of customer acquisition costs. This requires several leaps of faith for the visionary but then, if leaping once why not leap several times. None of the customers to date have shown a profit and most have not generated any revenue. Yet the corporation is reasonably certain they will still be around and profitable in the future. Much of investment is in advertising. William Hesketh Lever the father of consumer branding is quoted as saying more than a century ago that he knew he wasted half of his advertising spend but he did not know which half. Today with the help of modern technology the Internet and e-commerce corporations are certain that all of the spend is of permanent value.

The Internet technology revolution has also led to many participants selling on a no charge basis in order to build up revenue. The story goes as follows, 'My customers appreciate my product in comparison with my competitors because I provide it for free'. This is simply a modern twist on the well-established concept of the relationship factor in this case applied to revenue. A particular favourite is the loss making transaction made profitable by the relationship factor. Relationship is a specific goodthing by which unprofitable business can be transformed to profit. It is pure Antilogic. Because a relationship creates more value for a customer it is contended that they should be charged less than are other customers. It is also the extra factor in financial equations where the addition of relationship to two unprofitable products makes them profitable. The story goes like this: 'I know we know we make a loss on product A but we need to hang in there because of the relationship implication to the sales of product B made by our colleagues'. Meanwhile someone else is saying 'I know we make a loss on product B but we need to hang on in there because of the relationship implication to the sale of product A by our colleagues'.

So, loss A + loss B + relationship factor = profit.

Even if you cannot label costs as investment it is always possible to give them an attractive description and this will solve the problem today. Excessive expenditure of costs on a goodthing can have similar beneficial effects through the influence of the *Harvey Wallbanger School of Management.* Soon you will be in a position to compare the state of past high costs with the present position of no costs. When you stop pouring in the costs, the results look better, you feel better as you do when you stop hitting your head against the wall. No return on investment is required.

These accounting solutions do not go on for ever. One day mid way in the CEO credibility cycle the easy marginal costing and must-have essential projects environment will be over and replaced by a new process of financial rigour. The accounting manual will be rewritten and the planning zealots newly converted on the road to Damascus will send out the new message. All our business units must earn over our average return or they will be sold or closed. The harder the businesses try to respond the more frantic it becomes.

VI

BELIEVING THE NUMBERS: THE CONTRIBUTION OF THE STATISTICIANS

THE FINANCIAL cliché maybe the essence of Antilogic but it is statistical error that is the foundation. It is possible that statistical error is inadvertently made by the perpetrator but the effect is just the same on the outcome.

The economists are quick to attribute results divergent from their expectations as the fault of the accountant. They claim the bean counters cannot make their numbers stack up because of the inevitable simplifications of their profession. In the big boys arena of international economics with full panoply of statistics and computer power no such shortcomings are thought to be possible. Although the world is complex the hope exists that the application of analytical techniques to better and more copious data can explain all. The growth of computing power has been harnessed to process the wealth of data previously too extensive to tackle. New statistical techniques, improved mathematics and aids such as expert systems, fuzzy logic and neural networks give the prospect of untying the Gordian knot of too much problem and not enough explanation, let alone solution. We would hope that this would provide greater certainty and agreement as to cause and in turn give greater consensus and accuracy in predicting future outcomes. Unfortunately despite an explosion of effort the outcomes continue to disappoint. Although the cliché only talks about lies, damned lies and statistics, the contribution to Antilogic of spurious statistics is unsurpassed.

Spotting all the problems is not easy. All sources of information have various kinds of error for which allowance should be made if only the source and extent of the error were known. The problem is that error is the rule not the exception and applies at least as much in the social sciences as occurs in the natural sciences. The presence of statistical error therefore greatly increases the chance of Antilogic in the conclusions drawn. The problems associated with statistical error apply at all levels of business and financial use and go well beyond to the macro economic level as well.

Even after allowance for error in the information or data itself, its worth depends on its use. The idea of accuracy does not have much meaning unless we know how the data is to be combined with other information and a conclusion computed. The acceptability of statistics cannot really be determined until we know to what use the conclusion is to be put for there seems to be a human weakness about accuracy. We tend to pretend a level of accuracy that is out of reach and more than is needed. Keynes pointed out that this is particularly dangerous when statistics fall into the hands of economists, as they are over addicted to specious precision, making perfectly precise what is in reality vague and complex. Examples are when the statistics are irrelevant, functionally false as when the vast majority of transactions take place at rates different to the official statistics or meaningless as when an artificial relationship is computed. The danger from use of specious accuracy is that it looks impressive. With all those numbers after the decimal point it must be both important and correct. We are lulled into a false confidence.

Another human trait is to select the statistic that supports the theory. This is the lazy practice of finding the measure that appears to fit and adopting that without worrying if just as relevant statistics disprove the theory. The ability to select the index or statistic is crucial to the validity of the outcome and is part of the strength of political power. The erroneous use of official statistics is likely to go uncommented let alone corrected by other professionals because of the deference due to bureaucratic diplomatic relations. It applies just as much in business for exactly the same reasons. If public commentators in financial markets do become subject to criticism by professional rivals it is easily dismissed as competitive carping and market participants are unlikely to criticize their clients.

Karl Popper tells the story of being privileged to sit in during consultation by a noted psychoanalyst. During a consultation Popper was surprised when the Great Man claimed it as support for his theory whereas Popper could find no similarity in the symptoms. When Popper questioned the Great Man why he believed that the case gave his theory support the Great Man turned to Popper and replied 'A thousand-fold experience my dear Popper'. And concluded Popper ' I suppose that tomorrow in the same circumstances he will say, A thousand and one-fold experience'. So it is often that the belief in validity of predictions and worth of ideas is directly correlated to the importance of the person with the idea.

Popper's thousand and one-fold experience example is of the general case of a theory so loosely defined as to be supported by any evidence. This is particularly true of the apparent derivation of a conclusion from an impressive array of statistics when in fact there is no causal link. Marketing presentations and consultants' reports fall under this influence because of the difficulty of knowing the diplomatically acceptable conclusion before-hand. Often the conclusion is derived directly from the mathematical manipulation of the assumptions. The corroborating statistics included and then eliminated along the road are for effect and do not support the conclusion. This outcome is only marginally less reprehensible than reverse engineering of a model to generate the data that will prove the desired outcome.

Error has such a pervasive place in statistics that there are several precise and distinct uses of the term *error* for economic and financial analysis. It can be a precise numerical description as the standard or probable error in comparing various samples of the same population or measures of the same economic quantity. But it also has the wider and more generally used concept of incompleteness or imperfection of description or simply a mistake.

The difficulty of measurement in scientific experiments is well known due to the error of instruments. It might be imagined that no such problem would arise in economic or financial data as this only involves the adding up of money. Money is not as straightforward as you might think. Computation of money values has been made much more rapid by the use of computers but greater computing power has not made the models more accurate, not least because of complexity and confusion. The faster the computer, the greater the chance of computational errors. Powerful computing packages have also added to the dangers of the spurious correlations that are discovered through automated search but has not done as much to ensure the validity of the correlations chosen. If enough relationships are tested the law of large numbers will ensure that at least one will fit reasonably well even if it is totally coincidental. They say that if you torture data enough you will eventually make it confess anything.

The easiest way of making statistics show the results you wish is to eliminate any contrary information. This may be the simple elimination of rogue or outlying observations, to the more consistent culling of distortion right through to the not uncommon practice of ignoring all of the negative data and consequently finding that everything is now positive. Oskar Morgenstern was very severe on statistical shortcomings in his comprehensive book *On the Accuracy of Observations* published in 1963. Unfortunately the continuing presence of the errors he warns against suggests that it has become a *How to Guide* rather than a warning. He even went so far to suggest that some errors were deliberate and equivalent to lies.

Economic, social and financial statistics are frequently based on evasive answers and deliberate lies of various types. These lies arise principally from misunderstandings, from fear of tax authorities, from uncertainty about or dislike of government interference and plans or from the desire to mislead competitors, to mislead the boss, to please the boss and/or to get a favoured project over the line. This influence is not present in most scientific experiments. Nature may hold back information, is always difficult to understand but it is believed that she does not lie deliberately. Einstein 'Raffinart ist der Hars, Gott aber boshaft ist er nicht' 'The Lord God is sophisticated but not malicious'.[40]

It is not considered polite to refer to this sort of discrepancy as a lie and so references are generally to misunderstanding or inadvertent exclusion of data. The conclusion remains that statistics in social sciences are even more likely to contain error than the natural sciences because they are so much more complex and we do not know what answer to expect. The audience is likely to be concerned in verifying that portion that is easily understood but they are vulnerable to receiving literally correct but functionally useless or misleading statistics. This is especially valid when the really important aspects are obscured by vapour.

This is one step removed from the altering or suppressing sensitive statistics as has happened in totalitarian regimes and with regard to some financial statistics. It becomes really dangerous when interpreted by statistically literate individuals who succumb to the fallacy that reality only exists if it can be measured. If no measure is provided then it does not exist or even cannot exist.

Much of the incidence of error in surveys comes from the lack of definition of classification. The provision of false information could be for various reasons depending on the purpose of the survey and expectations as to its end use. With the frequency of surveys there is also error as a result of being familiar with another classification than that actually being requested. Confusion through familiarity is common. The recent Mars probe crashed because of a mix up between Imperial and Metric measure.

Many statistical errors are caused by haste. It takes time to correctly establish a reliable process and time to eliminate errors. The publishing experience is that it takes at least four to five reprints to eliminate all misprints and so achieve the perfect edition. In business, data generally has only one edition and probably is not proof read at that. The wonder is that any surveys turn out sufficiently accurate for their purpose. The survey constructor really needs to know the results beforehand to judge whether the results are satisfactory.

Time also has a period influence. Data that is attributed to a particular time period runs the risk that it is based on observations that have not been put in the right period. Even when the observations are counted in the correct period, if the cut off is significant, it is possible that the underlying system has been manipulated to cause it to fall in the desirable period by speeding up or slowing down. Financial observations are particularly sensitive in this regard as discrepancies can invalidate the matching concept if costs are in one period and the revenue is in another and is a prime source of adjusted reporting, that is the statistical term for window dressing. Interpretation of accurately attributed data is also sensitive to a time element such as seasonality or impact of a financial year end, etc.

Best Practice exercises are particularly vulnerable to all these influences. The implications of such studies are now well known and respondents try very hard to ensure that the results reflect well on their operation. With delegation it is very likely that those providing the data will have a very shaky knowledge of the operation but a very strong belief that the results should be good. Sometimes the lack of knowledge lies with those seeking to impose their will on the group and this can bring unexpected praise. One particular business where I once worked unexpectedly received the accolade for highest efficiency based on a mistaken idea of shift patterns. All operations were thought to be working the same length of working day whereas our operation was working a third longer due to extra overtime to make up for inefficiency. The data was correct but the interpretation was faulty.

The wish to show statistics in the best possible light is caused by an attempt to predict what the consequences of publication will be. This is what drives accounting window dressing but the impact of this window dressing or even accounting error goes beyond the first order provided to the reader of the accounting statements. That same information is then slavishly carried over together with distortions to any number of statistical returns.

A lie is in this context not a simple and obvious concept. It is unmistakable when a false cash position is fraudulently given or when physical inventories are reported that do not exist. But when a more optimistic attitude is deliberately taken in interpreting the success of a years' operation – e.g. by small amortization – it is hard to classify this statement as a 'lie'. Instead it may be viewed as an error of judgement and as such to be proved or disproved by later events. There is an intermediate category between the (subject) completely truthful reporting and outright falsification. It may be called 'adjusted reporting' one form of which is well known also as window dressing.[41]

Morgenstern again goes even further to suggest that the accounting errors were deliberate and that they were achieved by falsification. He sees this as a part of the normal commercial cut and thrust that he calls bluffing. It needs to be added that there may be multiple sources of bluffing, as there are more interest groups at work than just the corporation itself. The credibility or financial advantage of an individual or group may also be at stake. There are many ways in which the results may be influenced but there are three principle sources of false representation, bias, hiding or falsifying information to support a purpose or lying.

This sounds very sinister but may not matter, as it is quite likely that the recipient of the information is not listening to what is being said. He will be expecting to receive particular answers and it is possible that the questions are framed with that intent. Sometimes this may be done unintentionally by simply not posing the questions correctly.

With all the chances of information being dispatched and received erroneously it seems that the chances of hitting the correct answer are pretty slim. It cannot be assumed that businesses are always able to interpret their own actions if indeed they actually get the chance to express an opinion. With the growth of information requests it is very likely that the actual filling in of the questionnaire is delegated down the organization to a junior officer who has little idea of what the leaders had in mind if indeed they remember or comprehend. The current level of statistical inquiry covers such an array of subjects in such detail it is unlikely that any one individual will see the whole picture. It is also likely that if too many questionnaires arrive together the level of spurious, flippant or random answers will increase. The designers of questionnaires need to be able to check the validity of the answers but this implies that they already know the answer. If they know the answer there is little point in posing the question, which is why many questionnaires ask what the surveyor already knows.

The common answer to the criticism about the level of detail error in statistics is to claim that the errors are symmetrical and will more or less cancel out. There is no justification for this belief as every accountant knows when confronted with a balance sheet that does not quite balance. Errors may cancel out but they can just as well be omissions or counted double. Who is to say how many errors may be simultaneously present? Each has to be separately identified, quantified and established if they are interdependent. With the onward march of data there is no guarantee that the problem will resolve within a reporting period or that the subsequent correction will be on a consistent basis.

One popular way to make untidy statistical discrepancies disappear is to move to the first derivative, the rate of change. The computation of a rate of change from two or more uncertain observations has the look of precision that we think must be telling us something important. We hope that the discrepancies will cancel out and now you can't see them anyway. But unfortunately, rates of change pick up all the errors of the underlying data and depending on the method may have picked up a few extra. This technique is very popular with macro economists. A similar technique adopted in industry when confronted with gaps in data is to construct indices and by resetting to common base directly compare the different series. The tidier we make it look the more statistical gremlins creep in such as stationarity and autocorrelation where the errors in one period are related to the errors in previous periods. A spoil sport test is to check for correlation of the first differences. Many coincidental correlations caused by stationarity or time series effects fall by the wayside.

Business accounting itself is a rich source of statistics both for their own use and as input to economic analysis and forecasts. As we have seen business accounting is subject to a wide range of interpretation. Much of this variability comes from the separate role of the income statements that gives a result for a period of time and the balance sheet that is a statement of affairs at a point in time. These concepts frequently become blurred making it important to distinguish between those hard records relating to the handling of money and those softer entries that are based on opinion. Approaching from the technical statistical direction we reach the same idea as expressed elsewhere, cash is fact, profit is opinion. It provides a clue to distinguish fact from error and cash from Vapour. Management often relies on the use of statistics for decision making and as a basis of accounting but there is little linkage between the techniques of accounting and those of economics. Especially important is the impact of markets in financial results, the interlinking of values and other assumptions implicit in the addition of financial statistics to create economic statistics. In effect there is an implied assumption of non-disturbance of these markets and an overall consolidation of the interlinking shareholdings of insignificant magnitude as these influences are seldom corrected in the production of economic statistics. All of those assets are valued and added up on the basis that no business actually tries to transact them at that value and no attempt is made to extract the double counting of value arising by one business owning a share in another.

All of this boils down to the conclusion that by the time data is transformed to observation it has been selected, massaged and exposed to a myriad of possible distortions. It is difficult to be confident that anything reliable ever emerges for the use of the recipient and will he/she know what it signifies when he/she receives it. In this context we should distinguish observations from data. Observations are selected from data supposedly guided by theory and conducted in a controlled manner. Theory has to be invented supported by observations whereas data is just gathered.

The next step is receiving information, which is to be contrasted with noise. Noise is not much use especially when we confuse it for information. Noise is made up of extraneous data and observations and gets in the way of our theory. It leads people to adopting rules of thumb in decision making to help cut out the noise. Unfortunately this also tends to cut out the information leading to the problem of identifying insufficient variables to satisfactorily explain the effect. This might not hamper the acceptance of the theory as this is often achieved by persuasion rather than proof as pointed out by Fischer Black.

> No matter how many variables we include ... there always seem to be potentially important variables that we have omitted, possibly because they are too unobservable ... In the end, a theory is accepted not because it is confirmed by conventional empirical tests, but because researchers persuade one another that the theory is correct and relevant.[42]

The study of econometrics is aimed through the application of mathematics and modelling skills to identify and provide proofs of economic effects. The technique seeks to add further and further equations until a satisfactory explanation or proof is obtained. The econometricians are following down the same path as the physicists who discovered that their models did not adequately explain what they observed. Something was missing rather than there being errors and inaccuracies in the data. The missing bits are the hidden variables in the search for Antimatter. An explanation had to be found and the search went on until it was found. The discrepancy attributed to measurement error turned out to be valid because the hidden variable turned out to be valid. It shows again the wisdom of proceeding with caution in contrast to being too hasty to condemn that you cannot prove. There is no substitute for testing the model and tackling the results when they come.

It is the shortcuts to resolve the problems in the models that generate the Antilogic. Reconciliation becomes possible when there is a theoretical basis to compare with the actual survey results. All too often this gives rise to problems described as statistical discrepancies that are swept under the figurative carpet by assuming that they cannot exist or if they persist are ascribed to that phantom variable called dummy. The significance of this assumption is that it introduces the zero as the proof of accuracy. The pragmatic statistical solution relies on the assumption that all factors have actually been included in the balance. The existence of a non-zero discrepancy is assumed to be impossible. The balancing item tends to gain a dynamic life of its own. Nobody notices that the balance is not random. It moves in a consistent pattern as our example of the world imbalance of payments. It has become the compensating residual. It becomes the amount just enough to make up the difference. It is the statistical equivalent of the adjusting residual in discounted cash flow models.

Now why should we care about all this? Well, a lot of our financial assumptions are very dependent on the statistics upon which they are built. The financial markets are now very sensitive to the measurement of investment performance of mutual funds and share portfolios over long periods of time. The financial success of fund managers depends on how well they compare in surveys conducted by consulting firms specializing in the field. Naturally investors are impressed by high returns and are overly impressed by high past results. The accuracy of strategies based on these statistics is undermined by the bias that looks ahead expecting good past performers to perform well in the future. They might, but future performance is not driven by the past. The data is also subject to bias in that the really bad performers are no longer survivors in the sample because they have closed. The results can also be biased by the departure of funds through takeover but who is to say whether takeovers tend to be of good or poorly performing funds? I would be tempted to believe that the take-over of weakened performers is the more likely.

It might be thought that all these statistical quirks have little impact on the running of business. After all no one really pays attention to the statistics so long as they support what we want to do. However, for some business, especially in the financial services industry, their results are nothing but statistics. The profit only exists because the model computes that it does. Actuaries determine the fate of insurance companies as they balance future calculated benefits with future calculated liabilities. The same actuaries or their brother determine the worth of pension plans. They directly determine our ability to achieve our desired lifestyle in retirement.

Derivative operations are another case in point and profits can be totally transformed by the use of a spurious derivative cash flow formula. In the recent case at Natwest Markets, a derivative trading subsidiary, an announcement that the correction of the mathematical calculation of derivatives had reduced their value by £78 million, reduced the value of

Natwest, the parent bank, by £250 million. Apparently, valuation by fiction is acceptable so long as you do not change the story. We can never discover whether the fiction was the original model or the replacement as the result of the business will never be there to be counted at any point in time.

The delusion of statistics can reach monumental proportions generating Antilogic on an international scale that influenced world affairs. A grand recent example has been the varying estimates of the size of the Russian economy. The CIA conducted what was then touted as the largest social sciences research project to estimate the value of the communist system. Despite all the effort the CIA estimated the Gross Domestic Product of the Soviet Union to be equal to that of Japan and West Germany just months before the break down of the Iron Curtain. They made various methodological errors and so completely misread the available information despite contrary eye witness accounts of shortages and strain to the economy.

We should not have been surprised about Russia. Back in the 1960s Oskar Morgenstern had already identified the special problem that is offered by the statistics about the then Soviet Union especially through deliberate doctoring and double and multiple counting. Only the size of the error would have surprised him as he had long identified the prevalence of statistical Antilogic, or error as he politely terms it, and attempted to warn his readers of its presence. After a while the experts began to compute what should be there and began to adjust the official figures to correct for the disappointment factor. This became so institutionalized in Russia in the 1930s that lie co-efficients were established to adjust towards the actual numbers. Of course if this becomes known the numbers must be adjusted more and more by all parties to achieve the desired effect. Mining companies can vouch for the accuracy of this observation. Soon after the break up of the Soviet Union, a representative of an international mining company sought commercial arrangements for the supply of uranium. None of the twelve mines listed at the ministry were still in operation whereas four major mines not listed at the ministry were actually in production. The Soviet statistical handling of mineral reserves was an elegantly simplified method that avoided disappointment by only counting some discoveries and not depletion. This method implies that the known reserves are augmented at the same rate that reserves are mined. The result is not notably less accurate than Western oil producers who consistently discover new reserves at a faster rate in existing fields than they pump out.

What is especially interesting is the concept that we can make the economy bigger by adjusting the statistics to include the black economy.

Take Italy where the economists changed the methodology in the 1980s. At a stroke the Italian economy grew by 20% and proudly the GDP per head suddenly overtook that of the UK.

Forty years further on, the errors Morgenstern helps us detect are still present in economic, financial and business analysis. We can extend the concept by returning to a more modern Russia where the use of numbers can go beyond augmenting the economy to being the economy itself. The prestigious Brookings Institute dubs this the virtual economy. It is the economy where there is little or no money to measure in the conventional sense. It is tempting to equate virtual with vapour but the nub of virtual for them seems to be the presence of things but the absence of money. This greatly complicates the economists' job of measuring the economy and presumably that of the CIA earlier. I leave it to you to judge whether Russia is bigger or smaller than each set of statistics although I would expect the numbers of people, buildings, areas of land, etc. were just the same in each measurement.

> We call the new system Russia's Virtual Economy because it is based on illusion, or pretence, about almost every important parameter of the economy: prices ... The roots of the Virtual Economy lay in the largely unreformed industrial sector inherited from the Soviet period. At the heart of the phenomenon are the large number of enterprises that still produce goods but destroy value. The economy appeared to have a large manufacturing sector that produced value; in fact, manufacturing destroyed value, but this was masked by arbitrary pricing. The roots of the Virtual Economy lie in the maintenance of this pretence. It is the cause of the web of non-payments and fiscal crises from which Russia seemingly cannot emerge ... Very few negative signals are being sent about this state of affairs. Bankruptcy is still a rarity.[43]

It is intriguing that the absence of bankruptcy is advanced as the reason for the absence of money. This is the exact reverse of the situation in the West where it is the absence of money that is thought to create the bankruptcy. Bankruptcy is supposed to come from poverty and create further poverty but in the land without bankruptcy poverty abounds or at least seems to, if measured by Western statistics. The infrequency of bankruptcy limits the creation of Anticash and restricts the subsequent economic blossoming. The other intriguing contrast is the absence of banks in their role in the creation of liquidity. Again, in the Western system bankruptcy is caused by a lack of liquidity, i.e. the inability to pay bills and is only indirectly caused by inefficiency or lack of accounting profits. In Russia, without banking facilitation the lack of liquidity is solved by a level of barter that is unthinkable in the West despite all our financial markets and technology.

The discrepancy between the virtual and the real economy has become a problem for international organizations. Confronted with the choice between a tidy system and a larger economy the Organization for Economic Co-operation and Development has opted for tidiness.

> A particularly alarming trend of recent years in Russia has been the 'demonetization' of economic transactions and budgetary operations. This process is associated with the rise in prominence of various forms of money surrogates, including barter, debt offsets, and various bills of exchange (*veksels*). By early 1998, money surrogates had mushroomed to the point of accounting for a majority of industrial transactions and subnational budgetary operations (taxes and expenditures). The rise in money surrogates has been accompanied by an elaborate system of multiple prices for the same commodity depending on transaction type ... Neither state budgets nor firms have typically possessed enough cash to make basic wage, pension and other payments. The system of multiple prices also defies the basic logic of a market economy, as payment in kind is given a premium, as opposed to a discount, over cash payments.[44]

We are told that it is a bad thing for a system to continue to run without money and for the enterprise to continue after bankruptcy, in the unlikely event that it occurs. This is a rather Western perspective as the Soviet system was designed to operate without money. Money gave too much scope for business to do the wrong thing. The planners set up the system with central clearing accounts but no cash. Cash represented independence.

> The great bulk of commercial transactions is effected by means of credits and debit on the books of Gosbank, which operates as the centre of a general clearing system. The advantage of this procedure over that of direct commercial payment is the control exercised by the Bank over the operations of the enterprises; not only is the sphere of currency transactions greatly curtailed, but the Bank is authorized to scrutinize all transactions to ensure that they conform to the plan.[45]

Curiously the recent rush to establish business to business Internet exchanges is introducing a cashless exchange concept to Western business that is very similar to the discredited Gosbank.

It would seem that in Russia today there is official money, i.e. good money, and actual money that allows the system to continue to function.

The OECD would prefer the system to stop rather than admit the use of actual money. This actual money is probably Anticash.

Because of the existence of multiple price systems the natural monopolies in Russia are in a position to accept other forms of commodity exchange or money substitutes at inflated values. This works because of the difficulty in cutting off non-cash paying customers especially because of the interests of regional and local administrations and the management systems of the monopoly suppliers that do not properly account for the non-cash receipts. Proper accounting in this context is as determined by the OECD!

> In this context, natural monopolies, enterprises, and subnational state administrations all have an incentive to reach an agreement that implicitly reduces payment for a firm that is difficult to cut off from supplies, while at the same time not adversely affecting the balance sheet profitability of the natural monopoly. The later is achieved through a non-cash payment evaluated at an inflated price.[46]

We will ignore for the moment the strange concept of balance sheet profitability, as this must be a special OECD concept. But the effectiveness of the process would suggest that it is a valid response by the monopoly irrespective of whether the customer organization can be cut off or not. Self-interest is self-interest after all. The OECD however is not impressed and asks how a cash economy is to be restored.

> Part of this problem can be addressed directly through changes in accounting practice in natural monopolies. A heavy discounting of non-cash payments in balance sheet profitability would induce managers of local branches of the electricity and gas monopolies to prefer cash to non-cash receipts of equivalent value.

Here is proof that two negatives make a positive in the eyes of the OECD. Their solution to the virtual economy is to so distort the accounting that the result returns to reality! But they also propose the sanction of setting uniform rates of discount and demanding payment in cash that does not exist despite the natural monopolies and state organs having an interest in employing at least some money surrogates in budgetary operations.

In this land of virtual bankruptcy the use of non-monetary solutions (as defined by OECD but in reality Anticash) is an eminently sensible solution to bureaucratically induced problems. What is the difference between the settlement of tax obligations and barter and offset? Is there really any difference between these solutions and the derivatives and off-balance sheet transactions of the West? We also must note the similarity of this frontier society and the Cyberworld where Wall Street star performers swapped exaggerated advertising revenues between each other to meet market expectations of explosive revenue growth.

VII

BUYING THE FORECAST: FALLING FOR THE NON-FORECAST FORECAST

THE INVESTOR confident enough to look beyond the mechanical rule of thumb is likely to look for guidance from those who will tell how the future will unfold.

We now shift our focus away from words, numbers and action to concentrate on predictions about the future. We need beliefs about the future to guide us in our investments, to reassure ourselves and those that must provide the approval. To know the future obviously would give the investor a big advantage over those that do not, although the advocates of the efficient market would suggest that many would share the advantage. We need some help and I do not mean from fortune-tellers or astrologers. In this chapter we look at those that are willing, for a fee, to share with us their valuable predictions of what will happen in the financial markets.

If they knew, why should they tell you and me rather that save it for themselves? If we all followed their advice we would defeat their prediction by our influence in the market. Sceptics suggest that those who know the answer have already retired to Bermuda but this seriously underestimates the feeling of duty to public service that permeates the financial world. Fortunately there are those who are not only prepared to share the future but will also advise the investor of how best to take advantage of this information. That they are prepared to do this is not only altruistic but is itself a major category of Antilogic.

We all like reading market forecasts. It would reduce our uncertainty and help us make money for our well earned retirement. We avidly approve those forecasts that reach the same conclusion as us especially if the outcome would add to our well being. The only fly in the ointment is that overall these forecasts do not turn out very well. There are many academic studies that have established that professional investment managers do worse than the market index even before allowing for the cost of their service. This implies that the professionals provide a worse than random result. These findings are the genesis of the plethora of index funds that promise to do at least as well as the market and for a lesser cost than the active alternatives. Now if the professionals are doing worse than the average and index funds are getting the average who is beating the average? The amateurs? I think not!

The effort of the forecasters at the macro level trying to predict growth, prices and exchange rates is also not very encouraging as evaluated in a survey conducted by the Organization for Economic Co-operation (OECD) in 1993 of the forecasting record of the OECD and the International Monetary Fund during the period 1987–1992. The result showed that a simple rule that projecting growth and inflation as being the same as this year was more accurate than all the forecasts. Expecting no change was the best forecast and it also saved the trouble and costs of estimating a change. There is probably a good physical reason why turning points are so hard to predict and this relates to inertia and momentum that requires us to go in the same direction that we have been travelling. It is reinforced by the psychology of forecasting. If we are content with what we have we will predict that it will continue. No one likes to be a Cassandra so there is a predisposition against predicting disaster. Overall this must imply that we tend towards contentment as we overwhelmingly support continuation except for the less frequent situations when things are actually bad in which case the politicians will predict an improvement soon.

This is a not very reliable conclusion because things do sometimes change and cause a lot of inconvenience in the process. We would like to know what is going to happen for all sorts of good reasons but unfortunately the normal techniques do not work very well. Following the herd is no better. What is required is a better method of forecasting that incorporated both the propensity for the economy to go on the way it had been and also for the unpredictable changes that emerged out of apparently unchanged conditions. These are the times that the economy did not go on in a straight line and so was no longer amenable to rule forecasting, i.e. lay your ruler along a plot of the past numbers and see where the line falls for the future. It is a pity that the simple predictions do not always work. This is bad for the statisticians because linear mathematics is easier.

At the corporate level things must be even worse. Corporations do not publish the forecasts they use to support plans and investment projects but we know that they will certainly be no less optimistic than the official forecasters monitored by the OECD. There is also no published report of how the multiplicity of corporate estimates worked out in practice but we can be pretty sure from Antilogic that the sum total of corporate estimates will have totalled far in excess of the world estimates of the OECD. How could it be otherwise with all of the competitors all expecting to increase market share, lowering costs, buying better and all of those other projections that are necessary to get a corporate project approved. By definition an analyst justifying a business proposal has to find some basis for comparing the required effort or investment with what it will bring in the future. That is if a proposal is required at all. Our old friends the self-evident truth and the no-brainer need no justification although sometimes some token justification is created to placate the finance team. To ensure objectivity they probably get the finance team to do the creating. Here are some of the methods.

Start-ups and especially early start-ups may be expected to gain a major share of the fast growing industry in which they participate. The most recent examples are of Internet and e-commerce stocks. Because the present small state of the start-up would be misleading it is deemed better to look forward to future success and then discount for the time value for money. At present there are no limits to the prospects for the industry. The prospects are infinite. It is naturally in the future and so we apply a time value of money. So the project is valued as a discounted value from infinity. Starts ups are risky so the discount rate may be high but infinity gives plenty of scope. The net present value of infinity still gives a good basis for a business. This is analogous to driving a car and seeking to avoid the accountant's trick of driving by looking in the rear view mirror. Here we look forward through the windshield to an objective that is on a different continent.

An alternative to check the reasonableness is to extrapolate to infinity. The growth rates looks reasonable until it is compounded to exceed the total market, economy or the total world. The growth rate of Amazon.com looked achievable until it was realized that they would have to achieve 100% of the US book market within four years. This technique is more appropriate for a reasonably established company that actually has achieved some real growth and we can expect it to continue because what we have done to date was not so hard.

Exciting growth prospects are not the creation of the Internet. The combination of technology, speed and the ephemeral nature of the concept seem so well suited that it appears it was invented there but the reality is that each period has had its own Eldorado. They include some common themes. Bringing a new product to a huge market can be characterized as the *if each Chinese buys only one widget method*. This is a practical version of the discount from infinity concept. There is no need to project the future. There are a lot of Chinese, approximately infinity and they, with appropriate marketing and education, will like our product. Although there may be impediments and competition, the market is so huge that even if we only achieve a share well short of our natural share we will be very successful.

If there already is a market the version becomes *any fool could get one percent market share of a market as big as that justification*. Experience and marketing pride suggest that we will always be able to achieve a reasonable share and this relative to our aspirations will ensure certain success.

If the project is advocating a return to the scene of past unhappiness there is likely to be carping from some quarters not prepared to move with the times. *It's different this time* is the answer for the pessimists fearing disaster from a repeated mistake. If there is very determined resistance to repeated error it is time to intensify the explanation by referring to the *new paradigm* which translated means that it is *very different this time*.

Once the project is approved and up and running it is possible that there will be some form of matching between the forecast and the actual. A discrepancy will lead to manipulating forecasts and budgets to justify strategy instead of getting on with implementation. This may be overt in response to a disappointing outcome for a cherished project. The more elegant dynamic approach is to have already mastered the *what if analysis* so that the favourable forecast is established from the inception of the project.

There is always a risk for projects and so it is prudent to prepare the plausible explanation. It requires a fine judgement to be specific enough to be convincing but still vague enough to avoid any circumstances in which the explanation could be wrong. Such preparations are only required in fairly sophisticated organizations that actually try to find out why things go wrong.

If the market entry does not succeed so well as hoped it is time to apply Halstead's Law that states that market share is inversely correlated to the time in job of the Marketing Manager. It reflects the tendency of Marketing Managers over time to refine downwards the size of the market to achieve their target market share. The profits are still lower but the performance is to plan.

In very sophisticated organizations that actually conduct a post-mortem on all projects it is wise to avoid being associated with any project. It is impossible to predict either the outcome of the project or the post-mortem. It is a no-win situation. Even if the project is a success the credit will be given elsewhere so there is only downside. The project is very dangerous both if it is very successful, so engendering jealousy or unsuccessful needing scapegoats. It is particularly a problem in multinationals that regularly move staff, as those posted elsewhere are by definition to blame for problems with projects even if they departed before the project began. The only chance of a jackpot is to be present to steer through a very big disaster as this leads to promotion. As with all jackpots the odds are very low.

Underpinning any major project approval within a corporation are predictions not only about our market or our product but also those built on the same economic and financial variables that are key drivers of the financial markets. There is plenty of choice because the forecasters are legion with major followings and league tables rating the most popular with resulting benefits to both their employers and their remuneration. Although some are better forecasters than others they at least provide enough of a justification of future prospects to get our project approved.

Remarkably we continue to follow these systems even though overall they have proven to be inherently unreliable or, at least, worse than random. Suspicion that a system does not work or that news is inaccurate is never a reason for us to stop using it. We need something to base our decisions or to get our activity approved. Anyway we are smart enough to recognize the accurate forecasts. Those that we do not like we can easily discard. These puts a premium on those forecasters who ensure that their forecasts are believable. There are special techniques to aid this including, amongst some others that I will describe, the ability to accurately forecast.

Another way of checking out just how well the predictions work out can be tested by mixing a couple of metaphors. The proof of the pudding is taking your own medicine. In other words do the financial forecasters make money out of taking their own advice? Well of course they do or they would not continue. Well not quite. What we need to know is if they are successful because they follow their advice or because they persuade others to buy their advice. The specialist financial technicians can make money but not from following their own systems. They make money from giving or selling advice not from taking it.

Malkiel knew many purveyors of the technical forecasting systems and found that their poverty came from following their own systems and their wealth from selling them to others. He provides evidence of the Bermuda concept and its corollary that becomes *if you are still here you can't be that smart*. Alternatively as we have already learned *if you are rich you must be smart*.

'If you're so smart, why aren't you rich?'... The same question might be more appropriately addressed to the technicians. For, after all, the whole point of technical analysis is to make money, and one would reasonably expect that those who preach it would practice it successfully in their own investments. On close examination, technicians are often seen with holes in their shoes and frayed shirt collars. I, personally, have never known a successful technician, but I have seen the wrecks of several unsuccessful ones. (This is, of course, in terms of following their own technical advice. Commissions from urging customers to act on their recommendations are very lucrative.) Curiously, however the broke technician is never apologetic about his method. If anything he is more enthusiastic than ever. If you commit the social error of asking him why he is broke, he will tell you quite ingenuously that he made the all-too-human error of not believing his own charts.[48]

Within corporations it is possible that the actual outcome never sees the light of day so no embarrassing reappraisal is required. However, in the more open environment of financial markets and economic forecasting there is less chance that the outcome of the forecast will remain hidden, making obvious the faults. All this is a penetrating explanation of what the forecasters already know. They know that they do not know and so they resort to a few more techniques to overcome that impediment.

In analyzing these techniques we find further evidence that Ancient Greece has made a greater contribution to modern finance than is generally credited. We have seen how the ancient Greeks first identified Antilogic, how classical Greek drama contributed to the board structure and now we detect the very strong parallels between the modern financial forecaster and the Delphic oracles.

The everyday work of economists, analysts and pundits who as a group retain the same respect, at least with media, as did the oracles in ancient time. The rules to be a successful Delphic oracle are very straightforward and so their practitioners take care to disguise them. To be successful an oracle should have an impressive site and employ a recognizable guru who in theatrical parlance is the *talent*. The rest of the cast have their role but this is to support the guru and emphasis his brilliance. Again it is an echo of the character and the chorus. The site is very important and has to be impressive in its own right. Just what makes it impressive varies according to the style the guru adopts. It may be the opulent office fitted out with priceless antiques in the tallest newest building in the financial centre impressing the supplicant with worth of the guru. Or it may a minimalist high tech environment with the latest screens and news services indicating the information resources available. The annex of the White House might be calculated to give the promise of good political connections. The remote mountain top or the remote tropical isle might demonstrate the other world approach and tax efficiency.

Underlying this requirement for location is the same necessity to appear impressive and inculcate a respectful demeanour. This approach has been used since time immemorial by religion, secular rulers and more recently by judiciary, banks and regulators. We owe most of our most impressive architecture in our main cities to this need. The banking hall is a case in point. Ostensibly the elaborate security arrangements of thick walls with ornately obvious vaults and security grills were to demonstrate the impossibility of stealing the money from the bank although the main purpose was to disguise that most of the money had in fact been lent out again. In today's situation there is no physical money and a vault has no role in protecting an electronic pulse that actually may be located in the Cayman Islands. The bankers with new found practicality are rushing to dismantle the obsolete symbols but have forgotten the actual original purpose of impressing the parishioners. This objective was so transparent that contemporary descriptions of bank architecture of the early twentieth century include revealing descriptions as *architectural splendour, a palace of finance, a cathedral of finance* and *a uniform temple standard of building*. In trying to be modern the bankers are turning their back on their origins. The term *banker* derives not from what they do there or even from money. It is a description of where the transaction took place, at the *banco* or money changer's table. It is hardly surprising the decline in regard in which bankers are held despite the tenacious hope of the current generation of high priests to be liked. Fortunately the name has never been updated because *chip* or *ether* does not have a convincing ring to it and this would be fatal to the image of safety, security, success and association with money that the institution so keenly needs to maintain.

The guru must also sound impressive and will use special language to achieve this effect. The presentational tone of gurus, bankers and regulators has many of the attributes of mystery, magic and ritual. The Federal Reserve inhabits a Greek temple along Constitutional Avenue in Washington. Part of the mystique lies in a similar ability of their leaders to speak in language that is believable but that we cannot quite understand.

> The Federal Reserve was not a sacred temple. The seven governors were not high priests performing mystical rites. Yet the Fed inherited all the resonant feelings that surrounded money, the religious mood and the full freight of irrational meanings. The Federal Reserve's decision making was the essence

of secular rationalism, devoted to scientific theory. Yet it was still the modern equivalent of mysterious sanctification, for its officers performed the ancient priestly function: the creation of money. The central bank, not withstanding its claims to rational method, enfolded itself in the same protective trappings that adorned the temple – secrecy, mystique, an awesome authority that was neither visible nor legible to mere mortals. Like the temple, the Fed did not answer to the people, it spoke for them. Its decrees were cast in a mysterious language people could not understand, but its voice, they knew, was powerful and important.[49]

The pronouncements of the high priests of finance form a sort of institutional muzak that is an important part of the background of financial music but just like muzak we cannot quite recognize the song let alone pick out the words. Even if we think we understand we should not be too sure. It was reported that it was a concerned Dr. Greenspan who responded to an admirer who was thanking him for the information provided in an address: 'If you find my comments informative you must have misunderstood what I said'.

It is a good thing that regulators try and keep out of the prophesy business for they are not very successful. Unfortunately this does not stop politicians from joining the business but they are really trying to invoke the magical using forecasts as incantations because of the belief that the forecast itself could influence the actual outcome. In this example from the Depression it may have been magic but it was not strong magic as borne out by the unfortunate next few years.

> Andrew W. Mellon said [in 1929]: 'There is no cause for worry. The high tide of prosperity will continue'. Mr. Mellon did not know. Neither did any of the other public figures who then or has since, made similar statements. These are not forecasts; it is not to be supposed that the men who make them are privileged to look further into the future than the rest. Mr. Mellon was participating in a ritual which in our society is thought to be of great value for influencing the course of the business cycle. By affirming solemnly that prosperity will continue, it is believed, one can help insure that property will in fact continue. Especially among businessmen the faith in the efficiency of such incantation is very great.[50]

Business is not immune from the same influence with their predictions about share prices, exchange rate, profit estimates and so forth where they reflect what they would like to see happen. The technical term for this effect is *talking your own book*.

Typically the penitents seek the modern oracles at their temples approaching with due deference and bearing suitable gifts. The effect is sometimes heightened for the general audience without loss of prestige by the oracle through participation in much anticipated ceremonies such as economic briefings to Congress or well publicized comments at the Davos World Economic Forum. Such events are suitable occasions for pronouncements. The day to day work of the pundit remains the informal meeting and the luncheon briefing as networking is the technique to be preferred to forecasting. The briefings provided are likely to stick to being statements, commands and warnings. Sometimes a forecast is mandatory in which case it can probably be made conditional on events unlikely to occur in the future. The pundit if finally pinned down should frame an unconditional forecast in an ambiguous fashion that permits claim of success regardless of outcome. The use of certain mystical ambience provided by constantly updating jargon will preclude down to earth comparison.

From time to time the pundit will encounter a more accepting audience and can deliver a startling forecast, provided of course that the answer is known in advance. One such technique is the backfill explanation. It must be part of human nature to appear to have known all along what was going to happen and maybe even begin to believe it to be true. The advance of technology with real time information feeds and word processing and graphical presentational aids has greatly aided the facility by which explanations may be generated to match the event that has already taken place.

This comes close to providing the modern equivalent of the old story of the Prince when travelling in the outer reaches of his country comes across a number of targets with an arrow stuck right in the centre of the bullseye. The Prince commands that the marksman be found and brought before him to explain the secret of his marksmanship so that the army could be taught. Eventually a lad of twelve is found and brought before the Prince and asked for his technique. 'Well Sire, if it pleases you, I fire an arrow into the wall and then paint a target. You see Sire that way I never miss'.

Some of the most respected experts have such credibility that they achieve perfect results by the same technique as the archer lad. All outcomes can be safely described as conforming to their diagnosis. But most pundits do not have the luxury of painting the target. The outcome is the outcome and so to get a hit they fire many arrows. A certain number of times they hit and then they must confidently publicize the results of the forecast with a press conference that reviews the methodology in detail and forget the rest. If you must forecast then be sure to make them frequently. The advance of technology has also made it feasible for analysts to update forecasts almost real time and greater frequency of contact with the client has meant that they can always be given a fresh view that accommodates the latest news.

The downside of scattering of arrows around the countryside is the occasional need to explain unattended arrows but there is a technique for this too. Once the time frame of the forecast has past, the oracle should evaluate the accuracy before anyone else can comment on the miss. Statistics can come to the rescue in supporting the minor nature of misses relative to the high number of hits elsewhere or the trivial nature of this particular disappointment compared to the great significance of another perhaps temporarily forgotten great coup. This process is aided by making it difficult to evaluate whether there has indeed been a miss by using a new forecasting technique at each public meeting so that clients will spend their time evaluating the methodology rather than the oracle's past accuracy. In effect the audience is required to work out for themselves what target the forecaster was trying to hit.

The most reliable advantage the forecaster has is that all predictions, right or wrong are soon forgotten. There are many forecasts, each begins to blur with the other and with the memory bank soon full the predictions are forgotten. Given enough time most of the people hearing the prediction will be gone as well.

All of this archery would be very obvious if all the forecasters dressed up in William Tell outfits and tried to split the apple. The successful market forecaster showmen will have all adopted their own particular style to disguise the classic techniques. Some employ an approach very similar to their mentors, the oracle. This can be categorized as the mystic. Some effect a quasi religious doctrine. Others are the world person and for a smaller fee there is the cousin of the world person or his friend. There are the traditionalists who rely on some great historic figure or previously forgotten historical relationship. There are the mathematicians, correlation experts and contrarians who base their mystique on a never fail computed method. Yet others are the government source, the insider, the other world person who gain their information from somebody who knows. The list goes on as new techniques are applied. The individuals may change but the approach stays the same with an impressive demeanour that distracts attention from the non-forecast forecast. Each category is further differentiated by the personal characteristics of the individual who may be a showman, laid back, numerate, business-like, rapid fire or artistic. Theatre has room for actors of all shapes and sizes. In business terms this is called niche marketing.

We have seen that a lot of no doubt well meaning people have set up in the forecasting business and although the financial results must have been good to support the growth the quality of the forecasts have not. It would be uncharitable in the extreme to believe that this army has deliberately got it wrong. Yes there is a tendency to predict what we would like to see and a minority perhaps have forecast for their personal advantage but overall the forecasts are bad because it is very difficult to do and the mathematical techniques employed are inappropriate.

But no matter what their motivations it is no exaggeration to describe what we have today for financial and economic forecasts as chaos. It has come to be a technical term – chaos theory to describe a general class of non-linear systems. In the early 1960s the meteorologist Edward Lorenz came up with a mathematical model containing only three variables to explain thermal convection of the atmosphere and oceans.

> What he had discovered was a system which generated chaotic properties. Models which were virtually identical, except for very small differences, will eventually, when solved over many time periods, produce solutions, which are completely different...What is important to us is the fact that in chaos systems, practical long-range forecasting becomes impossible. ...Knowledge that the data being examined are chaotic rather than random can be of great benefit in improving short-term forecasting accuracy; there has already been a distinct improvement in the practical, everyday under-standing that physical and biological sciences have of the phenomena they investigate.[51]

Tvede approaches from the mathematicians' interpretation of forecasts in the face of fifty crashes in 500 years. He takes the position of the statistician in calculating our propensity for illusion from the high frequency of major crashes and our inability to learn from past problems.

> It starts slowly, then suddenly accelerates and become completely hyster-ical...well then, there is only one feasible explanation. That is, you have some frightfully strong positive feedback loops at force in your market. And they are possibly combined with some kind of fractal behaviour...It probably means that you can probably make short-term forecasts for these markets, if you understand the dynamics. But is also means that it must be impossible to forecast their long-term behaviour. Well, that is exactly what we have experienced. But is there a mathematical expression for such behaviour? There certainly is. In the mathematical world we call it chaos.[52]

He has his explanation of why it happens. The forecasts must be unreli-able because the actual systems have bifurcations of the feedback loops that amplify noise and end in unpredictable chaos. The multiple forecasts and back-fill explanations can only serve to accelerate and intensify the feedback loops.

> Feedback loops have fairly predictable effects in the short run. But over time they build up a forum of butterfly effects. The loops are accumulative...- Compounded over time they constitute an invincible barrier to prediction. They become the strongest component in our 'dark forces of time and ignorance'.[53]

The implication is clear. These forecasts do not work because we follow them!

VIII

THE AMAZING ROLE OF CASH

ADVANCED MONETARY concepts in primitive lands and primitive monetary concepts in developed countries. Or Buying the Label rather than the Contents.

No wonder it is difficult to explain and predict what is going on. Business is complex. Individual corporations may employ hundreds of thousands of staff over many different countries. The same corporation may produce a myriad of products and as our economy moves more towards services rather than physical things it is becoming more difficult to describe what is the product. The structure or organization is used to manage the complexity changes from time to time and one change might not be complete before the next change arises. When this corporate complexity enters the market place and the results are judged in the financial markets the complexity rises to a higher order. It gets worse when we then consider the whole economy and globalization. Individuals and organizations seek to bring understanding and order to this complexity by systematically applying labels to things, actions, concepts, etc. in the expectation that this will aid identification and hopefully prediction of the future that is consistent with the label. Unfortunately the label often fails to match the contents. This may be inadvertent but often it is deliberate.

Of particular interest is the way our understanding of the thing, the label and what is the basis of its existence drifts back and forth. Sorting this out is vital to the understanding of Antilogic and its influence on money. Our general concept of profit and money depend more on belief than on fact. In this chapter we pursue the difference between the token and the substance or put another way, between the money and the goods.

Back in Chapter V, the accountants taught us that profit was opinion and cash was fact. This so-called fact itself is very hard to pin down with many opinions and many commentators. We now discover that rather than money being the acid test of profits it is just part of the same concept. Money is the means by which we measure the inputs and outcomes of most economic and financial activities. It is divisible and provides the basis for ranking relative outcomes. Money is the label but brings its own complications because money is a label of itself. This changes from application to application and from time to time. Closer scrutiny reveals that there are many sorts of money.

What is money after all? Whence does it come and where does it go? If you think it is the dollar coin in your pocket, you would be very mistaken, as a few quotes from some eminent economists will reveal. The first is from Galbraith.

> There are three progenitors of money; mints, treasury secretaries or finance ministers these being the source of paper money: and banks of one description or another.[54]

> The process by which banks create money is so simple that the mind is repelled when something so important is involved, a deeper mystery seems only decent... The coin on deposit served no less as money by being in a bank and being subject to transfer by the stroke of a primitive pen. Inevitably, it was discovered...that another stroke of the pen would give a borrower from the bank as distinct from a creditor of the original depositor, a loan from the original and idle deposit.[55]

Here is another quote from Galbraith. It might be thought that some magical process is involved.

> Why is anything intrinsically so valueless so obviously desirable? What in contrast to a similar mass of fibres clipped from yesterday's newspaper, gives it the power to command goods, enlist service, induce cupidity, promote avarice, incite crime? Surely some magic is involved: certainly some metaphysical or extraterrestrial explanation of its value is required.[56]

Locke tells that mankind in accepting money with intrinsic value has used its imagination to ascribe a value.

> Locke was obliged to admit that there was nothing natural about the use of metal money: rather mankind had 'consented to put an imaginary value on gold and silver, by reason of their durableness, scarcity, and not being very likely to be counterfeited.[57]

Labordiére friend of Keynes was a prolific writer about money. He goes beyond imagination to the spiritual and introduces the indefinite, which suggests he means vapour.

> It is self evident that man will never be able to know what money is, no more than he will be able to know what God is, or the spiritual world. Money is not infinite, but it is the indefinite, an astounding complex of all sorts of psychological as well as material relations.[58]

He might not have known what money was, but he knew whence it came, that money is born in a deposit. Dennis Robertson, colleague, friend and ultimately critic of Keynes also found and named the source of money.

> We may think of the deposit as a kind of generating station or mother-ship for cheques: and though it is a bad and foolish practice as a rule to create new names for common things, it may help us to bear this relation in mind, and also to avoid some cumbrousness of phrasing, if we call a person's deposit his *chequery*, because it is both a breeding-ground and a homing-place for cheques, as a rookery is for rooks.[59]

He saw the humour in money and went as far as to describe the British monetary system as a somewhat eccentric contraption.

From these observations, you can see that there is nothing intrinsically very real about currency but magic is not necessary as all currency represents variations of a common theme. There is currency such as gold that derives its attraction from the pride of ownership. This obviously aids transferability as does currency that can easily be transformed into something desirable. This has developed into currency that is itself intrinsically worthless but is deemed to be valuable by some convincing authority despite not carrying a promise of redemption or conversion to something desirable.

Consequently physical manifestation tells us nothing that will distinguish between so called real cash and Vapourcash or Anticash. Indeed, we might as well conclude that real money only exists because we think that it does. Here are a couple more stories to illustrate this conclusion. First from Robertson

> It is said that there was once a mine manager in Johannesburg who had a glass eye. When business called him away he would take his eye out and leave it in a prominent place; and while the master's eye was on them the workmen continued to work like blacks, as indeed they were. But one day one of the workmen, more daring than the rest, stealthily approached the all-seeing orb and covered it up with an inverted cigarette tin: whereupon he and all his fellows promptly went away and got drunk. Which is a

parable of what might happen if all semblance of a gold standard were obliterated.[60]

Well, we will see how real the gold standard turned out to be. It took mankind quite a long time to work out how insubstantial money was and this complicated the choice between money and the goods. This choice is very much influenced by what we see reported as the situation rather than what actually is the situation. It goes right back to the start of international trade conducted on a commercial basis. The economic theory relating to trade became known as mercantilism and describes particular principles and mode of operation that through the centuries have been successively applauded and condemned. The doctrine of the mercantilists has been out of favour with academic economists since Adam Smith but has never really lost its sway with the business community and also can be seen in the policy of several western governments. This has included politicians such as Margaret Thatcher and Ronald Reagan seeking a justification for a smaller public sector.

Although the term mercantilist sounds like an impressive economic concept it simply means to act like a merchant. After all merchants carried out the international trade. It was not really a system as such but primarily a reflection of the attitudes of the statesmen, civil servants, and of the financial and business leaders of the day. The general philosophy is contained in the often-quoted comment from Johann Joachim Becher that it is always better to sell goods to others than it is to buy goods from others, for the former brings a certain advantage and the latter inevitable damage.

The mercantilist doctrine was subsequently spelled out but it is only what would come naturally to a merchant then or now. It pays little regard to national interests that might go beyond the pursuit of profitable trade desired by the merchant. The mercantilist approach is that only selling can lead to a profit, never through buying. The net effect of the mercantilist policy was that their kingdom had a big pile of cash while their impoverished neighbours enjoyed all the products. If they were advanced credit by their neighbours then it is even better; keep your money and still enjoy what money can buy. Keeping the money became an objective in its own right because of the possibilities it offered. Gold was seen as money and was pursued by highly motivated individuals such as Christopher Columbus who saw it as a means of possessing whatever the owner desired even to the extent of getting souls into paradise.

Thomas Mun (1571–1641), an East India Company director and pre-eminent of the English mercantilist writers defined the mercantilist objective as selling more to strangers than we consume of theirs, i.e. everyone should strive to have a permanent trade surplus. He set out the rules to maximize wealth and well being in a book for the better upbringing and instruction of his son.[61] These practical rules emphasized restraint in the consumption of foreign goods with the current preoccupation being food and clothing. If he was to be profligate he should at least do it at home so that the benefit could trickle down to the local poor. Exports were to be sent in his own ships which might well have long journeys as it was better to favour distant competitors than to give help to the competitor nearby. In any event one should always charge what the market will bear. If the foreigner does not have it sell dear and price sharply what they can otherwise obtain. He also had a most feared foreign competitor, the Dutch who represented best practice at that time especially in the fish business.

Mun allows himself one heresy where, in certain cases, it would be beneficial to allow the export of money itself. He argues that keeping money in the kingdom will not make a bountiful trade. That depends on the need others have for the goods so it is necessary to have faith that moneys invested in trade will come back as treasure.

The era of the merchant, also known as the time of merchant capitalism or mercantilism, lasted from the middle of the fifteenth century to the middle of the eighteenth century. This period of three hundred years is longer than the subsequent period of the industrial revolution or any of the periods that we would regard as modern economic history. It was a period that saw the development of trade on a commercial scale and its attendant financial techniques and the development of trade finance and banking that we would recognize today. More important, it brought social acceptability not previously afforded traders. The interests of state and individual became intermingled. As the merchants became influential in government the pursuit of wealth also became acceptable including the earning of interest.

The mercantilists were driven by self rather than state interest. Trade was all very well but it needed to be profitable trade and this led to a very forthright attitude to price competition so that prices should not be too low. Success was measured by the stock of precious metals the merchant could accumulate. It was assumed that what was good for the individual was also good for the state and this led to the granting of monopolies seen to be in the national interest. Today this is regarded as a fallacy of composition although its resounding simplicity makes it a contemporary political policy favourite that the government treats its receipts, expenditure and debt in the same manner as might the single household. Try as they might a legion of academics have failed to convince the world that a favourable balance of payments cannot be achieved by all countries simultaneously and the struggle to be the country to succeed in improving its balance has not diminished with time. Apparently practice makes perfect based on the evidence of the IMF statistics. The world in persistent surplus shows that more have succeeded than theory would indicate.

It is not only countries that can only buy and avoid selling. Current businessmen still grapple to decide whether the objective is to keep the money or own the investment. For example there are stock market mercantilists who buy shares that are too good ever to sell.

'Our family owns IBM, which is the greatest growth company in the world... If something happens to me, whatever you do, don't sell the IBM'. Mr. Smith himself never sold a share of IBM. Its dividends were meagre, naturally, so Mr. Smith had to work hard at his own business to provide for his growing family... The Smiths are now in their third generation of IBM ownership, and this generation is telling the next, 'Whatever you do, don't sell IBM'. And when somebody dies, only enough IBM is sold to pay the estate taxes. In short for three generations the Smiths have worked as hard as their friends who had no money at all, even though the various branches of the Smith family all put together are very wealthy indeed. And the IBM is there, nursed and watered and fed, the Genii of the House, growing away in the early hours of the morning when everyone else is asleep... Presumably the Smiths will go on, working hard, paying off their mortgages, and watching their IBM grow with joy, always blossom, never fruit. It is a parable of pure capitalism, never jam today and a case of jam tomorrow.[62]

Which just goes to show once again, that you never make money buying, only when you sell. It is also a warning about how the world's greatest growth story can quickly become the biggest restructure. Our friends the mercantilists lacked our forecasting techniques but they knew all about the time value of money hence their great interest in piling up heaps of gold here today. For them it was jam today rather than jam tomorrow. Gold was the way of keeping score and crystallizing success in monetary form.

Gold was a relative late comer for acceptance as the monetary symbol but it took a very strong hold when it came. So strong a hold in fact that as late as 1964 it was still seen as the ultimate monetary store and it was unthinkable that it could even be challenged by an international paper currency.

Humanity generally and central bankers in particular seem to regard the whims of nature as being more becoming than the whims of man, and for this and other reasons the development of a purely international paper currency is unlikely soon to appear as accepted reality. The interim is a difficult period, for in a world of imperfect understanding and co-operation, the evolution towards a more sophisticated international monetary system is subject to national interests and suspicions. It is not difficult to find many problems attendant on using national currencies such as the dollar as international money, and the world is essentially dependent on gold as the ultimate monetary store of value and medium of exchange.[63]

There is an extensive literature setting out how essential the gold standard was to world stability and economic growth. The subject was addressed then with such certainty that, only forty years on, we are duty bound to question any current pronouncements about money. The truth is that it only ever appeared to be impregnable. If it had been questioned at the time the cracks would have been soon revealed. The first question to ask was which gold standard? Even in its hey day during the forty years to 1914 there had never really been a single consistent gold standard. The final gold standard of the 1960s was actually the gold exchange standard where the central bank has no obligation to buy and sell gold. Older and purer forms were the pure gold or gold specie standard where the central bank buys and sells unlimited amounts of gold at fixed prices and the gold bullion standard where notes are not redeemable in gold.

It is a sad condemnation of the handiwork of monetary economists that there were pundits who realized that it was even worse than the random nature of gold discovery and production. Monetary growth was dependent on the availability of reserve currencies throwing the world at the mercy of the United States and previously the United Kingdom being willing to overspend. This would have been easy enough to predict and serves to emphasize yet again that all these monetary transactions must always have two sides.

One of the great problems of the gold exchange standard – and perhaps overlooked by its architects at Genoa – is that dollars and sterling can only be accumulated as reserves if America and Britain themselves run balance of payment deficits. The key currency component of reserves represents the difference between total receipts and expenditure on all international transactions. Under the gold exchange system, therefore, any additions to the total of international liquidity depend upon the fortuitous circumstances of the British balance of payments. Since the fluctuations in world gold mining output have tended to be less erratic than the net balance of payments position of the United States and the United Kingdom, this new technique of aligning the world supply of liquidity with world needs could scarcely be called an improvement on the old methods.[64]

So wrote Ian Shannon Managing Director of the Economist Intelligence Unit (Australia) in 1964. The situation is essentially the same today but with the role of gold further diminished and that of the exchange currencies augmented with the Euro.

The necessity for a continuing deficit of reserve currency purposes rather contradicts the mercantilists and much of current economic wisdom. A perusal of the IMF statistics would lay much of Shannon's concern to rest. The United States has stoically accepted the rest of world's goods in return for its paper making a great contribution to the structural surplus that the world has had with itself for many years.

Over the centuries mankind has had a number of different ideas of what represents real money. This might have been an archaic physical token such as stones, shells, tobacco, etc. The ideas developed along separate lines in communities cut off from developments elsewhere. Some of these ideas seem curious to us today although, to be fair, some of our own ideas seem curious today. The prize for the most concrete of all real money must go to the islanders of Yap although it is even better in being real stone rather than concrete. Strange though these enormous coins seem to us they are in principle no different to gold bars.

Henry Furness III an anthropologist who visited the island of Yap in 1903 was so struck by the monetary system of this community of five thousand that he titled his book about the custom and habits of the islanders, *The Island of Stone Money*.[65]

There is among the Caroline Islands an island called Uap, whose money consists solely of huge stones call fei, many of them are so large that they cannot be moved, so that even when they change hands in the course of business their physical location is left unchanged. In fact, the richest family in the island holds that position by virtue of being the owner of a huge stone, which was accidentally sunk from a raft while it was being brought to the island many years ago. For several generations this stone has been lying at the bottom of the sea, and none of the present generation of the family has ever seen it; but nobody questions that they are the richest family in the island. Some time ago the natives allowed the roads of the island to fall into disrepair, and steadily refused to mend them; and the Germans, who were at that time in possession of the island, had to devise some means of inflicting a fine. It was clearly useless to attempt to remove any of the stones from the island. At last by a happy thought the fine was exacted by sending a man to every failu and pabai throughout the disobedient districts, where he simply marked a certain number of the most valuable fei with a cross in black paint to show that the stones were claimed by the Government. This instantly worked like a charm; the people, thus dolefully impoverished, turned to and repaired the highways to such good effect from one end of the island to the other that they are now like park drives. Then the government despatched its agents and erased the crosses. Presto! The fine was paid, the happy failus resumed possession of their capital stock, and rolled in wealth.

Milton Friedman also tells the story of Uap (Yap) and adds the comment

Just so gold is a fetish, if you will, but it does the trick.

He goes on to explain how this isolated society had independently discovered many of the features of the twentieth century monetary system.

The ordinary's reaction, like my own, will be: 'How silly. How can people be so illogical?' However before, before we criticize too severely the innocent people of Yap, it is worth contemplating an episode in the United States to which the islanders might well have that same reaction. In 1932–1933, the Bank of France feared that the United States was not going to stick to the gold standard at the traditional price of $US20.67 an ounce of gold. Accordingly, the French bank asked the Federal Reserve Bank of New York to convert into gold a major part of the dollar assets that it has in the United States. To avoid the necessity of shipping the gold across the ocean, the Federal Reserve Bank was requested simply to store the gold in the Bank of France's account. In response, officials of the Federal Reserve Bank went to their gold vault, put in separate drawers the correct amount of gold ingots, and put a label or a mark, on those drawers indicating that the contents were the property of the French. For all it matters, the drawers could have been marked 'with a cross in black paint,' just as the Germans had marked the stones. The result was headlines in the financial newspapers about 'the loss of gold,' the threat to the American financial system and the like. The US gold reserves were down, French gold reserves up. The markets regarded the US dollar as weaker, the French franc as stronger. The so-called drain of gold by France from the United States was one of the factors that ultimately led to the banking panic of 1933.[66]

This fear of the financial panic is the nub of the monetary problem for the separated communities. At a stroke of a pen their hard won wealth in the form of the gold hoard or bank balance is transferred away. Where it goes they neither know or care. It might have been to the US as in the example or to Mars for that matter. They only know that they no longer command that wealth. The inverse is also true in that wealth can suddenly and inexplicably manifest itself and is the basis of the cargo cult followed in the Pacific Islands based on goods magically appearing from the sky.

Anyone who doubts the magical properties underpinning gold as currency should read *The Wizard of Oz* by Frank Baum. It provides a colourful and remarkably insightful allegory about monetary politics. Dorothy represents the stout hearted farming community and follows the yellow brick road (representing gold) to the Emerald City (representing Washington) where everyone looks through green-coloured glasses (representing money). She meets the Wizard of Oz (derived from an ounce of gold) who turns out to be a fraud. In the book Dorothy gets magic slippers from the Wicked Witch of the East (representing Wall Street) symbolizing the use of silver to ease the depression caused by low prices. As it turned out in the real economy the US remained on the gold standard but new discoveries of gold ended the period of tight money.

Our ideas of western monetary economics have led us to believe that traditional forms of currency, such as the stone coins of Yap, have disappeared or are no longer of use. This is not the case. These communities developed their own forms of exchange because they were useful or essential to support the social practices of their communities. In so far as these practices continue then the currency is also needed despite efforts of governments to suppress the traditional currency. The efforts to suppress came not because the traditional currency was ineffective but because it worked too well leaving too much of the profits with the locals and not enough with the foreign traders.

The Australian Broadcasting Corporation in the program *Pig Tusks and Paper Money* shown on 19 July 2000 provided evidence of the continuing use of traditional currencies. The main character is Henry, an inhabitant of the island of New Britain, whose ambition it is to establish a properly constituted bank for the handling of traditional shell money (*tabu*). Strings of shell money play a vital role in many important social activities of that society. The most important use of traditional money is its accumulation to be distributed at the owner's funeral and so gain admittance to the land of the dead. It is used in day to day transactions but it is difficult to accumulate enough by this means and so most stocks are obtained from organizing major ceremonies such as honouring the dead. Participants are required to pay admission fees, contributions and gifts. Weddings are the most formal occasions but other examples are fund raising for choir or church and the exorcising of bad spirits. When things go wrong tabu is needed to pay adultery fines and blood money. Modern money can be used up to a point but it brings no honour within the community.

Henry's ambition is to use modern techniques to overcome the inflexibilities of the traditional money by facilitating the deposit, safekeeping and lending of traditional money. In his particular community shell money holds sway but in other communities it is pigs' tusks and in the community of his friend Sarah on the Trobriand Islands the traditional money is made from banana fronds. We also meet Sarah on the program. She is a very well spoken and obviously very successful island trading store proprietor, familiar with modern business and products.

Henry's ambition has brought him trouble with modern society. The modern bankers protect the exclusive use of the term bank for their pieces of plastic and electronic pulses. We see a scene where Henry shows Sarah modern Papua New Guinea currency, which is illustrated with traditional symbols of wealth such as pigs. 'This is not real money, this is just a picture. This is real money', he says as he pulls a necklace of pigs' tusks out of his bag. Or should that be called wallet. Henry has a point here. The very name kina means shell money and the five kina note is illustrated with the kina shell. It is a full circle. Reality has become paper illustrated with pictures of the former reality.

Despite many obstacles Henry made progress through local government to get authorization for his shell money bank. But catastrophe came when the Rabaul volcanic eruption devastated the town and his bank. However the looters who broke into the bank during the confusion of the eruption and stole the shell money provided the ultimate test of the currency. It was worth stealing. Now the government is pursuing poor Henry for misappropriation of funds, being the paper kina used to buy the shell money that was stolen. We must await the outcome of the protracted litigation in a subsequent program but in the meantime Henry's clear logic explains to us why this traditional money is so enduringly popular and why the Islanders of Yap were so advanced in their understanding. Henry tells us 'The trouble with this paper money is that it goes away. Our community is very comfortable and can provide our needs for food, clothing and housing. We only need the modern kina to buy modern products. We get the kina from somewhere and buy the goods and then the kina is gone. Our traditional money is limited in its supply and always stays here in our community. When someone needs to buy pigs he goes and trades to get the shell money which goes around in our community'.

When Friedman goes on to describe the Yap islanders concrete manifestation of wealth he is describing the same process as Henry does. It is the means by which the community has decided who has wealth and importance and so has the claim on the bounty of that community.

The Yap islanders regarded as a concrete manifestation of their wealth stones quarried and shaped on a distant island and brought to their own. For a century and more, the civilized world regarded as a concrete manifestation of its wealth a metal dug from deep in the ground, refined at great labour, transported great distances, buried again in elaborate vaults deep in the ground. Is the one practice really more rational than the other?

What both examples illustrate is how important appearance or illusion or 'myth', given unquestioned belief, becomes in monetary matters. Our own money, the money we have grown up with, the system under which it is controlled, these appear 'real' and 'rational' to us. Yet the money of other countries often seems to us like paper or worthless metal, even when the purchasing power of individual units is high.[67]

The irony of burying money in the form of gold bars under the ground of the financial capital of the world goes even further. This very ground was purchased from the original owners using their shell currency, called in this place *wampumpeag* (shortened to wampum as peag means *bead*) or *sewan* (after the place where the shells were found). Wampum had been long established as the basis of trade between the coastal tribes and inland tribes when a Dutch fur trader Jacob Eelkes became the first European to realize its function. Soon there was a flourishing three way trade with European trade goods exchanged for wampum to be used to obtain furs from inland tribes. Wampum was so prevalent that it became legal tender in 1643 with a fixed exchange rate and acceptable for the payment of taxes. It was natural that when the Europeans negotiated the purchase of Manhattan the trade goods exchanged included wampum. Wampum remained in strong demand during the eighteenth century with a factory established in 1760 surviving in production for more than a hundred years, a survival period longer than achieved by the gold standard. Just as with tabu from half a world away wampum had a function that went beyond money and a means of exchange. It fulfilled the same function of blood money atoning for wrongs committed but also fulfilled an important role in cementing alliances and paying tribute. Further, it had a decorative function especially as the skill in stringing the beads was used to record the basis of the transaction entered into. In effect the wampum belts were an early form of written contract. Unfortunately the European settlers did not understand either the basis of the agreement or indeed the indigenous concept of native ownership of land. The use of wampum passed away not because of shortcomings as money but because of the inconvenience of the agreements it represented.

There really is no difference in mutually deciding that wealth and place in society is to be decided by the number of gold bars or stone coins or account balance at the local Bank of America. In this context it makes no difference if the stone coin is on land, under the sea or, changing the currency, safely deposited in Henry's Shell Money Bank of New Britain. For centuries communities determined wealth by inheritance and that generally through title to land. Quite why a particular family should have a claim to land is often not clear but in many cases it was related to service to some long forgotten king or overlord. On the Laccadive Islands in the Indian Ocean the idea of property in land was unfamiliar, and status was reckoned in the number of coconut trees possessed. This led to the overcrowding of trees. The very deep class division in that society was between the Koyas or patricians who owned the trees and the Melicheries, or plebians who climbed them.

Today the division of wealth within society may be as a result of participation in and prescient sale of shares in some sharemarket float. How much clearer and more honourable is wealth generated by an heroic journey across four hundred miles of open ocean bringing back the biggest stone coin that anyone has never seen.

IX

VAPOURCASH EXPLAINED: CASH, NOT AS REAL AS YOU THOUGHT

It is tempting to define real as having physical form but today the vast bulk of the world's money is already in electronic form made up of pulses in a computer somewhere and not much more than a particular form of electricity. This realization may come as a surprise but the concept is not new.

The idea of worth changed over time, as money became tokens of intrinsic wealth. Previous generations saw gold and silver as being the real money. When there was not enough cash of intrinsic wealth to meet the spending aspirations there came the growth of fiat currency where somebody of authority gave the currency worth. This started with coins of less intrinsic worth and has continued with an endless progression through paper and plastic notes, other tokens, traveller's cheques, debit and credit cards, stored value cards to electronic currency.

We will follow how money has become less substantial but more subtle in its functioning. Often the effectiveness of its functioning owes nothing to its physical form. Other attributes such as speed, security and flexibility can predominate. Various economic pioneers have identified key aspects from which I will piece together the various facets of money to provide as clear as possible a picture of such an indistinct subject.

Adam Smith, the original, noted that money lacked physical substance commenting that money is neither a material to work upon, nor a tool to work with. Long before the invention of the computer most of the money was made up from journal entries made in ink on paper. Even in the good old days of the gold standard the value of money was a multiplication sum of so many tons of gold times a computed value. When it comes down to it the bulk of the world's money is the belief that a specified ability to spend will be there when required. Human nature being what it is this belief often does not turn out to be what was expected.

Our generation is now used to paper money being the norm despite its peculiar behaviour in inflationary times. Even today greenbacks do strange things. US Federal Reserve statistics indicate that the Federal Reserve Bank of New York predominantly issues the mysterious United States thousand dollar bill. Ultimately they are mostly paid in again to the Federal Reserve of Los Angeles. The notes are seldom encountered in the United States. Where do they go? Are they like salmon or eels that travel the world but have to go back to their special place to spawn and to die?

We are also confronted with evidence that money is very unreliable and uncertain in fulfilling the payment role that we take for granted. Robertson observed a wide spread of performance of money.

> We decided...to fix our attention for the present on the flow of money onto the markets during a given period of time – let us say a week. But during that week some of the pieces of money in existence will not be available for work; they may be holiday-making in my pocket, or taking a prolonged rest-cure in the bank, or even being 'cooled a long age in the deep-delved earth'. Some pieces of money are very agile like pieces of scandal and skip easily from one person to another. Others are like an old lady buying a railway ticket – one would think they had lost the power of locomotion altogether.[68]

Loss of locomotion can go beyond the loss of velocity and also imply a loss of moneyness. Part of the idea of money comes from its ability to move from hand to hand and if this departs the token loses its value in just the same way that surplus Club Med tokens brought home from the holiday ultimately and regretfully end up in the rubbish. The idea makes James Buchan poetic in *Frozen Desire* as he explores the concepts of motion, and possession in the progression from value to pricelessness.

> Money must always be poised or in motion and must always be in some-body's possession, lest its moneyness evaporate: whereas the eagle remains the eagle whatever its activity or domicile. It is real as a father's kiss is real, precisely because it is not priced. I suspect that as the unowned elements of nature become more scarce, they will become not expensive but literally priceless; and will pass, like exhausted Old Masters, into communal owner-ship, which is no ownership at all.[69]

In contrast, the down to earth Robertson tells another little story to illustrate why transactions do not equate to value.

> On Derby Day two men, Bob and Joe, invested in a barrel of beer, and set off to Epsom with the intention of selling it retail on the racecourse at 6d. a pint, the proceeds to be shared equally between them. On the way Bob, who had

one three-penny-bit left in the world, began to feel a great thirst, and drank a pint of the beer, paying Joe 3d. as his share of the market price. A little later Joe yielded to the same desire, and drank a pint of beer, returning the 3d to Bob. The day was hot, and before long Bob was thirsty again, and so, a little later, was Joe. When they arrived at Epsom, the 3d was back in Bob's pocket, and each had discharged in full his debts to the other: but the beer was all gone. One single three-penny-bit had performed a volume of transactions which would have required many shillings if the beer had been sold to the public in accordance with the original intention.[70]

What is even more disconcerting than the variability of money itself is the way systems can function even when no real cash is present. Other forms of cash have taken the function. Anthony Jay came close to identifying Vapourcash in *The Corporation Man* when he describes *corporation money* as

A purely notional currency which appears on forms and memos, but never passed through pockets or wallets… The budget for a single (item) might be more than the workers annual salary… Corporation money, like corporation time, was simply something that was there. It had to be used up somehow.[71]

Jay was a pioneer in the analysis of forms of money and his groundbreaking work was based on experience in the operations of a government owned corporation. His judgement is inherently neutral in that the corporation money was there and it was to be used. It was clearly different to real money but he did not dwell on why it came, from whence it came and for what purpose it was to be used.

It was a small step to make in discovering that those objectives are the indulgence of the senior executives. After the excesses of the 1980s Saul spotted *Fancy Talk* and its objective as the justification for the consumption of resources to the benefit and indulgence of the corporate managers. It gave him a rather black and white view about money and according to Saul this is the more sinister motivation for the generation of Vapourcash, which he termed *apparent* money. The diversion of real cash to the sustenance of the participants as opposed to the necessities of the venture became so prevalent that he divided money into real and apparent with no other outcome possible. He contends that to achieve this end the corporation managers create and consume apparent money.

One of the most obvious innovations of the managed corporation has been the division of currency into two sorts – apparent money and real money. Apparent money belongs to the corporation but is used by the employees, directly or indirectly, for their personal lives. Real money actually comes out of the individual's pocket. Some people have only real money.[72]

However, it would be inaccurate and unduly harsh to attribute all Vapourcash generation as being motivated by or employed as apparent money. Apparent money is just a sub set of Vapourcash or more precisely it is part of the use to which it is put. His distinction between real and apparent is based on the nature, virtue, indeed worth of the spender rather than the characteristic of the purchase, although as he explains a certain pattern of expenditure can be observed.

> The executive classes of the West particularly from industry, but increasingly from government live large parts of their lives on apparent income. They eat, travel, phone and drive without even considering real cost, because that cost is limited only by their professional level.[73]

He has an extensive list of expenditure that constitutes apparent money and even suggests that it is so pervasive that some businesses are largely dependent on apparent cash for their sustenance. The list includes quality restaurants, city hotels, company cars, sports clubs and executive travel. Corporate governance, far from moderating the creation of Vapourcash and its employment, creates the environment that encourages its growth with access to apparent money increasing at the more senior levels of the corporate hierarchy. Apparent money shows how systemic the creation of Vapourcash has become in modern business. It reflects the mechanism by which Vapourcash is put to use by the participants of business and government bureaucracy for their collective benefit. One entertains the other and then the other reciprocates. Each can feel comfortable supported by surveys that establish that the practice in this particular corporation is comparable with the market. Those that fall behind are given the opportunity to adjust.

Strictly speaking, apparent money is not a different category of money but a label for its application, i.e. this expenditure is apparently for a justifiable purpose but it is not really justified. The importance of the link is the identification of the mechanism by which Vapourcash generated within an organization is applied for the benefit of the creators. It also reveals the circumstances in which it occurs and why it continues to flourish despite the damage it causes the sponsoring organization.

The generation of Vapourcash within the business cases of the organization is the mechanism by which the managers are able to justify the practices that Saul describes. The pervasiveness of the practice together with the remaining credibility of the corporation will determine whether the indulgences will be accomplished using real cash, Vapourcash or in the most extreme circumstances, Anticash.

Saul's idea of money having motivation goes too far as in this regard Vapourcash is no different to any other form of money. It does not know who owns it and it does not know why it was created. It is just Vapourcash to be used by whoever is around at the time. Money knows no stink (Cuniam non olet). Because it is fungible there is nothing to distinguish it from any other note or coin. It reveals nothing about how it was obtained nor about the motives of those who obtain it. You can do with it what you will.

Saul goes further than Robertson in revealing the performance of money by identifying wide areas of activity supposedly supported by money that turns out not to exist and by calling money that bears no relationship to reality, *imaginary* and *pure inflation*.

An imaginary market is one in which a multiple illusion of currencies is speculated upon without reference to normal agreements on value. The quantities of money traded bear no relationship to growth or production. They are manifestations of pure inflation. The international money markets represent the regularization, through a specialist technocracy and a revolution in technological communications, of the speculative economy. The South Sea Bubble and all the other great financial manipulations of the last three centuries have finally been normalized as standard business practice... The more sophisticated among us know that times have changed and that markets no longer need to be related to reality. These international money markets are a new truth. Of what and for what is irrelevant. Only the naïve would concern themselves with those questions. There is a market. There is competition. All the rest is idle chatter.[74]

Based on Saul's definition that money not grounded in reality is imaginary and pure inflation, apparent money is pure inflation. Yet it must seem very real to those who consume its benefits.

He relates pure inflation to lack of substance rather than to the movement of prices usually meant by economists. He has taken inflation to the next step in that prices without substance are inflation and those with no substance at all are pure inflation. No substance equals vapour and so it would seem to describe an extreme manifestation of Vapourcash identified soon before a violent condensation. For him there is no difference between a Weimar banknote, a junk bond or bank preferred share floated to cover non-recoverable loans. All are the same, pure inflation.

Mathematicians would recognize this concept of pure inflation as potentially being a finite process that has accelerated to its limit. If we use the

Bob and Joe example once again it just means that they are passing the coin back and forth so fast that we can no longer see it passing from hand to hand. This is a theoretical concept because in practice they could not drink the beer fast enough to match the money changing hand movements. This would lead to the normal simplification in these circumstances. They would agree to drink the beer first and forget the cash settlement until later.

The great economist Hume also noted the lack of substance but identified a role as a sort of production aid or catalyst. He called it the oil that eased the motion of the wheels of trade. For Bob and Joe beer, rather than money is the main lubricant. Playwright Henrik Ibsen found that money went beyond assisting the process. Perhaps it was the process or what made it happen. This process he described as being the outer or the packaging but money fell short of being the thing itself.

> Money may be the husk of many things, but not the kernel. It buys you food, but not appetite; medicine, but not health; acquaintances, but not friends; servants, but not loyalty; days of joy, but not peace or happiness.

All of these examples have illustrated why currency or so-called real money is proving to be very difficult to pin down. Not only does it have all these varied roles and flexibility in performance but it can also change its character. Hyperactivity can lead to Saul's pure inflation so that it does not exist or no longer exists. But we presume that it was there before. If that is the case then it must have changed its character. Saul also tries to explain how this might happen. Banks risk the evaporation or volatilization of their money through unnecessary speculation in international currencies, property or take-overs. Even lending to those who speculate is to risk volatilization or evaporation.

> If they speculate unnecessarily in the international currency markets and lose, then the real wealth created by investment, production and labour simply evaporates with that lost money.

> If they lend it to those who speculate in property, as has increasingly happened over the last thirty years, then the day the property boom collapses, the real value which the speculators had borrowed also evaporates. The same is true of the large merger and take-over speculations of the last three decades and of the international money-market binges.

> Speculators and corporate managers berate us for not working hard enough to create sufficient wealth to fuel growth. But a more reasonable explanation for the lack of solid money in our society is that repeatedly over the last

thirty years the citizenry have deposited the real wealth they created by investing, working and producing. And repeatedly their elites have borrowed that money and volatilized it.[75]

This description of volatilization of money is incomplete. Speculative losses occur all the time and there are also the possibilities the bankers dream up for the next banking crisis. But presumably the winner has received the proceeds. Saul provides another description in which he is even more specific both in the disappearance of wealth, the cause of poverty and in the mistaken belief that money is real.

> Volatilization; the act of causing wealth to disappear from an economy. This is most effectively done through speculation in areas unrelated to growth. Societies get into trouble when they begin to believe that money is real which it isn't. Those foolish enough to forget that money is in the nature of a working illusion based on a tacit agreement about value also tend to mistreat their currency. For example, they may shove it out onto an unregulated market-place where every punter can give it a kick. They may endlessly print it, which produces classic inflation. Or they may use it for speculation in an uncontrolled manner, which will cause the money to evaporate. All of this constitutes volatilization and causes poverty.[76]

Underpinning his idea of money being or coming closest to real is through the concept of reasonableness. It the goods are real, the prices are reasonable and there is no speculation then, for Saul, money is possibly real.

> Money comes closest to respecting the agreement on value when it is earned and multiplied through investment, labour and purchasing. Investment and labour produce real goods which can be bought. The money lent for investment earns interest for the banks. The wages earned by labour are deposited in those same institutions. If the banks in turn lend a reasonable multiple of this money out to people investing in real growth or in the sort of property which practical needs make necessary, there is a potential for real growth in value.[77]

Taken altogether his concept of volatilization conjures up the picture of the solid results of land, labour and investment being transformed by some petrochemical process into a gas and lost. This is reinforced with the image of wealth evaporating and just disappearing into the atmosphere. This view is consistent with his ethical view of society but tells only half of the story. In effect he has formed his view by observing only one side of the book-keeping entry. He has correctly observed the role of bankers of introducing volatility into a process where formerly there had been none. He also observed the making of rapid profits but also saw and concentrated on apparently inevitable losses. These together with the continuing or worsening state of disadvantage of some in our society had suggested that the volatiles had indeed been lost. Something of value had come from somewhere and through the process of volatilization it is lost.

Saul also explores the process by which volatilization takes place. This is his Fancy Talk. This is akin to the Vapourcash burner or generator. It is the mechanism by which Vapourcash is created through the processing or extraction of real cash or other value. Again this is just the difference between describing the process and the technique through which it occurs. There are similarities between Fancy Talk and Antilogic but Fancy Talk is more judgmental and restrictive than Antilogic. So we can conclude that Fancy Talk is a particular form of Antilogic. Many other Vapourcash generators have been identified. They all depend on Antilogic although their acceptability to the general public and the authorities differ widely from the highly respectable to the outright illegal.

My term vapour is very similar in emphasizing a gaseous nature but it is a rather more passive process with assistance required in the steps. I therefore prefer to refer to the generation of Vapourcash in a Vapourcash burner where real cash is consumed and Vapourcash is produced. The many examples of Vapourcash all share the common characteristic that the starting point is real cash that is processed so as to emerge extended as vapour. This vapour may expand further or it may subsequently condense. This process of condensation may be so violent that Anticash is created. No matter how violent the transformation, there is no loss of matter because of the physical laws and the necessity for double entry bookkeeping.

When Saul talks about loss he must also ask, 'who was on the other side of the transaction and so who won?' When he sees that the money has volatized and gone he must also ask, 'to where has it gone?'

'Adam Smith' is the nom de plume of a successful investor and writer. He is very certain and does not need the conditional about reality introduced by Saul. He takes the opposite position. He is positive that real money is not the *real* money.

Maybe they realize that the green stuff in their wallet is not the real money.[78]

His view is that *real* money comes from *Supercurrency*. What he is telling us is not really that real money is not real but that the money you really want is not real money. This begs quite a number of questions that I answer in this book. He identifies Supercurrency as the real money you really want but demonstrates that, although it is not real at all, it provides access to real money or more precisely, what money can buy. Supercurrency is an addition to the stock of wealth through capitalized income and is as any other currency *the fibre of the society*. He also explains that Supercurrency comes from gaining income and not from avoiding taxes. Supercurrency is the direct exploitation of Vapourcash to obtain goods and services. He looks at what can be done with the currency generated by the impact of market quotations and mark to market accounting on the earnings of corporations. These valuations make available today the cash flow that the corporation will earn in the future. More specifically it is the ability of the lucky creators of Vapourcash to syphon off a portion of real cash for themselves obtained by selling a few shares or more commonly by anticipating the growth in value that has been gleaned by the upwards valuation. Money, once created, can pass from hand to hand with no concern as to the nature of its origin. The circulation of money in whatever form is just that, circulation and it does not normally work in reverse.

> The most pure forms of Supercurrency are the great companies with broad markets selling at high multitudes of earning... The way to cash in is to turn the family business into Supercurrency, whether by selling to the public or to IBM or hopefully first to one and then to the other.... There are the impulses of the owners to cash in their business for a superior currency. Further the multiplier of the Supercurrency increases the distance between wage earners and capital owners.[79]

The best source is capitalized earnings which results in goodwill that is so unreal that bankers call it air or fresh air on the balance sheet, which I suppose is a particularly insubstantial form of vapour. We can make progress by putting these concepts together. Smith regards the real money to be so insubstantial as to be unreal.

> The capricious examples have lots of 'goodwill' in the Supercurrency (for goodwill some sceptics sometimes read 'air') but all capitalized earnings count as Supercurrency especially the legitimate broadly traded ones.[80]

And now Smith moves in for the kill. He claims that the really real money is unreal.

> Make no mistake this is real money... Economists start with a basic definition: money is M_1 all the coins and currency in circulation outside the banks plus demand deposits (i.e. checking accounts) in the banks. To this most economists add M_2 which includes saving accounts and time deposits in banks. This can be spent almost as easily as M_1. Everyone does not cash in his savings account on the same day but all you have to do is transfer your

savings account to your checking account to get M_2 to M_1 and that's pretty easy. Some economists add short-term government bills to this since they are also practically cash. (I would update this to include equity margin accounts and credit cards.) To this I suggest we add M_3 Supercurrency... To get M_3 to M_2 you buy at book, sell at market, peel off some stock, move to your checking account and presto! M_1 and you are rich.[81]

He has worked out the details and the numbers stack up so well that he has established a law called Smiths Increment that with special rules to stop double counting can also explain how Supercurrency works through to old-fashioned real cash in the hand. The final step in the process is to involve our friends the bankers in a process that confirms that there must be two sides of the transaction where one man's debt is another man's credit. He says that you can put it in the bank and write cheques against it. Merchants will sell to you as long as you are not bankrupt and in the US this means, so long as you are not bankrupt too much or too often.

There is also the geared exploitation of Supercurrency. Galbraith does not use the same terminology but this is an example of where Galbraith, Smith and Saul come close to describing the same effect.

> Thus came about two of the most spectacular financial developments of the 1980s; the corporate raids as they were called, to gain the power and rewards of management and the buyouts by management seeking to preserve its own position and income. Both were accomplished in essentially the same way – by the borrowing of money against the eventual credit of the corporation to buy up stock from the hitherto passive and languid stockholders. It would be hard to imagine an economically and socially more damaging design. Both exercises loaded a heavy debt on the firm: interest on this debt then had prior claim over investment in new and improved plant, new products and research and development.[82]

In effect the banks had granted the entrepreneurs a call over the corporation. If it succeeded the entrepreneur owned the corporation, if it failed it was the banks.

We can also call it the exploitation of gearing to achieve Supercurrency. When it succeeds it is Vapourcash and gives the opportunity for Supercurrency. When it fails the result is Anticash. Smith has identified some more of the elements of Vapourcash and circumstances that lead to its creation. Although he recognizes that there are two sides of the transaction he only describes the position of the party who passes on the Supercurrency. For them it is gain. It is the difference between giving and receiving. However, in the *Money Game* written earlier Smith discusses extensively the problems of investors whose portfolios suddenly diminished in value so we can see that indeed some recipients of Supercurrency find that it is Vapour that subsequently condenses and is lost. The other side is Vapourcash (as created by Volatilization or the Vapourcash generator), which implies that your Vapourcash is my Supercurrency.

When he writes about Supercurrency he is concentrating on the process of how large amounts of Vapourcash are created. The end result, Supercurrency, is Vapourcash although the perspective is different. You have received value for your Supercurrency by passing it to me but it remains only Vapourcash with me until I can use it for something else, i.e. pass it on. The process using Supercurrency may be the main means by which Vapourcash is created but it is not the only means as shown by reference to corporation money and apparent cash. No reliable research is currently available as to the relative contribution of or the extent of overlap between these forms of currency.

Although 'Adam Smith' identified the effect and coined the term Supercurrency, the phenomenon is not new and can be observed occurring whenever the generation of Vapourcash has become boisterous. The evidence is provided in the many booms and bubbles. Great attention is given to the prominent names and their spectacular failures and their discomfort is attributed to the insubstantial nature of the volatiles. The winners from Vapourcash perhaps came later in more unobtrusive ways as these same periods have also seen unprecedented consumption of real cash and what can be bought with that cash. The object of desire has changed with the centuries and so the booms have brought other fortunes built on lace, fine art, chateaux and corporate jets. This was no illusion because beyond contemporary reports we still have today the physical manifestation of this creativity in the fine houses and antiques that date from those times. We only need to look at the extensive production and enjoyment of luxury goods to know that not all volatiles were burnt off.

Sometimes it was temporarily uncontrolled enthusiasm for new investment that created the booms but often it was the boom that provided the means to implement otherwise unachievable dreams. Maybe the original owners did not ultimately enjoy the returns of their project but the Anticash provided benefit for future generations, as did the Vapourcash used before the moment of condensation. As well as these works of art, grand monuments, fine houses and other tokens of the boom days we find that many of our most indispensable items of infrastructure date from these same times and have come from projects that never paid a return on the investment. Whole industries that had been absent or moribund before the Vapourcash explosion sprang into a frenzy of activity. Here again is proof that Vapour-cash is no chimera.

Keynes was also hot on the trail of Vapourcash. He saw the flow of money in hydraulic terms of water flowing to its natural level. Some of his disciples led by Bill Philips, inventor of the Philips curve, became known as the hydraulic Keynesians and in 1949 actually built a working hydraulic model of the British economy with tanks, pumps, pipes and valves. This is now exhibited in the Science Museum in London.

> John Maynard Keynes writing in *A Treatise on Money* compared money to water in a reservoir. It was the function of the central bank to maintain the proper level of water. Yet there were many factors that could change the level of the reservoir – 'besides how much water is poured in – for example, the natural rainfall, evaporation, leakage and the habits of the users of the system'. Even as the Bunyan plumber, the Fed would have some problems, because its gauges measure what happened weeks ago, and the pressures have different intensities, as if part fluid and part gas.[83]

It is only a small step from this description to Vapourcash. Gas is after all the next stage of progression from liquid. There are additional problems if individuals discover their own private supply of taps or sink a money-well in the back yard.

So many in business are carried away with the upward drift of Vapour-cash that it brings to mind the image of some businessmen soaring ever upward in the basket of a Vapourcash balloon. The lifting capacity is only limited by the elasticity of the relationship canopy that is the means by which Vapourcash is converted into notional return. The interesting dilemma is whether a perforation of the canopy by the bullets of market reality can cause the Vapourcash to escape depriving the balloon of its lifting power. It might be argued that as Vapourcash does not exist it could not escape and that there is no onslaught of reality that could ever impede the upward progress of the illusion.

This is an error of Antilogic. Vapourcash does exist. The burning of real cash creates Vapourcash. It has no substance but is never the less real. The conversion of real cash through a Vapourcash burner creates the appear-ance of a greater total as defined by the nominal calculated value. This appearance can remain a reality so long as the recipients are prepared to accept the volumes created. All Vapourcash burners or generators require real cash to keep them going although high confidence may make this less than obvious. The largest and most obvious Vapourcash burners are the public markets with real time quotations, regulation, information feeds, etc. However, any market has the same effect where values are quoted and used as the valuation basis for assets. At the micro level there need not be a public market at all. A simple justification of value is sufficient within a corporate context to justify an action, to further a career or to allow access to corporate resources.

Vapourcash is vulnerable to several dangers, including too many passengers in the basket, the rupturing of the relationship canopy or most dangerous, the denial of continuing supplies of real money for the Vapourcash burner. Vapourcash is far more dangerous than Anticash in that it misleads people into the belief that it is something of worth, has substance and is something positive. In fact it has no substance (hence vapour) and is anti worth. The Thesaurus brackets vapour along with prate, rant and gas with all equalling 'meaning nothing'. Vapourcash is negative because it consumes a continuing supply of real cash to keep it going. The illusion of Antilogic fades over time, perhaps because of the credibility cycle, and so has to be constantly renewed with fresh supplies of Vapourcash produced by the burner. The relative position of losses and new supply will determine the fate of the venture.

Condensation is the process by which Vapourcash ceases to expand and then declines towards and then below the nominal real cash value from which it started. All Vapourcash must condense if it is denied new supplies of cash but this is often masked at the aggregate level by new sources of Vapourcash exceeding the decline of the old. Consequently it is difficult to be categorical but it is likely that the violent condensation, as evident in the aftermath of a financial panic is the exception and so that success in the low-level generation of Vapourcash is the rule rather than the exception.

Vapourcash can seep out of the individual corporation and uncontrolled Vapourcash generators caused many of the world's great financial disasters. Let me give you a couple of international examples of Vapourcash.

A first example comes from the world of Global Wholesale Finance. An English financial entrepreneur originated a plan for the retirement of the floating national debt of Great Britain. Under the plan, investment bankers took on the debt in return for government guaranteed annual payments for a certain period. This sum, amounting to six percent interest, was to be obtained from duties on imports. Certain rights to the British trade in the Pacific Rim were given to these bankers, incorporated a special purpose vehicle and extravagant ideas of the growth of the region were fostered. Subsequently, the company offered to assume practically the whole national debt. Companies of all kinds were floated to take advantage of the public interest in obtaining this stock. Speculation soon carried stock to ten times its nominal value. The chairman and some directors sold out, the bubble burst, and the stock collapsed. Thousands of stockholders were ruined. Parliamentary investigation revealed complicity by some company officials. Two members of the Government were also implicated in the scandal. About one-third of the original capital was recovered for the stockholders.

My second example comes from the world of biotechnology but the lesson is the same. The fascination with the new variety, its endless mutations and mystery, gave it immense value. Here was a product so costly that it was literally worth its weight in gold. Yet the seed was so unattractive that given a chance to steal it, a thief would probably pass it by. As a result of the rise in prices caused by speculation, the product was no longer sold by quantity, but by weight that was equivalent to about one-twentieth of a gram. The product was usually sold while it was still in the ground, so the weight had to be estimated. The buyer would often sell at a profit to a third party; the third party would sell to a fourth, at a profit; and so on. And all of this without anyone actually seeing the new variety.

It was trading in something as elusive as the wind – and it did in time come to be called the wind trade – and sometimes Tulipomania as you may have guessed for this early example dates from 1637. The Dutchmen better off for all this were the innkeepers, for it was in their establishments that many of the speculative transactions were carried out. The traders spent days and nights at the inns, eating and drinking the expensive foods paid for in real cash.

My first example was from a little later being the South Sea Bubble of 1711. It is remarkable how little has changed since those times. These financial disturbances are often called bubbles. This terminology was contemporary and so of course predates mankind's aeronautical achievements but the parallel between the bubble and the hot air balloon is obvious. The balloon is to be preferred as an image because of the more dynamic concept of lifting power over time as compared to static and mechanical inevitability of the bubble that expands to its limit and then explodes and vanishes. As will be seen the consequences are not all bad and not everyone loses. It is a process of transformation rather than of obliteration.

This burst of enthusiasm is probably a good thing. As Keynes said, wealth accumulates from enterprise not from thrift. No amount of saving will generate wealth. This creates the pool of money to spend on investments but unless there is the drive to initiate projects nothing will happen. For it is profit that is the engine which drive enterprise.

We have to reconcile this comment with another Keynes made when he denied that more capital can be invested than really exists. He claimed that in most cases more investment is made than really pays. I take him to mean that it is not really profit that provokes investment but the prospect of profit. He argues that it is only when there is willingness by the banks to create more credit than the community voluntarily wished to save that causes things to get out of hand and leads to booms. With the growth of corporations and the corresponding growth of Vapour it is the Vapourcash that provides the impetuous for investment. From this we can see that Vapourcash is not only present during the obvious conditions of unrestrained boom but also is increasingly becoming an integral component in encouraging investment. This must be the overall impact of Antilogic in provoking the approval of dubious proposals.

The change from emphasis on saving to investment was a long time coming. For generations because of Saws Law it was believed that saving and investment must be equal. If there was thrift first investment must follow. This was convenient not only for the mercantilists who measured success by money hoards but also meets the requirement of the religions that preached for the virtues of moderation.

It is not the miser who gets rich, but he who lays out his money in fruitful investment. Keynes theorizes that the engine of capitalization was driven by a neurosis which he calls 'love of money' but the neurosis is also the means to the good because it is the means to the abundance which will make capitalism unnecessary.

'Keynes links the power of money to disturb economic self regulation to the tendency for money itself to become an object of desire rather than a means to satisfy desires. Encroachment of money values on use values, the triumph of making money over making things. Depressions are the wages of sin, only the sin is not spending too much, but spending too little on the things which make for a good life.[84]

This idea links nicely to the parable of the talents. The three sons are all tested as to what they will do with the same sum advanced by their father. At the time the Bible was written the talent was a measure of gold or silver. A modern updating would be for the father to give the sum to his children to test their portfolio management. One would invest in bonds and do quite well. Another would invest in a diversified portfolio of shares and do very well. The cautious third would leave his in a bank deposit and be lucky to pay the fees.

The boost provided by unrestrained enthusiasm for money may be an essential element in the introduction of new and untested technology. It might also be the catalyst to provide turning points in economic cycles. The economists have had difficulty in agreeing as to the role of money in investment cycles. Does money matter or is it all determined by real economic activity? Keynes accepted Robertson's contention that the investment boom is usually triggered off by real factors. This comment was made many years ago and although management science has advanced it is still the situation today because of the influence of Vapourcash. The previously held assumption about the hard-nosed entrepreneur is no longer true because of the advent of the corporation man who has objectives very different to those of the corporation or shareholder. Most individual managers have an ambition horizon that is far shorter than the payback period of the projects they propose or approve. They expect to be gone long before the profits emerge for a project. It is unanticipated bad luck to be still around at such a time. This is also true of bankers who can work with probability, security and the time it takes for a loan to go sour. An analysis of corporate bond defaults by Moody's covering the period 1920–1999 reveals the elapsed time for the cumulative default rate for Investment Grade bonds to reach five percent is eleven years. Speculative grade bonds are quicker to reach a cumulative level of five percent but the average for all bonds is four years, which is an eternity for a loan officer.

Do not for one moment think that the world has lost its appetite for Vapourcash. Consider the values ascribed to gold prospecting companies that far exceeds the value of gold that could conceivably be discovered. Often the worst fate that can befall a gold prospector is to discover gold, but not enough. The find only serves to crystallize the market's disappointment. There is a similar issue for mining companies themselves for their market value is often greater than the total ore reserves the firm has or is likely to find and bring to the surface. The recent excitement over tele-communications, technology, media and biotech only serves to emphasize the effect. A new development according to *Lex* in the *Financial Times* is magic money, otherwise known as Internet equity. *Lex* appears to be applying this term to Supercurrency albeit in a particularly vaporous form. It would be unfair to specifically apply the term just to Internet equity just because this is the presently desired currency. Previous booms have all had their own particular magic currency. What makes this boom different, and provokes the ire of *Lex* is that the Internet is an environment where service providers cannot charge cash for their product. Most remarkable is that lawyers and management consultants are prepared to give up their fees.

> In the old days there was a simple rule in the services industry. First go to where the action is; if there are diamonds in Kimberley, go to Kimberley. Second, on no account join the suckers hunting for diamonds. Sell them sandwiches instead.

> It is not the least achievement of the Internet revolution to have stood this logic on its head. Today cyberspace is crowded with people offering free sandwiches. All they ask in return is the chance of the odd diamond in return. Management consultants, brokers and law firms are clustered around internet start-ups like barkeepers in the Yukon. But they do not want humdrum cash for their services. Instead, they want magic money, otherwise known as internet equity.[85]

No cash please is now the cry, that is, so long as the paradigm remains shiftless. Longer-term accepting Internet equity might give the same end result.

Vapourcash has become so prevalent that the accounting profession has begun to treat it as being the norm, insisting on marking balance sheets to market. This valuation is based on a flickering market quotation read off a screen or in the case of derivatives, some impenetrable mathematical model. Yet, we all know that only an infinitesimal part of the market could be liquidated at that value. The valuation has realism only so long as no one wants to realize it. Thus, the accountants are insisting on a value that is real, only so long as no one tests it. If events cause many people to test the value it will reveal that it is also Vapourcash.

The market trained by the accountants believes that reality is not what the asset will earn in the future but its price quote today. If enough people expect the speculative object to advance in price it will advance in price and attract more people with further expectations of further increases. It works well so long as prices are rising reliably. This gives the market a beautifully simple rule that states that if the market has gone up it will go further. There is also an inverse.

The Germans know about the dangers of vapour and have a descriptive name, torschlusspaniek, describing *door shut panic* with people crowding to get through the door before it slams shut. Speculation develops when people buy assets expecting the prices to rise because of a new theory or insight. The chances are that the rush to take action then serves to confirm their expectation.

It is not to be confused with Soufflécash, a particular form of Vapourcash that exists when an industry consumes cash throughout the rapid expansion phase despite good profits. As soon as the industry growth begins to slow profits are squeezed by the capital structure and cash flow remains negative despite a slowdown in investment as the industry restructures and downsizes. You have to eat a soufflé at the precise moment before it disappears before your very eyes. True to this analogy the cash is there only for an instant at the end of the growth phase before the downsizing begins. There are a surprisingly high number of examples including frozen food, automobiles and airlines where if totted up all the billions invested over the years greatly outweigh the cumulative returns ever earned by the shareholders. It is possible that these industries consumed cash in all phases of development; embryonic, expansion, stabilization and decline. When expressed in vapour terms it is seen that the soufflé expanded rapidly until it could expand no further and then condensed very rapidly.

Many causes of Vapourcash have been outlined but a common theme about its presence is the reality or otherwise of reported profits. The veracity of profits often comes into question at times of financial crises and a curious emphasis is given to reported losses if these occur. It could also be said that financial crises are caused by corrections to reported results especially if the corrections lead to losses. The media are likely to become excited. The most dramatic labels are those found in the headline exposés of enormous loss that occurs depressingly frequently in the financial markets. Billions of dollars are reported as being lost in some spectacular corporate crash or other. It makes dramatic reading but someone must have the money so why do we get concerned? Each loss is balanced by a gain elsewhere, yet we never celebrate the success on the other side and the balance of society would be undisturbed were it not for the intrusion caused by the distortion of bankruptcy. There is a long list of recent financial problem cases including the S&Ls, the junk bond bankruptcies,

Chase Manhattan and Drysdale Securities, Orange County, Bankers Trust, Long Term Capital and others

I have picked out just a couple of examples where the label of profitability did not turn out to match reality. We can start with paper losses that became real.

New York based MG Refining and Marketing (MGRM) was far less risky than the companies believed. Panicky liquidation of that business turned paper losses into real ones... When Metallgesellschaft (MG) nearly collapsed its supervisory board blamed reckless speculation in energy derivatives. To save the metals and services group, the board sacked its managers and hired new ones who arranged a $US2.1 billion bail out. Merton Miller and Christopher Culp argue that the derivatives business was far less risky than the company's new bosses believed. MG's panicky liquidation of that business turned paper losses into real ones and exposed the company to further losses as oil prices soared. Had MG's bankers responded by supplying sufficient liquidity, they could have nipped the crisis in the bud. Instead they concluded that MG had real losses of DM1.4 billion. The new managers installed by MG's supervisory board unwound the futures position. This would have worsened the cash crises by signalling to counterparties that MG was not credit worthy.[86]

The accountants also made a contribution. The prudent Germans followed the doctrine of conservatism and recognized potential losses as soon as identified but ignored potential profits contained in the contracts until realized. This indicated a loss of $US291 million. They might comment that it was just as well that they did so because in the event the profits were never realized because the contracts were cancelled. The Americans followed the matching principle and insisted on hedge accounting that matched both the potential profits and losses. For them there were no net losses to recognize as they saw a profit of $US61 million. It took the board to convert a problem into a disaster.

MG operated in the heaviest and grimiest of industries. There could never be any doubt that its businesses were real. Miller and Culp suggest that real cash was used to settle a Vapour difference. It is perhaps understandable that its board could feel uncomfortable about the Vapour feel of derivatives trading although energy and mining are traditionally heavy users of such instruments. Perhaps it was the bankers who were the most uncomfortable? Which result was the real result, the American profit or the German loss? We must take care to check the language of the label and the size it represents. This is like buying shoes and not knowing the difference between American and European sizes.

In contrast to MG, Cendant is a new age company that make much use of data mining techniques to obtain revenues from customer relationships. Its stock in trade comes from the use of intangibles. It was formed in 1997 from the merger of HFS Incorporated and CUC International. Both companies had similar philosophies and it might be thought that each would understand the other. This not how it worked out when they found that paper profits became real losses.

Cendant was formed with much fanfare from a merger of equals between HFS and CUC. The management of both businesses stayed with what is a very substantial corporation with revenues of $US4.2 billion, over 35 000 employees and a market capitalization in excess of $US9 billion. Cendant brands include Century21, Coldwell Banker, Avis, Sierra On-Line, netMarket, Travellers Advantage and Shoppers Advantage. Cendant is the largest franchiser of real estate brokerages in the United States, a leading provider of mortgage services, the world's largest franchiser of hotels and corporate relocation company.

Soon after the merger a problem cropped up in the accounts of the Membership Division of the former CUC. The Chief Financial Officer of CUC was terminated and when news of the problem reached the market the share price crashed. The Chief Financial Officer often has to go when there is bad news as he would be the only one to know anything about the troubles. He should have said.

It did not stop there. A couple of months later, Cendant announced that the accounting irregularities problem was much larger than previously thought. As a result the CEO and Chairman who had been the former CUC Chairman was paid $US35 million to go and all former CUC senior management and board members were also terminated. Trouble for the company and the CEO leaves with compensation for his trouble.

With the CEO gone things went from bad to worse. The new top management from the former HFS appointed new accountants to conduct a forensic accounting investigation of the former CUC business. These accountants discovered that despite a clean bill of health over many years from the auditors, Ernst & Young, there were accounting practices with which they disagreed. The accounting irregularities turned out to be a fraud of about $US500 million and Cendant had to revise its initial claim of a $US55 million profit to a new estimate of a $US217 million loss for 1997. The new management stated that the accounting fraud had not been discovered during the merger due diligence because of the expectation that the individuals with whom you do business are honest. After all they were about to become partners.

These accounting differences were stated to effect most business units, involve many staff at all levels, occurred in all the years studied and were expected to be followed in the future. The former HFS management was now in control and the former CUC management in exile. The HFS businesses were not included in the audit. The wrap up report by the surviving management looked very black indeed but emphasized the strength of the business and that the level of equity had not been materially effected! Once the decks are cleared of the past wreckage it became necessary to provide new executive incentives so a new executive option scheme was approved at a lower exercise price. The courts found in favour of the new management with a $US2.8 billion settlement of a shareholder action although they also required Cendant to institute corporate governance changes. Ernst & Young also agreed to a $US335 million settlement of a professional malpractice litigation relating to Cendant. All in all a very dramatic result to a disagreement about accounting.

Business has become so complex and normal financial transactions so involved that it has become difficult to distinguish the fraudulent from the normal. In the case of Barings the British investment bank brought down by a rogue trader, the hands off style of management and a desire to believe that unexpected profits were genuine led to many warning signs being ignored until it was too late.

At ISC, the UK corporation, a fraud involving £215 million siphoned off through offshore companies was not picked up because management was so used to funds moving through unusual accounts and domiciles they did not notice when it was undertaken for the benefit of fraudsters rather than the company.

It is not considered proper for industrial organizations to remove inventory entrusted to their care yet efficient management properly seeks to optimize the use of its working capital making it circulate faster and faster to such an extent that some businesses actually achieve negative working capital. The travel agent is an example of a business that receives its money from its clients long before it pays the airlines. Supermarkets receive stock on credit terms from their suppliers that are much longer than it takes to receive and hold the stock, effect the sale and receive the cash.

Sometimes it turns out that there is no stock as in the McKesson and Robbins, and Interstate Hosiery Mills cases from sixty years ago. Fred Schwed argues convincingly that the accounting was the state of mind releasing the potential to build on assets that do not exist. This allows the creation of virtual wealth.

For some time both corporations had flourished like the green bay tree, chiefly on assets that simply weren't there, but which everyone thought were there. Everyone, that is, save one man in each case, who had created the assets all by himself, using only a pen, ink, and a lot of skilful dishonesty. Presumably these corporations' securities would never have taken those two dives if only the non-existent assets had not been destroyed by having their non-existence discovered. At this point, the subject should be taken away from the accountants and handed over to the metaphysicians. Bishop Berkeley propounded the classic question: if a great tree falls in a forest, does it make any noise if no one is there to hear it fall? He decided it doesn't, which for all I know is the right answer. If the bishop was alive today, I believe he would be interested in this question: if a great corporation is toppling over, does it do anyone any financial harm if no one knows it is toppling over.[87]

In the past, lack of transparency, the possession of specialist knowledge or the control of funds during an extended transaction process often created wealth. The tendency for working capital optimization was sometimes augmented by exploiting structural inefficiencies of the payments system by drawing cheques on remote or obscure banks so as to enjoy the delay before the funds were ultimately called. For the businessman under pressure, it was only another step to cover these payments by drawing on further accounts that in turn depended on cheques drawn on the original accounts in a process variously known as *teeming and lading* or *kiting*. Everyone is happy and none disadvantaged so long as the cheques continue to arrive on time. This process can continue indefinitely and indeed structural arbitrages have been discovered and exploited. There is a distinction between these and the form of kiting where the money is real but the transaction is imaginary. Accountants working somewhat more ponderously have been able to achieve the same effect as kiting with the use of asymmetric balance dates, asymmetric accounting polices within the corporate group or by the use of off balance sheet constructions.

Teaming and lading can provide the ultimate in the velocity of circulation as the same money is required to appear to be at different places at the same time. The transaction is real but there is not enough money to go around if the music stops. Modern technology has made this more difficult as the process cycles faster and faster. The money arrives at almost the same time as it leaves although the banks still say it takes three days to clear. If we apply the principles of integral calculus we can reach a situation when the same money is indeed in two places at the same time.

The problems arise when there was not enough money to go around. A few hardy entrepreneurs acted selflessly to ensure that the money went a little further. Galbraith termed this the bezzle. If it is not discovered is it still a crime? During this period the embezzler has his gain and his victim knows no loss. According to Galbraith this gives a net increase in psychic wealth. The amount of this increase varies over the business cycle.

> To the economist embezzlement is the most interesting of crimes. Alone among the various forms of larceny it has a time parameter. Weeks, months or years may elapse between the commission of the crime and its discovery... At any given time there exists an inventory of undiscovered embezzlement in – or more precisely not in – the country's business and banks. The inventory – it should perhaps be called the bezzle – amounts at any moment to many millions of dollars. It also varies in size with the business cycle. In good times people are relaxed, trusting and money is plentiful. But even though money is plentiful, there are always people who need more. Under these circumstances the rate of embezzlement grows, the rate of discovery falls off and the bezzle increases rapidly. In depression all this is reversed. Money is watched with a narrow, suspicious eye. The man who handles it is assumed to be dishonest until he proves himself otherwise. Audits are penetrating and meticulous. Commercial morality is enormously improved. The bezzle shrinks.[88]

He gives us the Union Industrial Bank of Flint Michigan as the most spectacular example of the embezzle in the Great Crash with the unauthorized multiple use of funds that were sent on round trips between Flint and New York.

This example involving a bank is particularly appropriate in illustrating that embezzlement is as much a degree as it is of law. The way commercial banks make their money is little different except that it is the authorized multiple use of funds and float. The presence of regulatory approval provides the prime difference. It is the foundation of the banking industry to take deposits from all and sundry but give most of it out again in the form of loans or investments. In effect banking is a regulated form of teaming and lending. Everything is all right so long as enough money is available to pay out the depositor when he wants his money back. Nasty scenes can occur if not enough money is there. It is the same scene when the airlines provide aircraft with fewer seats than passengers with valid tickets.

The float is the other great support of the banks, credit card companies, travellers cheques providers and other financial institutions. Here they receive other peoples' money and hang on to it as long as they can. This is another form of increase in psychic wealth. The bank knows it has achieved a benefit and the customer doesn't realize that he has missed out. Add the two positions and the economy is better off.

Sometimes the float is created without a business. This is suspect as investors expected there to be a business or at least the prospect of a return. One example of a float without a business is the chain letter. The participant is invited to write to a lot of people in the hope of getting even more replies. The system works well at the micro level but when it reaches the macro it is difficult to handle the post. As in most business ventures the major rewards come for the innovator or entrepreneur and not from the late entrants. Pyramid selling is the selling equivalent of the chain letter. Each layer earns a commission from the sales of the lower levels so it is better to be a senior recruiter than to be a lowly seller. Another example of the business construction without enough money to meet the requirements of all participants simultaneously is the Ponzi scheme named after Mr. Ponzi a Florida land speculator who met the promised returns of early investors by new cash raised from subsequent investors. The only difference between a Ponzi scheme and an Internet float was that Ponzi knew that there wasn't a business. So long as money arrived when the investors expected it they did not question further what was happening. The recent rash of companies with unsustainable cash requirements and business models based on there being cash available are the financial equivalent of the early antique autos that depended on a total loss lubrication system. It worked perfectly well so long as you kept pouring oil in at the top.

If a means can be found to create money by the issue of stock then we have a scheme that is the next step beyond Ponzi where there is no continuing cash flow to satisfy investors. This is a system re-engineered to eliminate cash to create a virtual Ponzi scheme made possible by Vapour-cash with Anticash waiting in the wings. The other side of the situation (I avoid using *the other side of the coin* because there were no coins available) are the investors who will at some point suddenly encounter cash mirage. Others like them had thought that there was cash present but this turned out to be an illusion. This is not a new phenomenon as it is not only associated with share-market booms but prospecting booms and other scenes of excitement.

> The great investment trust boom had ended in a unique manifestation of Gresham's Law in which the bad stocks were driving out the good. The stabilizing effects of the huge cash resources of the investment trusts had also proved a mirage. In the early autumn the cash and liquid resources of the investment trusts were large. Many trusts had been attracted by the handsome returns in the call market. (The speculative circle has been closed. People who speculated in the stock of investment trusts were in effect

investing in companies which provided the funds to finance their own speculations). But now,... reverse leverage did its work.[89]

In the (old style) Bucket Shop, investment advisers promote stocks so speculative that it is almost certain that the investment will be lost. Naturally if the investment is lost the investor is unhappy. There will be complaints but there is a ready explanation so the repercussions are minor or non-existent. The bucket shop operators find it such a waste to actually put the punters' money into investments that will be lost so it is diverted to other purposes. In the unlikely event that an investor's selection actually is successful the bucket shop proprietors can make it good from other cash flow or depart for pastures green. The punter then realizes that his money has really departed to the wide blue yonder. The Vapourcash has condensed. The only hope remaining is to find the Anticash.

X

ANTICASH EXPLAINED: ANTICASH AND THE HISTORY OF MONEY

VAPOURCASH IS not to be confused with the expenditure of real cash to pursue unrealistic revenue targets that cannot, or are not obtained. The investment in a dud idea has the potential to be a genuine creation of Anticash.

Just what is Anticash? Anticash is created when an individual, entity or country has a deficiency of revenue relative to costs to the extent that it can no longer meet its obligations to provide real cash. Anticash is the contra entry created when the symmetry of double entry bookkeeping is disrupted by the artificial removal of an equity deficiency in actual bankruptcy or forced refinancing to avoid greater loss during financial distress.

It is not surprising that we have generally lost sight of Anticash amongst the rest of the uncertainty that has enveloped currency during its rich and confusing history. We might not yet be as familiar with the concept of Anticash, and miss a physical manifestation, but is this so very different from the so-called real cash? The abstract nature of cash has fascinated many writers. Buchan observed the duality of money that covers the real and the abstract.

> For from obscure beginnings, money has spread out to colonize the world, both in its forms as coin or banknote or book entry and as a notion of happiness penetrating the minds of men and women. Money was probably not invented in a particular place and at a particular era, but came into manifold being, for manifold purposes. Money permitted human beings to expand not only their possessions but their wishes beyond limits held ultimate by predecessors. By now, money has become a system, which we understood, by way of the simile of the railway shunting yard, as gathering the wishes of the most estranged and scattered populations and despatching

them to unimagined destinations. We also saw that money became indifferent to its physical form, and whether human beings revert to gold or cattle as money of account and payment, or pass into a realm of pure electricity, is a matter of indifference also to us.[90]

He also identifies the transition for abstract to become concrete but this concept may be taken further to includes moves in both directions. Money may make concrete the concept of wanting but if you do not have the money you can substitute the Vapour. In effect the image of the shunting yards works well, just as the real thing can move the wagons in both directions.

Money is one of those human creations that make concrete a sensation, in this case the sensation of wanting, as a clock does the sensation of passing time. It is that double aspect of money, airy and substantial, that has fascinated all civilizations. Human beings have never quite been able to decide whether money is a universal come down to earth or a daily thing forever aspiring to perfection.[91]

Buchan captures this evolution from real to abstract and explores the interaction with human ambition and aspiration. It is just one step further to analyze the rate of change and the reasons. When that step is taken we see the influence of the duality of double entry and can explore the inevitable consequences stemming from the dynamic influences effecting money and especially the effect of asymmetric distortions.

Current accounting practice does not handle well the creation of Anticash because of the inappropriate convention of discontinuing accounting in the case of bankruptcy. In bankruptcy it all becomes too hard for the accountants who abandon their cherished principles of double entry bookkeeping that have served so well since discovery by Father Pacioli. In bankruptcy the deficiency of shareholders funds is arbitrarily brought back to zero causing an equivalent amount of Anticash to be released to balance the real cash already in circulation. The principles of double entry would still work here as well if consistently applied.

The accountants may try and draw the line and say enough is enough with a failed entity. However, when they do, they are turning their backs on the laws of symmetry and denying their clients the very solution to their problems; the collecting up, intermediation and use of the Anticash created.

The recognition of Anticash is a natural step in the progress of money from unwieldy tokens such as cowry shells to gold, to coins without intrinsic metal value to scraps of paper and plastic to electronic records or ultimately the wish to be rich. A literary search could help in defining this state which could draw on the crock of gold at the end of the rainbow, the widow's cruse, and with the advance of technology to give greater customer functionality, Aladdin's lamp. The list goes on to include the hen that laid the golden eggs for Jack from the Beanstalk. Jack was one of our original venture capitalists who had the foresight to sell an outmoded technology, a cow, in return for a handful of beans in what turned out to be one of the all time biotech growth successes.

The history of currency is a fascinating story of both advancement and debasement with ample proof of Gresham's theory that bad money drives out good. Two examples of unusual currencies ending in debasement are first Wampum, which provided American Indians with an efficient currency with the rarer black shells, being many times the worth of the common white. With the arrival of the white man and commercial dyes, all the white shells surprisingly disappeared about the time that many more of the black shells were found in circulation.

The other example is of a remarkably efficient and self-regulating currency. After World War II, in occupied Germany there returned one of the classic currencies of the past, namely tobacco. This time it came in convenient denominations of singles, packs of 20 and cartons of 200. The coinage was hard to counterfeit and if the value for exchange got out of balance, the holder would smoke the currency. There was also some counterfeiting with the recycling of butts.

Despite the evidence of ultimate debasement these unconventional currencies were in their time the key currency of the region. Gradually they lost the support that is crucial for ongoing viability of currency. Gresham's law implies that Vapourcash drives out cash and in turn is driven out by Anticash. If it is correct that all cash is created by the fiat of Government, then I contend that Anticash is created by the fiat of the accountants at the time of bankruptcy. This they achieve in their attempts to balance their books, with the lawyers their willing accomplices. But it is just not possible to cancel existing money by withdrawing the fiat, because circulation of money has meant that it has already passed on several times. It was understandable in the old days of physical manifestation of cash as bullion, coin and note that the accountants would maintain the time honoured custom of ceasing to count cash value when it went below zero. Today with electronics and stored value cards it is old fashioned in the extreme to fail to account accurately for the asset of Anticash known to be created in the situation of bankruptcy. Electronics allow us to record the existence of the Anticash, segregate its storage and handle its exchange.

The present process of bankruptcy is so destructive of value and business resilience that a further analysis is warranted. Those who live in the common law system countries take the bankruptcy system for granted as though it is an immutable fact and has always applied everywhere. There is an unpleasant reality about bankruptcy that leads us to believe that it is always handled in the manner we see in our particular economy and assume it has always been thus. This is not so. Financial death shares some characteristics with its human equivalent. Nobody really likes to look at it too closely and it is only the specialists, the lawyers and the accountants taking the roles of undertakers and priests who are regarded as expert in what goes on. But there is no foundation to the view that bankruptcy has always been the same and is the same the world over.

Germany still has remnants of the traditional system of permanent liability that can be inherited. The debt goes on, passed down through the generations. The United Kingdom, the United States, Canada, Australia and New Zealand have had relatively recent experience with double and unlimited liability. Some of our western banks still function as unlimited partnerships as do many major professional firms. These systems have advantages of continuity that would be of benefit to us today. The recent Asian crises revealed the absence of any effective bankruptcy procedures in those countries. The debtors simply made the lenders wait until the economy recovered sufficiently to bring business back to a normal level and restore all parties to a state of contentment.

Lewis Evans and Neil Quigley[92] looked more closely at the impact of corporate organization on bankruptcy. They challenged the view that limited liability always represents the most efficient form of corporate organization. They found situations where unlimited liability prevailed, as when creditors are willing to compensate shareholders for bearing all of the costs of monitoring and the risks of the firm. Their study was based on data from Scottish banking in the nineteenth century, a market in which firms with limited and unlimited liability competed. They comment that limited liability is *at the heart of the legal and institutional framework* of the economic activity of our society because of the cost of monitoring the risk and likely liability in the case of business failure. But the general assumption by economists that limited liability is necessary for the efficient organization of the economy has no basis because limited liability has only recently come to predominate in several markets, such as banking, law and accounting.

As recently as the 1890s it was common for industrial firms adopting limited liability to voluntarily denominate shares so as to provide for large amounts of uncalled capital available in the event of liquidation. In banking this trend persisted much longer and had more explicit legal foundations. Variations of multiple rather than limited shareholder liability regimes were workable and durable: banks in the United Kingdom, and some large banks in Australasia retained multiple reserve liability until as recently as 1934, and in the United States double liability was mandatory for national banks and the majority of state banks until the introduction of deposit insurance in 1933.

Unlimited and multiple liability banks flourished in Scotland in the nineteenth century because the lower levels of equity and higher returns that made unlimited liability shares attractive to investors. Without limited liability the depositor needed to know who stood behind the bank and focused on the list of shareholders in the absence of independent auditing. Multiple reserve liability placed a limit on the calls on the individual and collective personal wealth of the shareholders, but it also shifted some risk to depositors, providing them with an incentive to monitor the performance of the bank directly.

The 1879 Company Act was a direct response to the failure of the City of Glasgow Bank. The ease with which the City of Glasgow Bank directors had defrauded the other shareholders prompted grave concerns about the stability of the banking system if some of the risk assumed by shareholders was simply transferred onto depositors. It is for this reason that the Scottish banks rejected the use of the modern form of limited liability, adopting multiple liability instead. The unlimited liability prevented the creation of Anticash by forcing the settlement of creditors' claims with real cash.

The lesson of Scottish banking in the nineteenth century is that there is nothing special about limited liability. Limited and unlimited liability can coexist in the same industry so long as equilibria in the market may be achieved by differences in formal information provision and alternative types of monitoring, as well as different returns to shareholders or depositors. The study shows nothing preordained about the regime of limited liability but that it evolved as a result of particular circumstances, risks and costs. Information was crucial in determining this trade-off. A move along the spectrum of liability regimes toward limited liability in any form represents a transfer of risk to depositors, while for shareholders it implies a reduced incentive to monitor bank management due to an increased tolerance of Vapourcash.

In this age of technology and the growth of the Internet and pervasive spread of Antilogic a case may be made to consider alternative liability regimes today. In considering this trade-off considerable care should be taken to ensure that the information given actually assists the investor in forming an accurate view of the risks of the enterprise. Our study of

Antilogic has revealed that this might not be the management's key objective.

Corporate bankruptcy is inherent in the current concept of limited liability. Recent United States academic research has cast new light on the justification for limited liability. The catastrophic failure of the Savings and Loan (also known as thrift) insurance fund and later the bank deposit insurance fund caused legal scholars to question the basic assumptions about the current United States system of bank regulation.

The United States is also a recent convert to the idea of limited liability for banks. Jonathan Macey and Geoffrey Miller[93] researched the three quarters of a century from the Civil War to the Great Depression where there was a regime whereby bank shareholders were responsible not only for their investments but also for a portion of the bank's debts after insolvency. This system was known as double liability and ultimately was rejected on the grounds that it had failed to protect bank creditors, did not maintain confidence and that deposit insurance was a preferable method to achieve regulatory objectives. Double liability was no passing fad as the succeeding regime is not yet so long lasting and has been subject to recent criticism especially following the Saving and Loan debacle of the 1980s.

Macey and Miller mount a spirited and convincing argument highlighting that deposit insurance created the perverse incentive to cause bank shareholders to use their control position to cause the bank to engage in increasingly risky activities to transfer wealth from creditors, depositors and ultimately the insurance scheme. In contrast, double liability encourages investors to decrease the riskiness of the firm. Their analysis revealed that the recovery rates on national bank assessments was remarkably good and did not deteriorate in the very difficult years. In addition the wish to avoid assessment prompted many bank managers to voluntarily liquidate their institution before insolvency. Overall the banks with double liability displayed better capital efficiency than banks without double liability by operating with a lower capital ratio in 1912 of 18.2 percent vs. 22.9 percent.

The analysis of the reasons given for change from the differing bankruptcy regimes reveal that the bankruptcy systems we recognize today in various jurisdictions are legal concepts rather than inherent economic events. Bankruptcy is a technical intrusion in the flow of monetary activity.

The Savings and Loan debacle that prompted Macey and Miller to undertake their research is a prime example of this intrusion and demonstrates how the potential problem of a liquidity impediment is crystallized into real losses and the generation of Anticash. Thus profit deferred is transformed in a realized loss. The Resolution Trust was the vehicle used to realize the assets of the failed thrifts. If the Resolution Trust had not acted so precipitately or rather had the liquidity to act more judiciously much better returns could in theory have been achieved. All those empty repossessed office buildings in cities like Houston were eventually filled as the 1980s recession turned around. Relative to the economy the financial problems were small and no lingering impact can be detected.

The economists have not been especially helpful either in distinguishing the legal concept from the economic reality. Economists are reputed to have a special role in the understanding of the mysteries of money. This is admittedly in competition with the bankers who have a role in both its creation and destruction. The banker may enjoy a beneficial association until the not infrequent credit problem undermines public confidence. Discovering the distinction between the theoretical and the eventual practical outcome may explain why economists have had constant difficulty in distinguishing accurately the precise sort of cash created in particular circumstances and indeed have trouble even recognizing the correct nature of Anticash.

Perhaps this lack of recognition has caused many of the divisions of opinion between economists this century. Here I particularly refer to the schism between the Keynesians and the Monetarists. This is uncomfortable for economists do not like identifying differences and increasingly need to flock together like fund managers and brokers' analysts. None can afford to be wrong. A shared orthodoxy has emerged amongst economists based on tolerating theories that were never grounded on any direct verification with reality.

> Such tiffs merely conceal the large body of shared belief which characterizes present-day economics. The old joke that twelve economists in a room could be guaranteed to hold twelve different opinions, and thirteen if one of them was Keynes, is becoming less and less true. An intellectual orthodoxy has emerged. Increasingly the subject is taught not as a way of learning to think about how the world might operate, but as a set of discovered truths as to how the world does operate... It can not be stated too often that very little of the content of such textbooks is known to be true, in the sense that many of the statements in textbooks on, say engineering, are known to be true.[94]

The whole of our market theory for example is based on the concept of competitive equilibrium but according again to Ormerod the proof is in the impossible category.

In a famous passage in *Alice in Wonderland,* the Red Queen declares that she often believes six impossible things before breakfast. The model of competitive equilibrium appears to be requiring us to move into this kind of world. And especially so in the case of companies, where the evidence from over a hundred years of economic history provides powerful evidence against the validity of the theory as a description of reality.

The assumptions of the competitive equilibrium model are not obvious on either a verbal or mathematical level and so the proof must rest on adding up the outcomes of all the individual decisions made and verifying the results as consistent with the theory. This rigorous approach would have pleased Popper but most economists simplify the impossible by not attempting verification. All the individuals who make up the competitive equilibrium also have a daunting task in that they have to process all known information and compute with everyone else the one optimum outcome that cannot be improved at that moment. In the absence of perfect foresight and infinite computational power the assumptions cannot be achieved with the result that conventional theory has never been proved and unconventional theories have not been disproved.

Lack of real world support has not diminished the belief of economists in the validity of their theories. Each school argues logically from their premise whether an economic fluctuation is real or pseudo. The Keynesians identify monetary influences as something that lays over reality and may impede the smooth functioning of the real economy. For the monetarists money is reality and any other basis is artificial or pseudo. They hold that if something happens, it must be real. This creates a gap in the logic as Kindelberger points out,

> In one monetarist view, a distinction should be made between 'real' financial crises, which involve a shrinkage of the money base and a 'pseudo' crisis in which it does not. 'Pseudo' strikes me as overkill, false, pretended, spurious, meaningless. It is legitimate to distinguish financial crisis in which money change occurs...from those in which money supply is not greatly effected, but for the monetarist to call the latter 'pseudo' is rather like a cardiologist finding a cancer patient only pseudo sick. Monetarists who insist on the distinction, do so because of a strong prior belief in monetarism more than empirical differences and the speculators and investors which were wiped out would...take little comfort from the thought that their experience was 'unreal'.[95]

It certainly would be some satisfaction for them to discover that their discomfort had been caused by Vapourcash or Anticash. Their financial health would remain unrestored but at least they would know the reason.

The proper explanation of the panic and crashes is, of course, the sudden condensing of Vapourcash. And, it is the unrecorded Anticash that creates the missing element in the models of both economic schools.

It would be no surprise to Saul that the economists are disunited in their analysis of monetary phenomena and have missed the presence of Anticash. He dismisses economics as a minor area of speculative investigation with econometrics as tinkering less reliable and less useful than car mechanics. Economic History which is the only useful branch tied as it is to reality has been downgraded. In his view the economists' advice has been taken and applied but in general it has failed to an extent akin to malpractice.

He is also very conscious of the tendency of institutions to lose sight of what is real and so permit loss of economic control. This is the profession on which we rely to gain insights into monetary affairs and here again their grasp on reality is far from firm.

> But most incredible of all is the abrupt illumination that money is something, when everyone knows perfectly well that it is just a notion, not even an abstraction, because we are unable to agree permanently what it is an abstraction of.[96]

Saul gives us a clue to solve the problem of lack of substance by pointing to conditions when substance is at its minimum, i.e. when conditions are most conducive to the generation of Vapourcash and Anticash. Putting the same point positively we interpret him as saying that a satisfactory inclusion of Vapourcash and Anticash will close the gap between the Keynesians and the Monetarist.

> This seems to work most successfully and for the longest period of time when there is some conservative relationship between real labour/resources/products and the quantity of money available. Within those limits a reasonable Keynesian and a reasonable monetarist are not very far apart. But people have difficulty remaining reasonable over abstractions. Instead they get so used to their arbitrary definition of the abstraction of money that they decide it is both real and absolute.[97]

It is interesting that he views the difference between the two economics camps as coming from being too definite and pragmatic about money that we just discovered to be at best an abstraction. He is very pessimistic about abstraction leading to the justification of speculation despite its consequences. A better understanding of the process will permit a better management of the outcome.

The impossibility of the assumptions implies a failure of the model rather than of the economy. Alternatively it is a failure of the economists rather than of the economy. After all it was Jean-Paul Kauffman who pointed out the similarity between economists and weather forecasters. Unfortunately the weather does not depend too much on the forecasters. Presumably, we had weather before the weather forecasters and carrying that analogy further I guess that there was economics before the economists? At least there was Keynesian economics before Keynes as could be the seen from the comment by economist Joan Robinson that Hitler had already found a way to cure unemployment before Keynes. Galbraith in reporting this comment also explained how it was done.

> There were Keynesians well before Keynes. One was Adolf Hitler, who exempt from any restraining economic theory launched a major program of public works construction upon taking office in 1933. The Nazis were also indifferent to the constraints of tax revenue, deficit financing was taken for granted. The German economy recovered from the devastating slump it had previously suffered. By 1936 the unemployment that had been so influential in bringing Hitler to power has been substantially eliminated.[98]

The German model depended on the excessive creation and ultimately total destruction of money. Buchan emphasize this theme that he equates with the destruction of the entire nation.

> In May 1933, two months after Hitler had come to power by election, a shell company (Mefo) was founded...its sole function was to create a form of money: it issued three-month bills to army suppliers and munitions manufacturers which could then be discounted – cashed – at commercial banks against a guarantee of acceptance at the end of the quarter by the Reichsbank. These bills were known under the general 1930's euphemism of 'job creation measures' but persisted long after the Reich had reached full employment in 1936.[99]

This represented an early form of off balance sheet financing or securitization of re-armament with special financial instruments that were made viable because of the centrally planned interlocking system.

> The armies and their equipment were paid for by the sale of paper obligations of the Reich to the public, amounting to around 380 billion Reichsmarks by the end of the war or about thirty times the debt at the time Hitler took power.

> The terms used to describe this financing in the secret documents are indescribably sinister: the goal was a 'noiseless', 'invisible', 'frictionless'

process. It was a closed system sealed without chink against reality... The Germans, all employed, all earning, received wages in banknotes that they couldn't spend; so they deposited the money at the banks; but the banks couldn't lend it, except to the government; so they bought the governments paper; which was converted into more banknotes; and round and round and round. Prices and wages were tightly fixed, so that inflation at first simply did not manifest itself...At Hitler's death, the Germans possessed 70 billion Reichsmarks in worthless coins and banknotes and 380 billion in obligations of a regime which no longer existed. Put another way, the expenditure on the war roughly equalled the cumulative national product of Germany since the mid-1920s. Germany had been converted into money and destroyed. Zero.[100, *]

I do not agree that the result was really zero because Germany undoubtedly still existed and through the Economic Miracle of the 1950s recovered very rapidly. This quibble aside, the Hitler period serves as a very good example of a forced vapourization of the economy, something like a pressure cooker in which heat was applied and the resulting vapour contained within. When the vessel was ruptured the vapour both escaped and condensed so rapidly as to form Anticash at a national level. Not everything was destroyed and the value was not zero. Spurred on by the generation of Anticash Germany entered a highly competitive and productive phase.

The image of a pressure cooker is not dissimilar to the attempts made to demonstrate the workings of hydraulic Keynesian economics with a system of tanks, pipes and pumps. Within a few years we could imagine the meeting of the hydraulic Keynesians with the atmospherics of the chaotic weather forecaster Lorenz.

In the hydraulic model, debt is more like a tank of water than a flow. A loan starts as a transaction and flows through the pipes but once received it stops. The interest is supposed to flow but is often added directly or indirectly to the loan. The dynamic concept of the flow stops and becomes static. It becomes a burden.

Saul worries about the growth of the debt burden without including the use to which those funds had been put. He distinguishes the position of the state from the attitude appropriate to the individual. Western economies are pursuing a dogma of paying down government debt, while simultaneously building up unprecedented levels of private debt. In seeking to debunk the current fear of public debt he refers to historic examples of

---

[*] Also John Weitz, *Hitler's Banker*, Warner Books, 1999, p. 157, if alternative quote needed.

societies that were crippled by debt burden but were reinvigorated when by one means or other the debt is removed.

He contends that the non-payment of debts represents no moral problem. The only moral standards recognized in Western society as being relevant to lending are those that identify profit made from loans as a sin. Loans themselves are contracts and therefore cannot carry moral value. As all businessmen know, contracts are to be respected whenever possible. When not possible, regulations exist to aid default or renegotiation. Businessmen regularly do both and happily walk away.

> Negative wealth. A quality proper to business leaders whose debt load is out of control. Less important people and governments do not have negative wealth. They have debt.[101]

It is not so easy for whole economies to have such attitudes and debt levels can build up out of control. Saul argues that debt is a burden despite money not being real!

> Civilisations which become obsessed by sustaining unsustainable debt-loads have forgotten the basic nature of money. Money is not real. It is a conscious agreement on measuring abstract value. Unhealthy societies often become mesmerized by money and treat it as if it were something concrete. The effect is to destroy the currency's practical value.[102]

Saul sees debt as fine as long as it can be repudiated and refers us again to those corporate finance pioneers, the ancient Greeks and in particular to the freeing of ancient Athens from public evil in the form of debt. This debt displayed an alarmingly active and mystical nature as it

> enters the house of each man, the gates of his courtyard cannot keep it out, it leaps over the high wall; let him flee to a corner of his bed chamber, it will certainly find him, out.[103]

In this guise money has become a ghost or an evil spirit. Solon is his fiscal hero for repudiating debt, thereby exorcising the ghost.

> Athens immediately began its rise to glory, spewing out ideas, theatre, sculpture and architecture, democratic concepts and concrete riches. All this eventually became the foundation of Roman and indeed of Western civilization. Today we cannot move a step without some conscious or unconscious tribute to the genius of Solon and of Athens – a genius unleashed by defaulting on debts.[104]

This process sounds rather severe on the creditors. We can only imagine that they had demonstrated a higher propensity to save but a lower inclination to cultural creativity than the debtors. How else could an internal transfer of wealth cause such an economic and cultural blossoming? Modern language usage equates money with Philistines who do not appreciate the finer things of life and here we find the Athenians exploding in cultural creativity as a result of the repudiation of debt.

He progresses through history with further examples such as Henry IV of France, Revolutionary United States, Brazil and Peru. In each of these cases economic salvation came from repudiating foreign debt. The subsequent improvement in economic conditions is not so surprising as it is the result of inadvertent development aid on behalf of the creditor nations. His final example is of modern Mexico where additional loans are arranged to tide the country through its financial crises. This is another variation that amounts to modern mercantilism as Mexico gains the imports but never actually repays the loans or interest.

Each example demonstrates the same tendency for economic renewal after a period of financial stress caused by various means such as hyperinflation, excessive borrowing or war. One example sees the solution as coming from the destruction or repudiation of the debt burden. Another looks at the other side of the balance sheet and sees the spur provided by the destruction of the monetary base of the economy. Both these influences are manifestations of the impact of Vapourcash developing into Anticash. The actions of these historic heroes of debt repudiation were no different than that of the present day judge presiding in a bankruptcy action. Their action led to the creation of Anticash and it is the Anticash rush that brought the economic and cultural resurgence that has so frequently followed the release from debt induced burdens. The economists have explained the recovery in terms of monetary policy with the repudiation of sovereign debt seen as something separate. But to the holders of the debt, especially if they are in another country and even if they are governments themselves, there seems to be no difference at all. Call it what you will, they have not been paid. The repudiation has brought the debtors negative artificially up to a zero.

Some economies have found alternatives to bankruptcy or repudiation by developing highly sophisticated systems of accommodation. A widespread inability to meet obligations in real cash is solved by the expedient of paying in kind. Russia has for years operated as a nation perilously close to the point defined as the creation of Anticash. In an economy where the inability to settle is endemic it becomes the accepted solution to take something instead of nothing. Remember that Anticash is created when an individual, entity or country has a deficiency of revenue relative to costs to the extent that it can no longer meet its obligations to provide real cash.

This is the daily situation in Russia yet bankruptcy is largely avoided and when it does occur it has very different consequences to bankruptcy in the common law systems. However, the role of Vapourcash and Anticash is still dominant.

The difficulties with that economy go beyond statistics to the whole process of grappling with chronic balance of payments problems. Clifford Gaddy and Barry Ickes contend that the difficulty of Western advisers to correctly determine a solution for Russia stems from a fundamental misunderstanding of how the Russian economy actually functions in the face of payments difficulties.

> At its heart is the ultimate pretence that the Russian economy is larger than it really is. It is this pretence that allows for larger government, and larger expenditures, than Russia can afford. It is the cause of the web of non-payments and fiscal crises from which Russia seemingly cannot emerge... On top of this is the notorious 'non-payments' or 'payments arrears' crisis. The way this story is reported is a familiar one. The enterprises don't pay their suppliers; they don't pay their workers; they don't pay their taxes. While the non-payment of taxes and wages attracts media attention, it is in a sense not the real story. Payments are made, just not in actual money. The share of barter in payments among the industrial enterprises is above fifty percent. Last year, forty percent of all taxes paid to the Russian federal government were in non-monetary form. The degree of non-monetization of local and regional budgets is even higher...in Russia today enterprises can operate without paying their bills. ... The Virtual Economy arises because of the combination of two fundamental facts (1) most of the Russian economy, especially its manufacturing sector, is value-subtracting, while (2) most participants in the economy pretend that it is not. Barter, tax arrears, and other non-monetary modes of payment turn out to be the main mechanism used to sustain the pretence... The relationship between the non-cash Virtual Economy and the cash-based market economy is a curious one. To some extent, the system described above is driven by an active effort to avoid cash. Cash transactions expose the pretense.[105]

All this is handled within something that sounds very much like a state administered CEO credibility account. If the performance is not good enough the managers are replaced but the company continues and no bankruptcy occurs. The Russians are not unique in having a Virtual economy. They have just taken it further. Other examples are the European common agricultural policy and the French solution to banking.

We cannot readily talk about the bankruptcy of a nation in the same way as we discuss the legal bankruptcy or corporation within our current legal system. Yet these examples drawn from far back in history and subject to a wide variety of legal systems show very similar characteristics. This suggests that some more general effect is at play. Very positive economic and social activities takes place when the participants are freed from the depressing influence of the payment of interest or the repayment of debt. This occurs not only in the situation of formal bankruptcy but also under several other distinct circumstances when the money does not return. This may be when the great confidence of lenders in the endeavour ensures further funding and no pressure for repayment. They believe in the self evident truth. This can lead to financial exuberance that defers the necessity for repayment. We recognize this as the bubble. Sometimes the activity is initiated by the speculator who has no intention of repayment. In the old days the princes eliminated the problem of repayment by the elimination of the debtor or at least his insistence for repayment. After a certain point this is insufficient and it is apparent to the creditor that there is a manifest inability to repay because of the fall of the past regime.

Formal bankruptcy is the purest example of the creation of Anticash because it provides the opportunity to observe the precise moment and precise amount created when the nexus between debit and credit is broken. But it would be incorrect to believe that this is the only example or that Anticash is distinctly separate from Vapourcash. It also occurs in circumstances of much milder forms of financial distress. The progression of examples from individuals to corporations to whole economies suggests a more gradual process, as does the evidence of creation outside the confines of the western legal liability framework.

If we pursue the notion of progression back upstream from before the moment of bankruptcy we discover evidence of creeping creation of Anticash. It is unusual for a corporation to plunge directly from corporate health into bankruptcy. Or put more precisely, it is highly unusual in the absence of fraud. Usually the sponsors of the corporation detect that it is under pressure and seek to raise further funds as borrowings or in new equity. As the conditions worsen it becomes impossible to rely solely on new borrowings and the raising of new equity becomes essential. The existing sponsors feel themselves compelled to kick in new equity as rights issues or often in specialized forms of convertible stock, preference shares or subordinated debt. This new equity has the effect of disproportionately diluting the existing holdings of the sponsors. These investors know that the new issue is not a good investment and merely adds to their exposure to an enterprise in trouble. In effect they are tipping in new funds that also have the effect of reducing the value of what they already hold. Never the less, they put in new money to try and save whatever they can of the original investment. The investors dilute themselves. They may also delude themselves but that is another story.

The new issue may look attractively priced but this is only an appearance made possible by the creation of Anticash by the original investment to the extent that existing value is given up. Realists might call this throwing in good money after bad but generally it is just called recapitalization, as the existing owners try to retain control.

With this in mind we can see that the formation of Anticash is a much more gradual process than first suspected. It is going on all the time as Vapourcash condenses. It is a process that is analogous to the weather systems. The atmospheric pressure is changing all the time creating air currents and presumably also ocean currents. Vapourcash is condensing into Anticash. It is unlikely that Anticash can revert to Vapourcash as distinct from new Vapourcash being formed. Occasionally with particular circumstances it has a spectacular and obvious manifestation as formal bankruptcy or destructive war in the same dramatic way as thunder and lightning do in weather systems.

The biological world has many examples of vitality in response to a life threatening experience. Indeed in the Australian bush many species of trees can only reproduce after the effects of a bush fire. Many species of fauna reproduce as a direct response to external threat. The idea that economic activity flourishes in the aftermath of bankruptcy or destruction does not sit comfortably with conventional or classical economic theory. In economics it is not clear what the true situation is but we can at least look to see how it has developed on a global basis. The destruction of assets or the repudiation of debt, on the face of it, reduces the productive capabilities of the economy and thus future output. It need not be negative. The rebuilding of the economies vanquished during the war was often used as an explanation or excuse for why those economies began performing better that those of the victors.

Fé, or stone money of Yap. © The British Museum. Reproduced with permission.

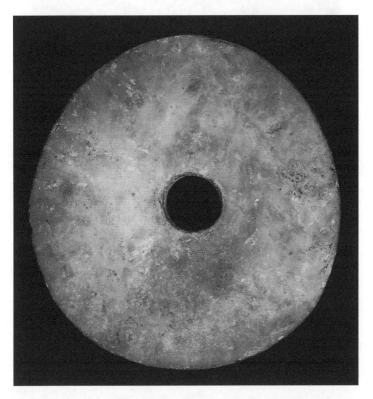

Yap stone money. © The British Museum. Reproduced with permission.

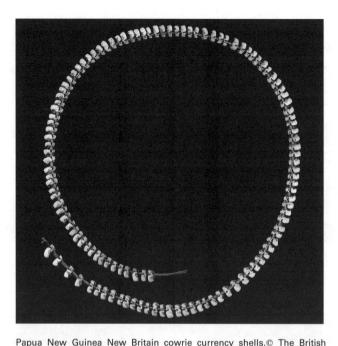

Papua New Guinea New Britain cowrie currency shells.© The British Museum. Reproduced with permission.

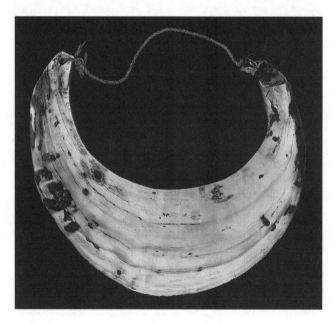

Papua New Guinea West Highlands Wahgi people kina pearl shell ornament. Kina pearl shells were used as currency prior to the introduction of paper money. © The British Museum. Reproduced with permission.

Papua New Guinea five kina note. The note features the kina shell from which the currency took its name. © The British Museum. Reproduced with permission.

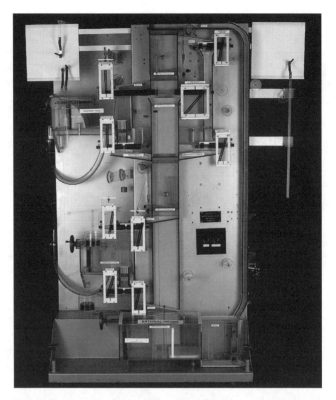

The Phillips Economic Computer. © Science Museum Science and Society Picture library. Reproduced with permission.

Burning bank notes which have been returned to the Bank of England, Britain 1872. © Mansell/Timpex/Rex Features. Reproduced with permission.

XI

ANTICASH: THE BANKERS AND THE ACCOUNTANTS

THE BANKERS are generally thought to have a priestly role in the mystery of creating and tending cash. Their banking halls are the temples for much of the ceremony surrounding money. Many parallels can be drawn between the traditional bank manager and the parish priest. This heavy responsibility does not guarantee popularity and doctrine does not guarantee infallibility. In contrast the accountants have had a blessed role with money right from the beginning when the Father of Accounting, the monk Luca Pacioli, first codified double entry.

In the view of most religions money itself is not supposed to be a religion and this has put the bankers in a difficult position. The money-changers were famously thrown out of the temple. Usury was a sin and even seen as Satan's secret weapon. Consequently bankers have not always been held in high regard but as it is only human to want the forbidden over the centuries the attractiveness of money made its high priests welcome. Earlier prohibitions that had been relaxed gradually have accelerated with a rush so that today the situation is largely reversed with respectability achieved through money. The dominance of money in influencing social position and economic thought has moved so far that bankers are now accepted as experts on many fields beyond banking. It is not surprising that these high priests of financial affairs have diversified into all aspects of the financial universe and play a key role in the creation of Vapourcash and Anticash.

But the tensions remain. Right through history there has been a consistent concern about the impact of bankers. The Ancient Greek dramatist Aeschylus in his play *Agamemnon* had a precocious understanding of bankers as demonstrated in the line, 'War's a banker, flesh his gold'.

The long standing and widespread religious aversion to money and in particular the charging of interest created a career impediment for the banker with persistent threats of exclusion and dreadful punishment. The Christian church long viewed the taking of interest to be a sin sometimes to the extent of threatening excommunication. Dante put usurers amid the fiery sands of the seventh circle of Hell. Temporal rulers regularly also discovered a distaste for bankers and interest although this was generally first discovered as repayment dates approached.

As a result the banker or moneylender was regarded with suspicions that linger to this day. Ways were found to get around the prohibitions. A religious arbitrage was discovered. The Torah while prohibiting the charging of interest to brother Jews is helpful in allowing the charge to the foreigner. As commerce developed Muslims and Christians borrowed from Jewish lenders free under their own beliefs to charge interest. Yet as late as 1571 English law refreshed the prohibition on interest taking. By this process of inter religious co-operation each group was able to proceed by means of a technicality that avoided divine retribution. This inherent banking skill continues to this day as a way is found around regulators who seek to impose their ill-considered restrictions.

Expectations gradually changed and actions previously thought reprehensible are now accepted and praised. Miserliness once seen to be the disease of money gradually lost its odium and became the condition of moral health when suitably relabelled as thrift. The suspicion about bankers also gradually moderated to the extent that the banker's family could be tolerated in the church and finally in 1658 in Holland the prohibition against bankers themselves was withdrawn. It is not clear when or if the other professions listed in this quote were also readmitted. The title of the book *The Embarrassment of Riches* says it all. Wealth was suspect, those involved with wealth were treated with suspicion and the enjoyment of wealth was to be discrete.

> The predikants would not stand idly by while the Golden Calf was erected amidst Israel's tents. Far from tacitly endorsing finance capitalism, the Dutch general synods did their level best to proclaim their disapproval. Bankers were excluded from communion by an ordinance of 1581, joining a list of other shady occupations – pawnbrokers, actors, jugglers, acrobats, quacks and brothel keepers – that were disqualified from receiving God's

grace. Their wives were permitted to join the Lord's Supper, but only on condition that they publicly declared their repugnance for their husband's profession! Their families shared the taint and were only permitted to join communion after a public profession of distaste for dealing in money. It was not until 1658 that the States of Holland persuaded the church to withdraw this humiliating prohibition on 'lombards'.[106]

The process of relaxation was slow and as late as the eighteenth century England, Samuel Johnson still defined bankers as someone who traffics in money. Gradually the tide turned so that previously condemned professions are now sought after. It all became a matter of degree as the magical properties of money began to overcome the scruples of religion. So long as the impact of the pursuit of wealth or the display of its accumulation were not excessive it became acceptable.

> Since the merchants were patently in pursuit of wealth in a society where they were influential, perhaps dominant, such pursuit lost its evil or dubious connotation. The merchants were easy in their conscience. Protestantism and Puritanism may have helped, but as ever, religious faith was accommodated to economic circumstances and need. As wealth and the pursuit of wealth became respectable, so if it was not immoderate, did the taking of interest.[107]

Over time the view was taken that if a little was acceptable then a little more would be better.

> Professions that in earlier ages seemed barely legitimate, let alone honourable – stockbroking, consumer credit, futures trading, risk arbitrage, all types of parasitic commission business, kiss-and-tell – are now celebrated as manly and ladylike. Money wealth, though it is as colourless as celebrity, appears to many to be good. Actions are good that bring money.[108]

Religion has retreated and today money dominates. The change has become rapid and dramatic but it is not yet a stable domination as views fluctuate with the economic cycle. Bankers have continued to make a major contribution to cycles over the centuries. Imprudent lending is often linked to forgetting the cause of the previous crisis although this is probably underestimates the ability of the bankers to discover a new cause for each crisis. The inability to remember old crises or more particularly for younger bankers to learn from their predecessors provides the basis of an underlying cyclical pattern as tried and true disasters repeat. One theory suggests that the length of cycle is determined by how long it takes for the bankers to forget the cause of the previous crises. Another theory is based on how long it takes to develop enough gullibility to accept the new financial exponents as having the Midas touch.

Sometimes it is said rather unkindly that bankers never learn and so repeat their mistakes. This is inaccurate. Individual bankers generally never again get the chance to repeat a mistake for they are gone. By banker we mean in this case, someone who makes loans. It is not for nothing that the bankers themselves take the elephant as their mascot. It is not because they are big, grey, lumbering and smelly. It is because they take pride in never forgetting and in particular never forgetting a loan that goes bad. This may be observed in the tendency for bankers to wear elephant decorated ties and cuff links. The more culturally sensitive remembers only to choose elephants with their trunks upraised. A trunk depressed is bad luck.

The lending institution is not supposed to make the same mistake again. The cyclical nature of banking would suggest that although they may not forget the loan that goes bad they have trouble remembering why it went bad. Banks distinguish small losses from large losses and pursue the former more rigorously than the latter. This is felt internally within the bank as well by the troubled borrower.

> The larger the sum that you owe, the more considerate the banker will be, for after all it is the bank's money that is being considered... If your debt is small, they will, in all probability, put you into liquidation. If your debt is very large, they will engineer your affairs so that for years you work only for the bank, until you reach the moment when the value of your business is greater than the money that you owe them. At that point despite all the hard work of paying off your debts, they will destroy both your business and in all likelihood, you as well. A bank should not be blamed for such conduct – it is the very nature of their trade and those that engage in business should know this.[109]

Most banks will pursue not only the borrower to try to recover the outstanding loan but also the lending officer with the dreaded Review of Personnel Consequences. These consequences are often unhelpful for a happy career. If the loss is very large there will still be personnel consequences although these generally will involve the rapid promotion of the lending officer involved. Middling disasters have unpredictable consequences for personnel and are determined by the state of internal politics that always seeks just this sort of ammunition.

The bank will try not to forget the cause of the disaster. The small disasters, no matter where they occurred in the world, will be diligently investigated and the findings incorporated into the bank's risk management model and rigorously enforced until the last member of the current management has departed. So if the bank has ever lost money on, for example, garden centres anywhere in the world it is self evidently true that no garden centre should ever be financed in the future. If it was the big disaster that caused the big promotion then the successful Mr. Big will have learned from this experience and he will be busy to ensure that the corporate memory recognizes the folly of that sort of lending and the role of his rivals in its occurrence. Big disasters have a very beneficial effect in provoking change and delivering up scapegoats. This helps to explain the hard edge displayed by bankers in hard times. As well as the legitimate concern to recover the bank's money, the bankers must deal with their own vulnerability and the need to act correctly in the newly emerging political environment.

None of this will stop the bank from making a new mistake. The first mistake is the negative act of ceasing to make loans to industries that are now quite safe or to firms without problems in troubled industries. The follow-on mistakes are many and varied. We cannot predict what they will be. Every banking disaster has been followed by another quite different disaster. This must continue as banking is a risky business that makes its money by accepting risk. There is little return in banking in the absence of risk. When the banks recoil from a disaster and lick their wounds in the safety of riskless banking they find that not only have the losses of the disaster gone away but so has the underlying profits of the business. After a while steps have to be taken to build the business in new areas away from the ever growing list of old disasters. In due time after a diligent search a new disaster will be found.

Some recent disasters follow a different pattern. No longer are banks restricted only to the taking of deposits and the granting of loans. Transaction banking brought experience with the international currency and debt markets and many banks have begun trading for the own account. The use of mathematical models, the discovery of arbitrage, the exploitation of tax differences and the low usage of capital (or high usage of gearing) have opened the prospect of high profits. The junk bond, Barings, emerging markets debt and Long Term Capital are a few examples that suggest that these activities are not always successful for the banks. However, in these markets the consequence for the individual might be very different.

The nature of these markets demand that the participants be paid a very high salary, receive a high proportion of the profit as a bonus and be recruited and retained with the golden triangle (hellos, handcuffs and parachute) also known as the socially acceptable trifecta (come, visit and then say goodbye). If the business prospers all is well for the individual and the business. If the business hits trouble it is still good for the individual, who is paid to leave and is likely to emerge with a golden hello at a competitor to repeat the process. In effect the profit share has an upward ratchet effect that is paid in good times and cannot be recovered in bad times.

The Accountants have a much more Spartan existence based on their mentor and role model Luca Pacioli. Their vocation reflects a more benign religious guidance in the affairs of finance. Luca was a religious man who dedicated his system to God and endorsed profit so the business man could sustain himself in God's work. What a contrast with usury. His contribution still appears miraculous in its completeness and vision. What great connections he must have had. Luca sent the accountants off in the right direction and we are still discovering the full significance of his contribution.

Luca was born about 1445 or at least between the years 1445 and 1450 probably in Piero della Francesca's hometown of Borgo San Sepulcro. He was known as Luca Pacioli or Paccioli or Paciolo or Paciolus. Although Luca's family wanted the boy to prepare for a career in business he was apprenticed to Piero who taught him writing, art, and history. He used the famous library at the nearby Court of Urbino to lay the basis of his fame as a mathematician. At the age of twenty, he moved to Venice as tutor to the three sons of the rich merchant Antonio de Rompiasi. He went abroad with them on business.

He received private tuition in mathematics and attended public lectures in philosophy and theology. He learnt about architecture and military affairs from his uncle Benedetto, a military officer stationed in Venice. Luca moved to Rome in 1470 to continue his studies and at the age of 27 he became a Franciscan monk. Paccioli's masterwork, *Summa de arithmetic, geomettia et proportionaliti* was published in 1494. It has five sections, of which the third is a treatise on bookkeeping called *Particularis de Computis et Scripturis*. This became one of the most widely read books of the Renaissance and was translated, imitated and paraphrased into Dutch, French and English. Thus another perceptive observer of the ways of money Sir Thomas Gresham learned well the lessons from Pacioli. In 1546 he opened his journal, in exactly the fashion prescribed by Luca in his treatise. No doubt guided by the infallible rigour of double entry Gresham was able to gather the data that led to the law that bad money drives out good. The origins of bookkeeping pre-date Luca but his treatment, reproducing the practices of the Venetian merchant houses where he served was the most extensive to date and brought the basis of order to economic activity. It was one of the first business best practice guides. Peter Bernstein compared the economic consequences of Paccioli's contribution to the discovery of the steam engine three hundred years later.

Luca became a close friend of Leonardo da Vinci who supplied complex drawings for Paccioli's other great work, *De Divine Proportione*. This title indicates that he had a strong belief in the source of his ideas. Luca is known to have been a religious man and there is much that is magical, mystical or even supernatural about his achievements that were so extensive that he must have received special help. Contemporaries must have shared this impression as revealed in this description by Buchan of a painting thought to be of Luca called *A Demonstration in Mathematics* attributed to Jacopo de' Barbari, a painter active in Milan in the 1490s.

It shows a burly friar in a grey Franciscan habit, pointing with a wand to a construction drawn in chalk on a slate, labelled on the side with the word EUCLIDES. To Luca's right, suspended in air, is an object that takes the breath away. It is a crystal polyhedron. It shimmers, drenched in light and yet impenetrable in its mathematical perfection. It seems to be made of some unearthly material, brighter and more translucent than diamond. All its twenty-six faces, eighteen squares and eight equilateral triangles are simultaneously visible. Some of the faces reflect images of buildings, standing no doubt beyond an open window outside the picture frame.

It is as if the painter thought there was something miraculous about his subject, and many people from Thomas Gresham to Goethe, were later to agree. Across the interval of time, Luca does indeed seem admirable not simply as an overlooked hero of a celebrated age but even, as Goethe thought, one of its greatest. If his master, Piero della Francesca, and his friends, Leonardo da Vinci and L.B. Alberti, still astonish us with their notions of a mathematical order underlying phenomena – think of the Arezzo frescoes, Leonardo's sketch-books or Alberti's Tempio Malatestiana in Rimini – Luca identifies that order with money.[110]

Buchan implies that money springs from that order and that it perhaps is unearthly or miraculous in origin. Indeed that order may be the prerequisite for money. Despite society's attempts to unsettle that order, the symmetry of money is preserved by the unrecorded presence of Anticash. Luca recognized that the philosophical and spiritual transcended the physical manifestation of order. He could recognize what was needed to understand money and value and he was only defeated because the technology had not yet been invented, just as Leonardo was unable to give effect to his plans for flying machines. The philosophical basis for money set by Luca has been proven to be completely sound now that electronics allows physical manifestation to go beyond note and coin. The technology of money is at last catching up with philosophy identified five hundred years previously.

The accountants have a major role in the modern financial world not only in the mundane recording of costs and revenues but also in the determination of profit. This can be a miracle in itself and so the accountants often also act as referees for business at difficult stages in their development. This can be seen in their role as valuers, auditors, administrators and receivers. It is only a short step to be the arbiter in the formation of money in all its many forms. Buchan distinguishes the role of accountants (or the less prestigious bookkeepers) in creating money from that of the economists who merely describe.

From the bookkeepers, we learned that money can be written or rather forged into a written language which can express reality after a fashion; but at the price of a compulsion and the ludicrous, almost grotesque, restriction of the personality. We learned from the economists that money is an avenue to both choice and prosperity, now redefined in civil language.[111]

Over the years the tools of the accountant have become more complex and with the encroaching role of bankers it is easy to lose sight of the original philosophy and objectives set out by Luca. His work laid the foundation of the modern conception of profit and identifies order with money. He was a brilliant mathematician who also set the basis of modern risk management although it has taken us centuries to realize the full significance of his contribution.

There are fashions in the professions and sciences just as there are in the more every day activities of clothing, food and hairstyles. Accounting is no exception. The classical symmetry of double entry bookkeeping is so deceptively simple that it is easy to take it for granted. Familiarity, the changing fashions and bogus sophistication have caused the accounting profession to underrate the power of the philosophy of double entry and forget its purpose. Unfortunately, the financial community seduced by its own technology and short-sighted pragmatism have fallen for the same error. It has been a classic case of not seeing the wood for the trees. The fog of Vapourcash has caused the market to blunder away from the true solution, probably because the flexibility of Vapourcash provided an easy cover for any discrepancy in the balance. The denial of his double entry rules creates the Anticash required to reassert symmetry and order.

As we start the twenty first century we have seen the shift from bookkeeping to accounting; the move from trade to profession; its study from night school to trade college and on to university; the move from philosophy to art and even to a science. The emphasis has changed as well. When the fundamental principles were applied to more complex situations the practitioners encountered problems and turned to the academics for help. Inevitably, the resulting complexity provided opportunity for the entrepreneurs and the speculators. Taxation has contributed its own particular logic and complexity.

The combination of these factors put great pressure on the basic accounting structure both when periods of success brought booms, take-overs and derivatives and during the troubles with bust, bankruptcy and depression. Big trouble brings lawyers and simplistic solutions based in the past. The problems that we encounter today come from the crude forcing of pragmatic solutions. These heavy-handed solutions caused accounting asymmetry as courts attempted to remove the inconvenient negative in the shareholders funds. These actions have damaged the original philosophy that would still be relevant today if consistently applied.

This gradual slide away from the essential symmetry has seen premature netting of entries and even the abandonment of one side of the double entry. Over several generations this created the conditions to permit the release of significant quantities of Anticash.

Buchan is intrigued by Luca's impact on the history of money.

> To be able to keep books in double entry is to have a machine for calculating the world. …its influence on our thought has been almost without parallel. Our conversation is replete with assets and liabilities, depreciations, profits and loss, balance sheets: all echoes of Luca's system. Above all, Luca laid the foundation of the modem conception of profit, not as some vague increase in possession, as in antiquity, but as something hard, even crystalline, mathematical and open to empirical test *at any time whatever* through an interlocking system of books.[112]

The full impact of double entry is less apparent to us today because of the numerous modern accounting modifications of the basic system. When you strip away the passing fashions you find that the true value was in the original features all along, just like the restoration of old houses. Some of the greatest observers in history did not lose sight of this solid virtue.

> Goethe, the last person successfully to inhabit the worlds of business and poetry, was entranced by double entry. In *Wilhelm Meister*, a character calls it one of the 'loveliest inventions of the human spirit' and 'a reliable, daily measure of accumulating happiness'.[113]

How could it ever be justifiable to step aside from such a commendable objective?

> Stephen Monteage, an English merchant writing in 1682, used the language of alchemy: 'This way of accounting which we Treat of, carries with it its own Proof, and here lies the Supreme Excellency and Usefulness of this mystery. Werner Sombart, wildly enthusiastic even on a bad day, was duly ravished:

'Double entry bookkeeping was born from the same spirit that gave rise to the systems of Galileo and Newton and the teachings of modem physics and chemistry. It uses the same methods as they to organize phenomena into an artificial system: indeed, it is the first cosmology on the basis of mechanical thought'.

He went on to detect the influence of double entry in the theories of gravity and the conservation of energy and even of the circulation of the blood, itself the chief metaphor of the profession known as economics.[114]

We cannot fail to be struck by the comprehensiveness of the method. When we compare this elegance with the capricious arbitrariness of the bankruptcy system we have to question whether we are throwing out the baby instead of the bathwater.

Luca was not a simple practitioner, nor did he believe that double entry evolved in isolation. He had had special help. It brought an altogether more significant message.

You begin, says Luca, 'with the name of God. Your first journal should be marked with a cross'. Luca is a religious (of some sort, at least) and the world of business is still subordinate to religion: 'The end and object of every businessman is to make a lawful and satisfactory profit so that he may sustain himself. Therefore, he should begin with the name of God... Luca permits some latitude as to how the accounts are kept, but insists on one indispensable condition: that every journal and ledger entry must be made twice, as a *debit* on the left-hand side and a *credit* on the right-hand side. That means that at any moment a trial balance can be struck, which will reveal error, incompleteness or fraud; and the entries accumulated and cast off through a profit-and-loss account to give a notion of worth without the need for repeated inventory-taking.

Luca explains

The Profit and Loss account shall be closed in this way. If the loss exceeds the profit (may God protect each of us who is truly a good Christian from such an eventuality), then credit the account in the usual manner. 'Credit Profit and Loss on such-and-such a day, debit Capital for loss sustained in this account.' Here is, without doubt, a rational framework for the pursuit of 'sustenance' and Sombart is no doubt correct to accord it a place in the capitalist pantheon.[115]

Nowhere does Luca instruct us to change the method if losses continue, if capital becomes negative or in response to some court issued directive. No freedom is permitted because consistency is the key to the system and the whole basis of capitalism depends on it.

> One cannot even imagine capitalism without double entry bookkeeping: they are as intimately related as form and content. There is a legitimate doubt whether capitalism created double entry as a tool in its realization or whether double entry bred capitalism out of its inner spirit... Sombart was surely misguided in thinking that capital, which we define as property capable of generating profit, did not exist as a notion before Fra Luca's treatise (or, rather, the accounts of the Genoese *massari* and other pioneers of double entry in the century before). Capital and profit existed in the antique mind: it is merely that in, say, the Roman manuals of estate management, or Cicero's forensic speeches, they are not defined with any precision. Indeed, what seemed in antiquity to be profit would sometimes be what we now call loss.[116]

Poor Buchan is in somewhat of a tangle to claim Sombart is in error by justifying the existence of capital while suggesting that profit existed but was really a loss! Are we to believe that capital was to be serviced by losses in the days before Luca's treatise? Perhaps Sombart is correct after all or perhaps the identification of the symmetry of double entry reveals the presence of other influences to maintain capital in the face of losses. Sombart's position is very modern in its pragmatism. If the numbers do not suit then a little window dressing will save the day and by this pragmatism the balance is flawed.

> The world is dissolved into numbers, and the undissolved residue – values that cannot be expressed in money – will ultimately be denied existence: *quod non est in libris, non est in mundo* (nothing exists unless it is in the books).[117]

How easy it is to criticize Sombart for emphasizing the books yet this is exactly what happens in bankruptcy when the court seeks to eliminate the deficiency of shareholders funds from the books. Naturally it cannot succeed and reality continues in the form of unrecorded Anticash.

> The double entry account is not merely objective and rational and public, in the sense of being comprehensible to others: it is also mechanical. Once started, and Luca is quite firm about this, it proceeds in a predictable and

specific fashion. The accounts become compulsory. Though mere sheafs of figures, they acquire a dominion over the individual who casts them up or has them cast up: 'Next to being prepared for death, with respect to Heaven and his soul,' wrote Defoe, 'a tradesman shall be always in a state of preparation for death, with respect to his books'.[118]

Double entry is a discipline. Not even the judiciary can stop the process once started. Once it proceeds it must continue to completion. We should not be surprised that the system of accounting set out by Luca has had ramifications far beyond those expected by those who lack his great foresight and sophistication. Luca was no ordinary scribe diligently recording what already was the practice of business. He was the greatest mathematical thinker of his age. Peter Bernstein attributes much of the stimulus for mathematics in the Renaissance to the publication of the *Summa* in 1494. He goes on to explain the impact of a puzzle set by Luca in the *Summa* that baffled mathematicians for two hundred years. Its solution by Pascal and de Fermat led to the discovery of the theory of probability, the mathematical heart of the concept of risk.

A and B are playing a fair game of balla. They agree to continue until one has won six rounds. The game actually stops when A has won five and B three. How should the stakes be divided?

This brain-teaser appears repeatedly in the writings of mathematicians during the sixteenth and seventeenth centuries. There are many variations but the question is always the same: How do we divide the stakes in an uncompleted game?

The puzzle, which came to be known as the problem of the points, was more significant than it appears. The resolution of how to divide the stakes in an uncompleted game marked the beginning of a systematic analysis of probability – the measure of our confidence that something is going to happen. It brings us to the threshold of the quantification of risk.

...Their solution to Paccioli's puzzle meant that people could for the first time make decisions and forecast the future with the help of numbers.[119]

What a man Luca was. The list of his accomplishments is almost too extensive to be the work of one man or at least of one man without special assistance. His contribution has at the most fundamental level laid the foundation of the modern conception of profit. The method he built on this foundation is a machine for calculating the world with a set coded money value for all possessions and professions. This over time has provided a reliable, daily measure of accumulating happiness and this was not achieved in the manner that might be expected in the rather base and passive term, bookkeeping. Luca soared over the mundane and with the symmetrical, complete and subtle workings of double entry created one of the 'loveliest inventions of the human spirit'.

The interpretation of the output of his machine gave structure to analysis so as to permit the identification of money with order and order with money. This identification made possible the separation of possessions from the individual personality. The method of determining what should be there and what category gives the basis of comparison with what is there and if not, what is the nature of the difference. This created the basic framework for internal control and the prevention of fraud.

He also provides the element of self perpetuation that makes the resolution of accounting differences both automatic and inevitable. This he achieved by establishing the double entry account as being not merely objective and rational and public, in the sense of being comprehensible to others: it is also mechanical. Once started it proceeds in a predictable and specific fashion. It has a life of its own. The accounts become compulsory. They are the first cosmology on the basis of mechanical thought.

As if this was not enough for one man he also provided much of the stimulus for mathematics in the Renaissance and set by his puzzle the path that has led to modern risk management and probability. This contribution not only dominated his own life time but was of such depth and subtlety that it took several hundred years to work out the implications of his contribution and who is to say that we fully understand the ramifications today. We tamper with his message at our peril.

Luca has not only set out the philosophy necessary to separate possessions objectively from the individual but has had the vision to recognize the consequences that would develop from the dynamic and unstoppable process that he described. This perception grounded both in spirituality and his knowledge of the commercial world of his day allowed Luca to pose the questions that signposts the path to probability and risk based management.

It is ironic that generations of accountants and businessmen who have tinkered with the basic philosophy of double entry have been grappling inexpertly with the concepts of risk and value to which Luca had already hinted.

Today's accountants abandoned too easily the fundamental principles of double entry. It makes no sense at all to record a deficiency of shareholders funds, the contra to Anticash, while an entity continues in existence and then somehow pretend that the Anticash has been destroyed when bankruptcy is declared. The courts may hope that their decisions might put the genie back in the bottle but Luca and his symmetry guides us towards a different solution.

Accountants were right to believe in balance. We know from the laws of chemistry that no net increase in matter is possible and that what we see is the transformation of what we already have. It is the same with cash. There must always be two sides of a transaction. If someone is buying, someone is selling. Similarly when you buy you use cash and when you sell you receive cash. The old joke of stockbrokers is that the share price falls because more people are selling than are buying gains its humour because, of course, there always has to be precisely as many buyers as there are sellers.

When we see the headlines about the $US10 billion lost in a property crash or bank failure or entrepreneurial flop it can only mean that $US10 billion has already been made by someone else. This amount is passed on to others by means of the multiplier and accelerator. If the cash associated with that transaction is already with other parties and the unsuccessful party fails that cash cannot be returned. Double entry must prevail. Luca was put here to show us the way. There is no escape. It can only mean that Anticash has been created.

XII

ANTICASH MORE REAL THAN YOU HOPED

WE ARE coming to the end of our journey exploring the strange phenomena encountered in the world of business and finance. We have discovered many curious things and many entrenched positions. Many of these examples provided by eminent experts are curious, comic or contentious in the sense of being incorrect, not of use, or not of value. Experts point to the 'facts' but we do not need to agree with their conclusions.

A single 'fact' does not represent truth. G.K. Chesterton the creator of the detective Father Brown pointed out that many facts are contradictory and we have to look at the whole picture if we are to detect the solution.

> How facts obscure the truth...I may be silly – in fact I'm off my head – but I never could believe in that man – what's his name, in those capital stories? Sherlock Holmes. Every detail points to something, certainly, but generally to the wrong thing. Facts point in all directions, it seems to me, like the thousands of twigs on a tree. It's only the life of the tree that has unity and goes up – only the green blood that springs like a fountain, at the stars.[120]

Maigret, the detective created by Georges Simeon, also had difficulty with the problem of interpreting contradictory facts. The clues led to no definite conclusion so he developed the elegant solution of plying the suspects with food and alcohol and talking to them until eventually the one true villain capitulates and confesses. Facts or science were too contradictory for these two detectives who found the solution in a return to first principles.

Maigret's method has its attractions and if applied to me I would confess to adding a few new phenomena amongst those presented. Mostly, I have just used new language to give emphasis to what was always there. This new language might look unfamiliar but the ideas it expresses could nevertheless be valid. This is quite likely being simply the converse of the all too common situation we encounter where apparently sensible things are not in fact valid.

How can this be? The perpetrators of Antilogic are not fools or at least we trust that they are not. Maybe they adopt their actions because they know no better or get swept along by conventional wisdom, applying ideas that were valid somewhere, sometime but are no longer valid in today's situation and facts. This can only explain some of the examples. People are too smart to follow blindly conventional wisdom for too long. Their interests are more direct and personal than the interest in the firm assumed by the theorists. They have their own particular interest that might be pride, survival, comfort, career or money. This explains much of the role of managers, brokers, forecasters and media commentators. Their actions are sensible in their light and meet their ends but are not of value to you and me. We must look out for ourselves to determine what will serve our purposes. The study of Antilogic will help you sort out fact from vapour. Chesterton used the term 'atmosphere' but the idea is the same.

> The philosophy of the world may be founded in facts, its business is run on spiritual impressions and atmospheres.[121]

If only the accountants and bankers return to first principles we will see the reality of Anticash and its manifold uses. Of course its obvious use has always been as a convenient means of giving change against large denomination notes but the most likely breakthrough will come in the facilitation of stored value cards. The move to stored value cards such as Mondex will make the use of Anticash essential. The use of stored value cards has to be closely controlled to prevent the unauthorized addition of value to the card. Such unauthorized addition would in effect allow individuals to create their own money. This would be a popular development for cardholders but is not likely to be encouraged by monetary authorities. In order to prevent an outbreak of individual initiative the card system is structurally arranged to ensure that merchants (i.e. the shops that have accepted the transfer from your card) can only upload and never download value from the bank. Unfortunately mistakes are made and goods are returned so the merchant has important and valid reasons to want to retrieve value from the bank. As this is not possible for security reasons the banks instead will solve the problem by reducing the upload of value by the inclusion of an appropriate amount of negative value, i.e. include enough Anticash to achieve the appropriate net transfer. Banks have an ample availability of Anticash because of their frequent involvement in the bankruptcy process and additional sums can be obtained from the Anticash exchange.

The recognition of Anticash as being an irrevocable obligation makes it likely that a whole new market will be developed based on the transfer of irrevocable obligations operating in exactly the same manner as the world's financial markets do with the transfer of rights. Conceptually there is no difference. These are just the opposite side of the same transaction. It is purely an historic convention that the right has been used in financial markets. The same motivations of profit maximization and risk avoidance will be present as the participants make choices consistent with their own preferences as they manage their way through the bankruptcy situation. Investors with an aversion to risk will try to cut their losses and sell out for whatever real cash they can get from other holders who have a bigger risk appetite. The incentive for these hardy souls is that they gain a greater share of the enterprise and benefit when perceptions of the perfect market changes in their favour. Establishing a marketplace for irrevocable but transferable obligations brings several economic advantages. The recognition of the obligations permits the retention of the full original asset obviating the need for a provision or write off so ensuring a marked reduction in the loss of value currently being caused by the too frequent destruction of the business and the careers of those working within. The deliberate retention of the two sides of the transaction avoids the netting off that currently provokes precipitous action with resulting unnecessary loss of value. Better processes will introduce a self-regulating characteristic to help solve one of society's most persistent problems. Better to trade the obligations between those that can value them than to insist on the destruction of the entity. The use of modern electronic exchanges supplemented by the use of Stored Antivalue cards provide the means by which the risk preferences of the, sometimes reluctant, holders of securities can be transferred between the parties in an orderly manner, rather than in a panic rush to the exits. Ironically the recognition and flexible use of Anticash is therefore likely to reduce the circumstances in which it is created. Modern electronics can solve the previous problems of lack of liquidity and administrative complexity. The basis of an electronic exchange to handle the trading of these obligations already exists and any stored value card that can keep separate different categories of information, would have no difficulty in facilitating the storing and transfer of Anticash. Present functionality permits the secure storage of incompatible currencies as well as non-monetary information such as passport and driving licence details that must never be corrupted by inappropriate combination.

The growth of capital markets with the use of powerful computers, complex mathematical models and globalization has exacerbated the torschlusspaniek effect. In the old days there was always the hope that the main lender was a bank that would rather not take the loss. There was always a risk that banks would decide that their first loss was their best loss but generally in the absence of a financial panic a bank would try and nurse the troubled debtor to the safe haven. Safe for the bank that is! After all, the most profitable customer for the bank is the troubled customer that approaches but does not enter bankruptcy. They have no choice, cannot refinance and have to pay maximum fees and penalty interest rates. Whole businesses have been established to specialize in lending to this category of borrower. It can be highly profitable but unpredictable, as the lender has to reckon not only with the fortunes of the debtor but also with the attitude of the other lenders.

Today if trouble begins, the ultimate holder of the loan paper may be our old friends the banks but from anywhere in the world and without any local affiliations. It could also be held by conservative and nervous insurance companies and mutual funds through to junk bond investors and scavengers. This is a powerful and unpredictable mixture driven by the desire to get out of the investment and not by the desire to retrieve value.

The commitment required to nurse the company back to health is likely to be overwhelmed by the impact of politics within and between the creditors. Although a lead bank still is supposed to manage the process there is now an inherent tendency provoking bankruptcy. The lead manager is likely to have sold his initial holding into the market long before the debtor has got into trouble so the direct incentive to solve the problem is reduced. Within each bank, the lending officer, if he is still there, will be distancing himself from the problem that will have been passed to a risk department and the lawyers. They will seek to protect their institution from loss by initiating a process that leads inevitably to litigation and bankruptcy. There is a big internal incentive to remove the situation from the list of problems. The feared outcome becomes the inevitable.

The investors will come from an increasingly wide spread of countries and will have different amounts at risk. The smaller investors using implied or actual threats of bankruptcy typically seek to depart early by encouraging the larger investors to buy them out. This has become so pervasive a practice that no one wants to run the risk of being pre-empted. This leads to the destruction of value and the needless loss of a productive enterprise. The banking industry has tried to impose a greater discipline on the club of lenders but this simply further encourages participants to seek to depart even earlier before sanctions can be applied.

The use of Anticash is presently held back only by convention and our lack of familiarity with the concept. I have set out a wide range of examples of the uses of Antilogic and some ideas of the technical manner in which it might be handled. People need to get used to the idea to discover all of the possibilities. This same process has occurred at each step of monetary evolution, as each new innovation seemed strange at the time. Once we have passed through this stage it will gradually become clear to us all that Anticash can be used the same way as most applications of real cash. The concept of Anticash is the same as for real money but in reverse, giving the possibility of action and reaction in monetary affairs that is so common in many aspects of the physical world.

Although monetary uses will become increasingly prevalent, its real importance comes in the better reflection of symmetry as we achieve harmonization of financial, chemical and physical laws. The inclusion of Anticash will permit a more reliable reconciliation of national financial flows by capturing value now being allowed to escape from the records at the time of bankruptcy. Overall, the total economy should now balance on a double entry basis and lead to statistics that are more accurate and to more honest politics. It should also bring improved information technology processing by eliminating current artificial simplification. Finally, the statistical task force at the IMF will find the basis of a well earned retirement with their books properly balanced.

Much of economics is taken from the myopic viewpoint of personal self-interest. The viewpoints of individuals and groups are not consistent and may be contradictory. If we could add up all these positions it is not likely that it will equal the total of the world. Even when we try and measure present reality it is only an estimate and subject to all sorts of error. It is little wonder that economic forecasters starting with an inconsistent and largely estimated present have difficulty in accurately forecasting the future or even robustly advising the appropriate policy remedies. There is so much slop in the working of world economic flows that it is not surprising that experts fail in balancing the world's book of accounts. It is easy to dismiss this as accounting error or not of significance but the level of discrepancy is so large that almost any micro economic error can safely be accommodated within the overall discrepancy without attracting attention. No doubt this is convenient for the economists to have this degree of flexibility but it means that their theories are never satisfactorily proved. Other less fashionable theories cannot be disproved either. It is my contention that some alternative theories may meet the evidence more closely than the convenient theories conventionally accepted today.

Pragmatic business people, regulators, accountants and lawyers have to make the best of the system in which they operate and exploit it to their best advantage. After all that is the assumption of the free enterprise system. The centrally planned economies tried to resolve all economic conflicts in the interests of their society but these systems were overwhelmed by complexity. The pragmatists therefore resort to the best decisions they can come up with in circumstances but these are inherently arbitrary. There is no reason to expect that these decisions are even approximately correct. The presumption of correctness based on the invisible hand did not take into account the self-satisficing tendencies of individuals revealed through the identification of Antilogic. From this we must conclude that the mere prevalence of a pragmatic micro economic activity does not indicate that it is valid on a macro or global level. As we have seen at the IMF, the simple adding up of all the micro economic activities does not result in a global balance. We must look to science to find a robust proof to validate monetary activities. This book does not pretend to explain advanced mathematics or quantum physics but developments in the fields have great relevance for the solution of the monetary discrepancies.

Establishing a proof on the basis of the absence of discrepancy is an inherently unsatisfactory process. We use a mathematical trick to establish that there is not a discrepancy but this falls short of proof. The absence of discrepancy exists when there is no difference between the two numbers chosen for comparison, as in double entry bookkeeping. The establishment of a zero is supposed to make the proof. In the case of bankruptcy a zero seems like it is a good outcome as the starting position is a big negative with the debtor having a surplus of liabilities over assets. The object of the bankruptcy process is to bring the discrepancy from negative back up to zero. Unfortunately, if this cannot be naturally achieved by settling the debts the courts resort to an arbitrary process designed to force the outcome back to zero. The application of force or arithmetical shortcut is fraught with danger because of the fundamental linkages that exist in the double entry bookkeeping journal entry. The physical world has the same limitations because of pervasive interrelations.

> The physical reasons for our interdependence stem from the laws of conservation, especially the conservation of energy. Regardless of its form – solar, heat, light, gravity, wind, mechanical, chemical, nuclear, or electrical – when energy metamorphoses from one state to another, the total quantity does not change. In one of the first efforts to explain the duality, mutuality, reciprocity and [double entry] of the properties of matter, W.R. Grove, in *The Correlation of Physical Forces,* wrote 'There are for example, many facts, one of which cannot take place without involving the other, one arm of the lever cannot be depressed without the other being elevated – the finger cannot press the table without the table pressing the finger. A body cannot be

heated without another being cooled or some other force being exhausted in an equivalent ratio to the production of heat; a body cannot be positively electrified without some other body being negatively electrified... The probability is, that, if not all, the greater number of physical phenomena are correlative, and that without a duality of conception, the mind cannot form an idea of them; thus motion cannot be perceived or probably imagined without parallax or relative change of position.' [122]

So it is you cannot have debit without credit and cannot expect to have bankruptcy without Anticash. It is likely that the archaic bankruptcy system of the accountants and lawyers, with its origin dating back several centuries, accommodated a lack of familiarity with or indeed fears of negative or anti numbers. When they even suspected the presence of such numbers it was with a feeling of unease about something untidy or perhaps mystical. They have sought to bring the difference between liabilities and assets back to zero. No difference is supposed to mean no problem but this has been a bad choice. There is no more problematic number to have as the basis for balance. The history and quirky nature of zero gives an important history lesson to the courts as they try to replace the inconvenient negative represented by deficiency of shareholders funds with the unstable fiction of zero.

At least the mathematicians realize that the rules relating to zero are necessarily arbitrary whereas the lawyers and accountants try to pass them off as self evident truths whose origins are lost in the mists of time. Well, the vapour is true enough but the truths are open to question. The problem started with the difference between nothing and zero where there is a definite discrepancy. Nothing is nothing, a void and an absence of anything. Zero is a number and so it is a thing. It is what you count and do not have anything. Originally zero was a symbol for the concept of emptiness but by AD 800 an Indian mathematician established that zero could be used in the same way as other numbers for addition and subtraction where the number always stayed the same. Multiplication was also possible but always gave zero. It became more troublesome with division with dividing zero by a non-zero number always giving zero but there was no number for the result of dividing by zero. This could be forbidden but dividing zero by zero was harder because of the multiplicity of possible answers. This too was forbidden but found its way back as the basis of calculus. Just what the zero discrepancy represents remains a matter for conjecture.

Zero is bad enough for the accountants leading to artificial solutions but the concept of positive and negative causes them far greater problems, perhaps because the rules do not even contemplate the mirror image of the traditional entries. The accounting terminology tries to encompass the different sides of the same transaction by the use of the terms 'debit' defined as the recording of an item of debt in a account, and 'credit' which should be the acknowledgement or an entry of payment of value received in an account. Whether the precise implications of credit are generally understood is very doubtful as this bookkeeping definition was listed as definition 18 among 27 definitions in the Macquarie dictionary. It is generally understood that the system is based entirely on the premise of incurring or imposing debt. In other words it is based on enforcing a right. But this is just convention. The system could as easily be based on accepting obligations and so create a wholly different perspective on business finances.

The science of Physics also cut its teeth on the positive but has come to recognize the unexpected presence of the negative. The physicists have been forced by physical evidence conflicting with previous theoretical models to contemplate the idea of negative and anti worlds. Generations of physicists found that their theories were undermined by inconvenient results emanating from their experiments. The numbers just would not add up. The numbers were blamed but for some time there has been widely held acceptance of the concept of antimatter and further concepts of anticomponents are emerging. Paul Davis explains the existence of negative energy (anti-energy) and negative gravitational force (levitation or antigravity). He concludes that the deep principle that protects the second law of thermodynamics from negative energy abuse (e.g. perpetual motion) stems from the concept of information. Reducing entropy (the state of disorder or the measure of unavailable energy) is like creating order, which is equivalent to creating information and naked singularities are a source of gratuitous information.

If information is the source of the solution to the second law of thermodynamics then we should remember that money is only a particular subset of information. As we have seen, money is nothing more than the means of conveying information as to claims, obligations and desires. Consequently it is feasible that cash displays the same characteristics of real/actual and vapour/virtual/ghostly/anti as the generic case of information. Because of the force of entropy it becomes inevitable that such monetary phenomenon must be present.

> (N)egative energy really does exist. The trouble is, generating and manipulating large enough quantities of negative energy could threaten some of nature's most sacrosanct laws – the second law of thermodynamics, for

instance. It is easy to dream up scenarios that produce unphysical or para-
doxical consequences – building perpetual motion machines, or even
travelling backwards in time. ...Intriguingly, if you look carefully at any
of these scenarios, some effect always seems to intrude in the nick of time
to stymie the would-be law-breaker. It is as if there is a deeper principle of
nature at work that permits negative energy, but proscribes its worst
effects.

...The secret lies with quantum theory. According to this, what appears to
be empty space is in fact teeming with all manner of 'virtual' particles that
exist only fleetingly. The so-called quantum vacuum state cannot be
stripped of these countless ghostly entities, but they reveal themselves
only when something disturbs the vacuum state.

It is these ghostly particles that hold the key to creating a flux of negative
energy – in effect a beam of cold and dark, rather than heat and light...[123]

This presence of anticomponents would appear to be much more plausible than the short-cut pragmatism that occurs when we try to eliminate
inconvenient negativity by forcing it back to zero. By observation we have
seen that the simplistic idea of wiping the slate clean and returning to zero
does not work. The chips must lie where they fall. The act of moving to the
troubled nil position simply creates new forces including the formation of
Anticash.

When it comes down to it, money is just an idea, sometimes with
physical manifestation. This idea is made up of a subset of information
about value, obligation and ownership. The history of money has revealed
that we have long moved on from money as being a physical manifestation
to being a record of right or obligation often carried as an electronic pulse.
The effectiveness of this information has been shown to be greatly influenced by confidence and belief in its worth. This belief is in turn determined by a whole array of information that guides the individual
corporation or country to form its opinion as to the worth of the money
in question. It is inconceivable that money should avoid the general rules
that apply to information in totality. Information is not as straightforward
as we might imagine and recent discoveries suggest wide-ranging new
possibilities. Investigations in the quantum world are revealing weird
characteristics of information that is opening the path to teleporting and
the simultaneous presence of matter in two locations. The concept of
negative or anti particles plays an important part in these discoveries by
a growing band of physicists who believe that

Information is a super-weird new substance, more ethereal than matter or energy, but every bit as real and perhaps even more fundamental. ... perhaps the quantum landscape is the way it is because it must conform to the laws of some deeper level where information is supreme. If so, information would truly be the most fundamental level of reality.

Ordinarily, we think of space as being empty. And yet according to quantum theory, it is in fact filled with 'virtual' pairs of electrons, positrons and other quantum particles which flit constantly in and out of existence. A virtual particle is not real, because it must borrow its energy from the vacuum. By Heisenberg's uncertainty principle, it can do this for a short time only, and must then give its energy back and vanish. As a result, these particles only exist briefly, and only make their presence known if they interact with a real particle before vanishing... In traditional information theory, information is always real – just as energy is in classical physics. In quantum theory, however, information can become virtual. The act of entangling a pair of particles corresponds to creating a virtual pair of information particles – a qubit and an anti-qubit – out of the information vacuum.[124]

As demonstrated by this article, money also must be made up of qubits and anti-qubits that would seem to support the likely existence of Anticash also made up of qubits and anti-qubits in different proportions.

We now know that antimatter is real and it has been isolated and measured. This will remind the reader of the occasions where the so-called monetary experts have been inconvenienced by unexplained influences in their equations and national statistics. These have often been blamed on the accountants and explained as accounting or measurement errors. The equations were always correct as far as they went but failed to include the vital element, Anticash. The physicists grappled with the same problem of trying to prove a theory before the necessary tools were available as shown in this quotation from 1960.

Now the idea of antimatter arose as a direct result of mathematical considerations which had come to replace what were felt to be inadequate visual representations of the atom. These mathematical considerations were:

– Relativity theory, which introduced a new expression for the energy of the particle.
– Quantum theory which lead to the consideration of negative energies
– Relativistic wave mechanics, which gave a correct representation of the properties of the electron.

We have seen how the theory of holes, by giving a definite meaning to electrons of negative energy, was able to predict the existence of new particles and to give a precise definition of their properties. Particle and anti-particle only differ in the signs of their charge and of their magnetic moment.

Theoretically predicted in 1930, anti-particles were soon to be demonstrated experimentally. The first to be detected was the anti-electron, or positive electron. Further progress had to await the construction of giant accelerators, when $\pi-$ and $\pi+$ mesons could be produced in the synchrocyclotron, and anti-protons and anti-neutrons in the bevatron. More recently still, atomic piles have been used to prove the existence of the anti-neutrino, and by the end of 1956, all the anti-particles necessary for building a model of antimatter had been observed. The present-day picture is then as follows. The central anti-nucleus is made up of anti-protons and anti-neutrons held together by the exchange of $\pi°$, $\pi-$ and $\pi+$ mesons. The anti-nucleus is surrounded by anti-electrons which often revolve at considerable distances from it and envelop the central negative charge with an atmosphere of positive electricity.

Does this picture of the anti-atom represent a physical reality? In other words, does antimatter exist? One way to find out this would be to create it out of anti-protons and anti-electrons, but unfortunately this is a very difficult task. Though the dematerialization of matter has long been achieved, its creation demands temperatures beyond our normal reach. Now such temperatures do in fact exist in the stars where such reactions may easily take place.

We have seen how matter can be created from its constituent elements. Is antimatter to be constructed in the same way? If we could fuse an anti-proton into a positive electron, we might well have created the simplest anti-atom (anti-hydrogen), but what would we do with it once we had it? Our laboratories and the world in which we experiment, are made of matter, and the anti-particles are characterized by the fact that they become annihilated in contact with their sister particles. How could we prevent the positive hydrogen element from meeting one of the negative electrons of which all matter is constituted? How could we preserve anti-hydrogen so that we might use it for synthesizing anti-helium? How, in short, could we do experiments with antimatter at all?

Antimatter probably has a structure identical to that of matter, and it is not unreasonable to assume that some stars and even galaxies are made up of it. But we also know that the coexistence of the two types of matter, is in the present state of our knowledge, an unreasonable hypothesis, and that antimatter cannot be produced experimentally at present. We may however talk about it theoretically or mathematically.[125]

So wrote Maurice Duquesne, Director of Research in Nuclear Physics at the Radium Institute Paris in 1960.

In less than half a century the practical impediments that prevented Duquesne and his colleagues from creating that which they had discovered were all removed and antimatter has been manufactured in the laboratory. Who knows with pace of scientific achievement where this will lead us? It would be a bold economist indeed who would question mankind's ultimate ability to capture the Anticash that we already have on a theoretical basis proven to exist. It is only a matter of time before our technological ingenuity will permit us to capture Anticash and put its manifold benefits to work for our society. This breakthrough might not be so far away.

We have explored many examples of Antilogic and seen how pervasive it is in the corporate and financial world. We have referred to many authorities that have been included because of their own expertise in Antilogic or their perception in pointing out the proficiency of others. We have seen the interrelation between Antilogic and Vapourcash and Anticash. We have seen how Vapourcash and Anticash depend on Antilogic for their effectiveness but also how the generation of Vapourcash has provided the scope for Antilogicians to achieve their objectives.

The full implications and benefits of Anticash are only now becoming fully known. The dangers of Vapourcash and other forms of Antilogic are not always recognized for what they are. I have indulged myself a little bit in demonstrating how far the application of Antilogic can take us and how the addition of a series of apparently logical steps does not bring us to the conventional outcome. But I have not exaggerated the prevalence of Antilogic.

We have seen that Antilogic may lead to strange outcomes and certainly not to those predicted by conventional finance theory. This is not a random outcome. Antilogic is revealed not as a lack of logic or an absence of sense. We have found that Antilogic is a perverse logic, a reverse of what you might expect, not solely because it is faulty but because it is seeking a different outcome than we have been taught to expect.

Yet, when we dig deeper we have found that the outcome is not as perverse as it first appears. It all depends on your point of view and what is being attempted. Many of the intriguing examples we found were created by a personal view of self interest. This is not always obvious and the true motive may have been disguised to meet conventional expectations. At the end of the day the direct interests of the individual in the world of finance will have more influence than the indirect workings of the invisible hand. Often the individuals do not achieve their objectives and these may be in competition with those of their colleagues but you cannot blame them for trying. We have found so many examples of unfortunate outcomes for individual investors, corporations and communities as to suggest that the adverse effects are endemic. However, there is no need to be pessimistic as every expected disaster is likely to be matched by an undeserved windfall. The correlation between reward and virtue does not look to be either very strong or positive.

Who are the winners? I hope that we have made clear enough that this question has no automatic answer and each case must be judged carefully on its merits according to the individual's logic at the time.

Unfortunately the outcome may not be in your interest. This need not imply ill will or bad intentions by anyone. It is the application of the law of unintended consequences as identified by Pierre S. du Pont, a deputy from Nemours to the French National Assembly in the eighteenth century. Speaking on a proposal to issue additional assignats – the Vapourcash of the French Revolution – he said

> Gentlemen, it is a disagreeable custom to which one is too easily led by the harshness of the discussions, to assume evil intentions. It is necessary to be gracious as to intentions; one should believe good, and apparently they are; but we do not have to be gracious at all to inconsistent logic or to absurd reasoning. Bad logicians have committed more involuntary crimes than bad men have done intentionally.[126]

It is up to each financial participant to protect value by being always vigilant in the evaluation of ideas presented. It is vital to be alert to the differences between logic, paradox and Antilogic. By this means it is possible to gain true value from Vapourcash and Anticash. Beware the false prophet but be open to new ideas.

REFERENCES

1. Keynes. J.M. (1970), *General Theory of Employment, Interest and Money*, MacMillan, New York, p. 155.
2. Skidelsky, R. and Keynes, J.M. (1994), *The Economist as Saviour 1920–1937*, Papermac, London, p. 526.
3. Janis, I.L. (1972), *Victims of Groupthink*, Houghton Miffin, Boston, MA, p. 3.
4. Janis, I.L. (1972), *Victims of Groupthink*, Houghton Miffin, Boston, MA, p. 12.
5. Galbraith, J.K. (1994), *A Short History of Financial Euphoria*, Penguin, Harmondsworth, p, 15.
6. Schwed, F. (1995), *Where are the Customers Yachts?* Wiley, New York, p. 162.
7. McAlpine, A. (1998), *The New Machiavelli. The Art of Politics in Business*, Wiley, New York, p. 138.
8. McAlpine, A. (1998), *The New Machiavelli. The Art of Politics in Business*, Wiley, New York, p. 139.
9. Galbraith, J.K. (1994), *A Short History of Financial Euphoria*, Penguin, Harmondsworth, p. 23.
10. Janis, I.L. (1972), *Victims of Groupthink*, Houghton Miffin, Boston, MA, p. 45.
11. Jay, A. (1969), *Management and Machiavelli* as reported by C. Northcote Parkinson in Big Business, Hodder & Stoughton, London, p. 157.
12. Galbraith, J.K. (1992), *The Culture of Contentment*, Penguin, Harmondsworth, p. 68.
13. Galbraith, J.K. (1992), *The Culture of Contentment*, Penguin, Harmondsworth, p. 68.
14. Jay, A. (1969), *Management and Machiavelli*, Hodder & Stoughton, London, p. 148.
15. Townsend, R. (1970), *Up the Organization*, Michael Joseph, London, p. 48.
16. Janis, I.L. (1972), *Victims of Groupthink*, Houghton Miffin, Boston, MA, p. 123.
17. Janis, I.L. (1972), *Victims of Groupthink*, Houghton Miffin, Boston, MA, p. 7.
18. Sampson, A., (1996) *Company Man*, Harper-Collins, London, p. 218.
19. Sampson, A., (1996) *Company Man,* Harper-Collins, London, p. 314.
20. Janis, I.L. (1972), *Victims of Groupthink*, Houghton Miffin, Boston, MA, p. 13.
21. Little, G. (1999), Why it was time, *The Age*, 23 October, p. 18 (newspaper article).
22. Radzinsky, E. (1996), *Stalin*, Hodder & Stoughton, London, p. 335.
23. Pyatakov quoted in Radzinsky, E., *Stalin*, Hodder & Stoughton, London, p. 231.
24. Radzinsky, E. (1996), *Stalin*, Hodder & Stoughton, London, p. 328.
25. Lewis, C.S. (1996), as reported in Sampson, A., *Company Man*, Harper-Collins, London, p. 80.
26. Saul, J.R. (1997), *The Unconscious Civilisation*, Penguin, Harmondsworth, p. 125.
27. Saul, J.R. (1997), *The Unconscious Civilisation*, Penguin, Harmondsworth, p. 19.

28. Bernstein, P. (1993), *Capital Ideas*, Free Press, New York, p. 136.
29. Bernstein, P. (1993), *Capital Ideas*, Free Press, New York, p. 137.
30. Bernstein, P. (1993), *Capital Ideas*, Free Press, New York, p. 149.
31. Keynes, J.M. (1970), *General Theory of Employment, Interest and Money*, MacMillan, New York, p. 155.
32. Smith, A. (1987), *The Money Game*, Vintage Books, New York, p. 133.
33. Smith, A. (1987), *The Money Game*, Vintage Books, New York, p. 200.
34. Smith, A. (1987), *The Money Game*, Vintage Books, New York, p. 15.
35. Smith, A. (1987), *The Money Game*, Vintage Books, New York, p. 22.
36. Buffett, W. (1981), *Berkshire Hathaway annual report*.
37. Sombart Liebe, W. (1997), *Luxus und Kapitalismus* quoted by James Buchan, *Frozen Desire*, Picador, London, p. 70.
38. Schwed, F. (1995), *Where are the Customers' Yachts*, Wiley, New York, p. 11.
39. *Heard it on the Grapevine* – Discussion Paper, Australian Companies and Investment Commission, November 1999.
40. Morgenstern, O. (1963), *On the Accuracy of Economic Observations*, Princeton University Press, Princeton, NJ, p. 12.
41. Morgenstern, O. (1963), *On the Accuracy of Economic Observations*, Princeton University Press, Princeton, NJ, p. 81.
42. Black, F. (1986), as quoted by Peter Berstein, *Capital Ideas*, p. 124.
43. Gaddy, C.G. and Ickes, B.W. (1998), *Beyond a Bailout: Time to Face Reality About Russia's 'Virtual Economy'*, Brookings Institution, Washington, DC, www.brook.edu./fp/events/gaddy, unpublished paper, June.
44. *OECD Policy Brief Economic Survey of the Russian Federation*, March 2000.
45. Berliner, J.S. (1988), *Soviet Industry from Stalin to Gorbachev*, Cornell University Press, Ithaca, NY, p. 3.
46. OECD (2000), *OECD Policy Brief Economic Survey of the Russian Federation*, March.
47. OECD (2000), *OECD Policy Brief Economic Survey of the Russian Federation*, March.
48. Malkiel, B.G. (1996), *A Random Walk Down Wall Street*, Norton, New York, p. 138.
49. Greider, W. (1989), *Secret of the Temple*, Touchstone, p. 240.
50. Galbraith, J.K. (1992), *The Great Crash 1929*, Penguin, Harmondsworth, p. 44.
51. Ormerod, P. (1994), *The Death of Economics*, Faber & Faber, London, p. 175.
52. Tvede, L. (1999), *The Psychology of Finance*, Wiley, Chichester, pp. 39–41.
53. Tvede, L. (1999), *The Psychology of Finance*, Wiley, Chichester, p. 234.
54. Galbraith, J.K. (1995), *Money Whence it Came Where it Went*, Penguin, Harmondsworth, 2nd ed., p. 17.
55. Galbraith, J.K. (1995), *Money Whence it Came Where it Went*, Penguin, Harmondsworth, 2nd ed., p. 18.
56. Galbraith, J.K. (1995), *Money Whence it Came Where it Went*, Penguin, Harmondsworth, 2nd ed., p. 63.
57. Buchan, J. (1997), *Frozen Desire*, Picador, p. 99.
58. Skidelsky, R. and Keynes, J.M. (1994), *The Economist as Saviour 1920–1937*, Papermac, London, p. 312.
59. Robertson, D.H. (1928), *Money*, Cambridge University Press, Cambridge, p. 50.
60. Robertson, D.H. (1928), *Money*, Cambridge University Press, Cambridge, p. 147.
61. Mun, T. (1664), *England's Treasure by Foreign Trade, or, The Balance of Our Foreign Trade is the Rule of Our Treasure*, as reported in Gray, A. (1931), *Development of Economic Doctrine*, Longman Green, London, pp. 85–90.
62. Smith, A. (1987), *The Money Game*, Vintage Books, New York, p. 62.

63. Shannon, I. (1964), *International Liquidity: A Study in the Economic Functions of F.W. Gold*, Cheshire, Melbourne, p. 2.
64. Shannon, I. (1964), *International Liquidity: A Study in the Economic Functions of F.W. Gold*, Cheshire, Melbourne, p. 121.
65. Furness, W.H. (1910), *The Island of Stone Money*, J.B. Lippincott, Philadelphia, PA and London.
66. Friedman, M. (1994), *Money Mischief*, Harcourt, Brace and Jovanovich, New York, p. 5.
66. Friedman, M. (1994), *Money Mischief*, Harcourt, Brace and Jovanovich, New York, p. 5.
68. Robertson, D.H. (1928), *Money*, Cambridge University Press, Cambridge, p. 33.
69. Buchan, J. (1997), *Frozen Desire*, Picador, London, p. 281.
70. Robertson, D.H. (1928), *Money*, Cambridge University Press, Cambridge, p. 33.
71. Jay, A. (1972), *Corporation Man*, Jonathan Cape, London, p. 13.
72. Saul, J.R. (1993), *Voltaires Bastards*, Penguin, Harmondsworth, p. 369.
73. Saul, J.R. (1993), *Voltaires Bastards*, Penguin, Harmondsworth, p. 369.
74. Saul, J.R. (1995), *The Doubter's Companion*, Penguin, Harmondsworth, p. 206.
75. Saul, J.R. (1995) *The Doubter's Companion*, Penguin, Harmondsworth, p. 207.
76. Saul, J.R. (1995) *The Doubter's Companion*, Penguin, Harmondsworth, p. 206.
77. Saul, J.R. (1995) *The Doubter's Companion*, Penguin, Harmondsworth, p. 206.
78. Smith, A. (1972), *Supermoney*, Michael Joseph, London, p. 14.
79. Smith, A. (1972), *Supermoney*, Michael Joseph, London, p. 18.
80. Smith, A. (1972), *Supermoney*, Michael Joseph, London, p. 23.
81. Smith, A. (1972), *Supermoney*, Michael Joseph, London, p. 23.
82. Galbraith, J.K. (1992), *The Culture of Contentment*, Penguin, Harmondsworth, p. 56.
83. Smith, A. (1989), *The Roaring 80s*, Bantam, New York, p. 22.
84. Skidelsky, R. and Keynes, J.M. (1994), *The Economist as Saviour 1920–1937*, Papermac, London, p. 236.
85. Lex (1999), Column in *The Financial Times*, 23rd December.
86. Miller, M. and Culp, C. (1994), reported in *The Economist*, 24 September.
87. Schwed, F. (1995), *Where are the Customers Yachts*, Wiley, New York, p. 58.
88. Galbraith, J.K. (1992), *The Great Crash 1929*, Penguin, Harmondsworth, p. 152.
89. Galbraith, J.K. (1992), *The Great Crash 1929*, Penguin, Harmondsworth, p. 144.
90. Buchan, J. (1997), *Frozen Desire*, Picador, London, p. 268.
91. Buchan, J. (1997), *Frozen Desire*, Picador, London, p. 269.
92. Evans, L. and Quigley, N. (1995), Shareholder liability regimes, principle–agent relationships, and banking industry performance, *The Journal of Law and Economics*, October, Vol. XXXVIII (2), pp. 497–519.
93. Macey, J.R. and Miller, G.P. (1992) *Wake Forest Law Review*, 27.
94. Ormerod, P. (1994), *The Death of Economics*, Faber & Faber, London, p. 4.
95. Manias K. (1996), *Panic and Crashes*, Wiley, New York, p. 3.
96. Saul, J.R. (1993), *Voltaires Bastards*, Penguin, Harmondsworth, p. 399.
97. Saul, J.R. (1993), *Voltaires Bastards*, Penguin, Harmondsworth, p. 399.
98. Galbraith, J.K. (1991), *A History of Economics*, Penguin, Harmondsworth, p. 222.
99. Buchan, J. (1997), *Frozen Desire*, Picador, London, p. 253.
100. Buchan, J. (1997), *Frozen Desire*, Picador, London, p. 255.
101. Saul, J.R. (1995), *The Doubter's Companion*, Penguin, Harmondsworth, p. 218.
102. Saul, J.R. (1995), *The Doubter's Companion*, Penguin, Harmondsworth, p. 91.
103. Saul, J.R. (1993), *Voltaires Bastards*, Penguin, Harmondsworth, p. 402.
104. Saul, J.R. (1993), *Voltaires Bastards*, Penguin, Harmondsworth, p. 402.

105. Gaddy, C.G. and Ickes, B.W., *Beyond a Bailout: Time to Face Reality About Russia's 'Virtual Economy'*, Brookings Institution, Washington, DC, www.brook.edu./fp/events/gaddy, unpublished paper, June.
106. Schama, S. (1988), *The Embarrassment of Riches: An Interpretation of Dutch Culture of the Golden Age*, Fontana Williams Collins, UK, p. 330.
107. Galbraith, J.K. (1991), *A History of Economics*, Penguin, Harmondsworth, p. 37.
108. Buchan, J. (1997), *Frozen Desire*, Picador, London, p. 270.
109. McAlpine, A. (1998), *The New Machiavelli. The Art of Politics in Business*, Wiley, New York, p. 139.
110. Buchan, J. (1997), *Frozen Desire*, Picador, London, p. 65.
111. Buchan, J. (1997), *Frozen Desire*, Picador, London, p. 271.
112. Buchan, J. (1997), *Frozen Desire*, Picador, London, p. 67.
113. Buchan, J. (1997), *Frozen Desire*, Picador, London, p. 68.
114. Buchan, J. (1997), *Frozen Desire*, Picador, London, p. 68.
115. Buchan, J. (1997), *Frozen Desire*, Picador, London, p. 69.
116. Buchan, J. (1997), *Frozen Desire*, Picador, London, p. 70.
117. Buchan, J. (1997), *Frozen Desire*, Picador, London, p. 71.
118. Buchan, J. (1997), *Frozen Desire*, Picador, London, p. 70.
119. Bernstein, P. (1996), *Against the Gods*, Wiley, New York, p. 43.
120. Chesterton, G.K. (1995), *The Club of Queer Trades*, Wordsworth Classics, Ware Hertfordshire, p. 10.
121. Chesterton, G.K. (1995), *The Club of Queer Trades*, Wordsworth Classics, Ware Hertfordshire, p. 22.
122. Niederhoffer, V. (1997), *The Education of a Speculator*, Wiley, New York, p. 297.
123. Davies, P. (1998), Paradox lost, *New Scientist*, No. 2126, March 21, pp. 26–30.
124. Buchanan, M. (1998), Beyond reality, *New Scientist*, No. 2125, March 14, pp. 26–30.
125. Duquesne, M. (1960), *Matter and Antimatter*, Hutchison & Co., London, pp. 118–121.
126. Friedman, M. (1994), *Money Mischief*, Harcourt, Brace and Jovanovich, New York, p. 265; Pierre S. du Pont speaking, 25 September, 1796.

INDEX